V

Georg Lukács

Verso

Record of a Life
An Autobiographical Sketch

Edited by István Eörsi
Translated by Rodney Livingstone

Photos on front cover, clockwise from top, centre: Lukács in 1917 (Lukács Archives of the Institute of Philosophy of the Hungarian Academy of Sciences); decree on the working conditions of apprentices, Budapest 1919; Commissar Lukács thanks the proletariat for its help in overcoming the counter-revolution (from a newsreel in the Hungarian Film Institute); Lukács's membership card of the Soviet Writers' Union (Lukács Archives); Commissar Lukács ninth from the left, second row, among the troops of the Hungarian Commune, July 1919; drawing of Lukács from *Friss Ujsag*, April 1919 (Lukács Archives); Lukás with Béla Balász and friends, April 1909; Lukács at the age of 11 (Lukács Archives).

Photos on back cover, clockwise from top right: Hungarian Communist Party poster of 1946 'Intellectuals! You should join us!' (Institute of Party History); stills from the film *Our People Want Peace* (1951), showing Lukács addressing the Third World Peace Congress in Budapest (Film Archives of the Hungarian Film Institute); Lukács, on the left, welcoming Pablo Neruda at Ferihegy airport, Budapest, in 1951 (Photo Service of the Hungarian Telegraph Agency); Hungarian CP poster, 1946, proclaiming 'We are building the country for the people, not the capitalists' (Institute of Party History); Georg Lukács in 1971, very shortly before his death.

Grateful acknowledgement is made to Corvina Kiadó, Budapest, whose *György Lukács: his life in pictures and documents*, edited by Fekete and Karádi, is the source for all the photos listed above.

This edition of *Record of a Life* is a translation of the German edition, incorporating corrections, additional footnotes, and emendations and further entries to the Biographical Notes prepared by the editor.
    The interview with *New Left Review*, published here as an appendix, originally appeared in *NLR* 68, July-August 1971.

Translated from the German edition.
This translation first published by
Verso Editions, 15 Greek Street, London W1
© Verso Editions 1983

Interview with *New Left Review*
© NLR 1971

Filmset in Bem by
Comset Graphic Designs

Printed by The Thetford Press Ltd
Thetford, Norfolk

ISBN 0 86091 071 7
ISBN: 978-0-86091-771-7

CONTENTS

Editorial Note

When Georg Lukács was told that he was suffering from an incurable disease, he made extraordinary efforts to speed up his work on the corrections to *The Ontology of Social Being* so as to complete them. However, the rapid deterioration of his condition prevented him from attending to this task, which was of such overriding importance to him, with his customary intensity. It was at this time that he embarked on a sketch of his life, partly because of the relative freedom from theoretical effort which it entailed, and partly to fulfil the wish of his late wife. But once the sketch was finished, it became obvious that he lacked the strength to elaborate it further. The sheer exertion of writing was something to which his physical powers proved increasingly unequal. Since he could not endure the idea of a life without work, however, he followed the advice of pupils close to him and, with his strength rapidly fading, he recorded the events of his life on tape in 1971 by answering questions put to him by Erzsébet Vezérs and myself which we had based on the sketch *Lived Thought* (*Gelebtes Denken*). We had frequently made such taped interviews with Georg Lukács, particularly in 1969.

In assembling and editing these materials I had two aims in view. In the first place I wished to give a complete account of the *contents* of the interviews, to record everything Georg Lukács felt to be of value about himself and his age. Secondly, I was at pains to produce a readable and coherent text. For this reason, in addition to the usual stylistic corrections, I also made a series of structural changes. As far as possible I have ordered the material chronologically. Where passages are repeated I have opted for the more trenchant and complete version. In a number of places I have preferred earlier phrases and formulations to those of the 1971 interviews, chiefly because in 1969 Georg Lukács was still in full possession of his powers of expression. In places I have modified the questions to fit the answers and have treated the questions of the two interviewers as though they were one. I have also woven a number of theoretical statements into the biographical narrative where I felt that these convey better than any others an accurate picture of Georg Lukács as he was on the threshold of death.

It follows that in strict philological terms the present text is not 'authentic'. However, it is authentic in the sense that every utterance recorded is guaranteed by the statements on tape. I have resisted the temptation to publish anything I cannot actually document, even where my recollection of what was said is accurate in every detail. A further aspect of the authenticity of the text is that I have not made any 'selective' use of the material. Neither political nor any other considerations have induced me to censor Lukács's words in any way. During my work on the text I felt encouraged partly by the fact that I had performed similar tasks for Georg Lukács during his lifetime, and partly by my belief that I was proceeding very much in his spirit. Throughout his entire life he had felt a greater esteem for the sort of fidelity that is concerned with an accurate reproduction of the essentials of a form or a process than with literal fidelity and philological pedantry.

István Eörsi

Translator's Note

István Eörsi's introduction, 'The Right to the Last Word', has already appeared in English, in *New German Critique*, Number 23, Spring/Summer 1981. The present translation is new, although I have consulted the version by Geoffrey Davis and am grateful to *New German Critique* for permission to use the occasional turn of phrase.

Most of Lukács's own books referred to in the text are available in English translation. I have added some references where appropriate. I have also added some footnotes to the text where clarification seemed neccessary. These are marked: (*Trans.*); other footnotes are the editor's.

I wish to express my thanks to Professor Peter Evans of Southampton University, for providing me with useful information about Bartók; to Mrs Ilona Bellos, for help with some Hungarian words used in the original; to Andrea Reiter of Southampton University, for resolving some of the ambiguities of the German text; and to Alison Hamlin, for having typed the manuscript so efficiently at short notice.

Rodney Livingstone
Southampton

István Eörsi
The Right to the Last Word

After Georg Lukács was given his party card back in 1967 after ten years in the wilderness, he had the feeling that this new turn of events in his life made it desirable for him to make a statement. After all, he had been Minister of Culture at the time of the popular uprising in 1956 and he had not publicly dissociated himself subsequently from the Communists who had been abducted to Romania along with him. Despite official promises of good treatment, some of those men had not managed to survive their period of internment—to put it tactfully. Lukács himself was permitted to return to Budapest in 1957, but found himself type-cast for the role of 'chief ideological risk'. His writings could not be published in Hungary and everything was done to ensure that they would not appear abroad. This was how matters remained until preparations began for a reform of the Hungarian economy. In a new climate of destalinization it evidently became impossible to continue treating Georg Lukács as the carrier of a contagious ideological disease. In addition the conviction appears to have gained ground in leading party circles that it would be prudent to bring about a reconciliation before his death in order to avoid a repetition of the case of that other outstanding Hungarian Communist, Attila József,[1] who had been expelled from the party in the early thirties and with whom the reconciliation had been brought about after his death by means of all sorts of lies and falsifications.

'I don't know whether you have already heard that I have become a party member again?', Lukács said to me with that sly sidelong glance he used to have. I nodded, whereupon he began to list the reasons for his decision to join. First, there was the economic reform, which made a rapprochement objectively possible, even though he viewed the planned reforms, which the party considered extremely radical, as merely the first step on the road towards a genuine socialist transformation. And as a Marxist, he added he thought the economic infrastructure could not be modified significantly unless there were accompanying reforms on the political plane. For its part, the party wished to confine the changes to the economic sphere. Yet Lukács thought that the proposed reforms would provide some scope for dialogue.

In the second place, he had acted out of a sense of obligation towards his students. He himself could make a living from philosophy and was able at least to publish his writings abroad without serious administrative repercussions. His students, however, were for the most part condemned to silence, chiefly on account of his position, and hence forced to earn their living in unsuitable fields in which their talents were unable to thrive. The party had now promised to resolve their problems along with the question of his membership; they were to be offered academic posts as well as publishing opportunities.

Lukács was particularly proud of the third reason. He had received an assurance that he would be permitted to maintain his special ideological position and to voice it as the occasion arose. This opened up a new perspective, a new opportunity to exert influence that would enable him to function as an ideologist and also a party member without having to make any compromises. Having listened to all his arguments I said to him: 'It sounds to me as if it is not so much that Comrade Lukács has rejoined the party, as that the party has rejoined Comrade Lukács!' He gave me another of his sly glances and said, 'Unfortunately it would be premature to claim as much.'

* * * *

We both knew full well that, however seriously he took them, these three reasons simply represented a deeply buried human need whose articulation had now become historically possible. When he returned to Hungary from Romania in 1957 Lukács had written to the Hungarian Socialist Workers Party, saying that he continued to regard himself as a member. He never received a reply to this letter. Obviously no one had the courage to sign a letter expelling him even at the time when the propaganda campaign against him was at its height. 'I have stuck in their throats,' was Lukács's description of such situations: 'They can't swallow me and they can't spit me out.' Later he read in the official encyclopedia that he had been expelled from the party. The encyclopedia article had been written by a former pupil, József Szigeti. 'He only had one idea that he hadn't stolen from me, and that was that I ought to be pensioned off,' was Lukács's opinion of him.

The encyclopedia article cannot be regarded as an official reply. Although Lukács joked about it, there is no doubt that he felt slighted. He needed to be accepted by the party. 'My party, right or wrong' seems a strange sentence in the mouth of a philosopher, but he used it to explain why he had never resisted Stalinism, even during the purges. Not even inwardly! And of course he justified this on historical grounds—for example, in the interview he gave to *New Left Review* which did not appear until after his death.[2] He explicitly reiterated here his conviction that 'one could only fight effectively against fascism within the ranks of the Communist movement. I have not changed in this.' As a perceptive admirer of writers like Attila József and the Mann brothers, Lukács could only have stuck to his belief as late as 1970 from some deep psychological need which allowed him to place the facts in abeyance. He frequently explained his attitude by maintaining that, while the conflict between Stalin and Hitler was still unresolved, it was a moral necessity to postpone any criticism one might have of the Soviet Union. But even if that were defensible, why did he not break his silence subsequently? Why, even after his return to Hungary, in the inner circle of Hungarian Communists who had no personal experience of the Soviet Union, did he behave as if he were ignorant of the monstrous restrictions on physical and intellectual existence, of the atmosphere of universal fear, of the labour camps which also functioned perfectly as death camps, in a word, of the whole phenomenon of Stalinism in the Soviet Union? The answer to this question can be found in the continuation of the quotation from *New Left Review*: 'I have always thought that the worst form of socialism was better to live in than the best form of capitalism.' He expressed the same view even more categorically in the May 1969 number of the Vienna *Neues Forum*: 'But even the worst socialism is still better than the best capitalism. This only appears to be a paradox.' A man who defends such an opinion has no need of particular historical circumstances or moral considerations to justify his joining a party which is directing the establishment of a socialism as vaguely defined as this.

Lukács's psychological, one might even say his religious need is, in my view, a consequence of his origins, on the one hand, and of his intellectual position on the other.[3] The son of an immensely wealthy banker, he soon ceased to have any illusions about the moral and intellectual atmosphere in his parents' house or about the conventional attitudes that prevailed there, the 'spirit of protocol' as he termed it. He must have experienced a profound desire to become part of a large, meaningful community. The party as the 'bearer' of class consciousness—or, if you like, of the World Spirit—creates, albeit sometimes in a roundabout way, the 'conscious realization of one's species essence'. This gives the individual, as a component in this process, the best opportunity to raise himself to the consciousness of his own species essence. On the other hand, Lukács had won an international reputation for the books he had written in his idealist phase and, given the general level of his cultural and intellectual attainments, it must have been impossible to fit smoothly into a hierarchical movement based on discipline and sanctions. Thomas Mann, whose character Naphta in *The Magic Mountain* is known to have been based in part on Lukács, gave a very sensitive account of the subtle and even insoluble contradictions implicit in such a man and such a situation. Naphta is a Jesuit; that is to say, he is the ideological champion of an organization which is striving for world domination. But at the same time, his keen intellect places him outside the movement to which he dedicates his life. Although the movement guarantees his freedom, it views him with constant mistrust, provoked in the final analysis by his bold ideas whose rigorous logic leads him to the brink of heresy.

Lukács was no Jesuit and never managed to come to terms with the problems imposed by this inevitable intellectual remoteness. It constantly brought him, the theoretician, into conflict with a movement that was guided by tactical considerations and demanded discipline on tactical matters of the moment. It was hard for him to reconcile himself to a situation in which he was constantly being driven to the verge of an excommunication which in his eyes was tantamount to a sentence of death.

Since he was a theoretician, he responded to this situation with an idea, the so-called theory of the partisan. The most explicit statement of this theory dates from 1945 and is to be found in the context of a discussion of party literature. 'The party author is never a leader or a simple soldier, but always a partisan. That means that if he is a genuine party author he will experience a profound sense of identity with the great historical vocation of the party and with the great strategic line determined by it. But within this strategic line he must reveal his views with his own methods and on his own responsibility.' The pathos of this text, the generality of the formulations, make us suspect that they apply not just to literary authors, but also to the philosopher, to Georg Lukács himself. In another passage he speaks explicity of himself. 'I was compelled, therefore, to conduct a sort of partisan war on behalf of my philosophical ideas.'

The partisan theory aroused very little enthusiasm in party circles. Instead of narrowing the gulf between the philosopher and the movement, it widened it. In 1949, after the creation of a Communist monopoly of power, the partisan theory was an insurmountable bone of contention in the debate whose ultimate purpose was to eradicate Lukács's ideological position and influence. As usual, Lukács reacted to this debate with a formal act of self-criticism so as to forestall his excommunication. The partisan always concealed his weapon behind his back when the gaze of his leaders focused too sharply upon him.

What he calls 'loyalty' in his discussion of party literature, is something he always places above his own life's work and its moral and intellectual reputation. In bourgeois literature, Lukács writes, loyalty is often nothing more than a pathological, kitschy emotion. 'Party discipline, on the other hand, is a higher, abstract level of loyalty. A public figure's loyalty involves a deep and ideological relationship to one or other historically given tendency—and it remains loyalty even if, on a particular issue, there is not complete harmony.'

But what becomes of loyalty when the essential determinants of a particular historical tendency change or are even inverted? What happens, for example, when the revolutionary system of workers' councils, which the philosopher has loyally supported, is replaced by a bureaucratic police dictatorship? In such an event his steadfast loyalty has to confine itself to remaining true to the continuity of names and slogans. But if this loyal person chances to be a highly gifted philosopher of immense intellectual powers, he finds himself forced to insert this loyalty into a perspective of world history and to bridge the gulf between that perspective and reality by means of will-power and faith—by means of religious values, in short.

In Lukács's case, his critical sense was too highly developed to enable him to perform this intellectual *tour de force* in a way that was disagreeable to the dominant power. On two occasions in his later years, in 1956 and again in 1968, history even presented him with a painful reckoning, but he was unwilling to declare himself bankrupt. Only once, in autumn 1968, not long after the entry of the Warsaw Pact troops into Prague, did I hear him concede as much: 'I suppose that the whole experiment that began in 1917 has now failed and has to be tried again at some other time and place.' It is true that he never repeated this sentence, never wrote it down and never even mentioned it in his last interview, even though that interview was not destined for the public. He may partly have been unwilling to contemplate the fatal consequences this would have had in retrospect for the last five decades of his life.

This did not prevent him—and this is why the Lukácsian version of 'loyalty' is so unacceptable—from elaborating a theory about the Soviet Union which maintained that it was an atypical transition to socialism and led him to appeal for a 'reform' and 'renaissance' of Marxism. This appeal culminated in the slogan, 'Back to Marx!' It was an historical perspective designed to confer a meaning on the decades he had spent in the movement. But at the same time it forced actually existing socialism into an uncomfortable confrontation with Marx. The fulfilment of Marxist theory under modern conditions is a challenge that, with the best will in the world, actually existing socialism has simply been unable to meet. But by the same token it is a challenge that cannot be openly opposed. This is the reason why Lukács could be neither swallowed nor spat out.

Thus when he responded to the terrible hammerblows of history with the slogan, 'Back to Marx!', even attempting to specify some of the important tasks implicit in that slogan, he thereby developed a critical point of view tailor-made for himself and in complete harmony with his life and work. Extending his sense of loyalty back into the past (to Marx and to the Lenin-phase of the Revolution) as well as projecting it into the future, he assigned to faith a single yet decisive role in this critical project: that of providing the encouraging assurance that ideological, economic and organizational reforms from above could open a route from the austere Marxist present into an authentic Marxist future.

* * * *

In the last few months of his life, when Georg Lukács attempted to commit his autobiographical sketch *Gelebtes Denken* to paper, his intention was to depict his life as one that had been dominated by these aspirations over a period of decades. The circumstances in which he set about writing his memoirs were quite extraordinary. He was eighty-six and had known for some months that he was suffering from cancer. When the doctor broke the news to him, he wanted to know how long he would be able to continue to work. He wanted at all costs to revise the *Ontology*, to which he had devoted his last years and which had been severely criticized by some of his pupils. The labour of revision proceeded very slowly. This was not due primarily to his illness, but to the structure of the book itself, and in particular to the strict division into historical and systematic chapters, which confronted him with absolutely insuperable problems. A further complicating factor was the disastrous shift of perspective that resulted from the events of 1968. For Lukács it was like being a photographer whose subject suddenly moves. The effect was to intensify the already marked dichotomy between (conservative) system and (progressive) method so characteristic of his last phase.

Furthermore his illness undermined the harmonious functioning of his hitherto admirable constitution. It was not the cancer that wreaked the worst havoc, but the rapid progress of arteriosclerosis that made the greatest inroads on his physical strength and his powers of concentration. Some months later, at the beginning of 1971, he had to admit to himself that—in his own words—he was 'no longer competent to judge the *Ontology*'. But since he could not survive without work, his pupils suggested that he should write his autobiography.

This thought had long been in his mind. After all, his wife, Gertrud Bort-stieber, who died in 1963, had urged him to write such a book. He now set to work on it, albeit somewhat tentatively, because he did not wish to produce anything unreliable or to rely simply on his own memory. But he no longer felt strong enough to refresh his memory by research and to reinforce it with material from archives, libraries and journals. Finally, conscious of the increas-ing urgency of the task, he began to write. In a short time he completed in note form a fifty-seven-page typewritten text in German. There may have been two reasons for this solution to the problem. In the first place, it was his custom to produce a draft of every major piece of work, and so he was simply using a proven method. But also he may have been influenced by his realiza-tion that without proper access to libraries, he would not be able in any case to produce a thorough and factually reliable book. A draft in note form would enable the reader to research the details for himself.

This research began even before his death. For when it became apparent after he had produced the draft that he was no longer capable of the physical effort of writing, it became necessary to think of a new activity. This was how it came about that Erzsébet Vezér and I recorded onto tape the conversations we conducted with him between March and May 1971. The subject matter of our talks was *Gelebtes Denken*. We had the typewritten text before us and we questioned him on specific hints or turns of phrase which called for explana-tion or expansion. This resulted in a substantial Hungarian transcript some hundred pages long containing numerous repetitions and uninteresting details. The May conversations reflect that process of decay that was heart-rending to see, and which Lukács was also able to witness with his last spiritual strength. Nevertheless, many important issues were clarified by these conversations. The draft text was expanded, interpreted and concretized at many points. The labour which we had thought up out of sympathy and compassion for the dy-ing man was made meaningful not by our efforts, but by Lukács's own as-tounding mental exertion and will-power.

* * * *

I do not think it is necessary here to give a systematic chronological intro-duction to *Record of a Life*. I would like only to select some of the passages which highlight the author's last word on controversial and important issues. But I would like to preface these with a few comments on the personality which confronts us in this fragmentary record.

'In my case everything is a continuation of something else. I do not think that there are any non-organic elements in my development.' Lukács uttered these proud words in the course of our interviews. His autobiographical sketch is in fact organic and homogeneous in character. Even as a child Lukács rebelled against the conventional ethos of his upper-middle-class family. At the start of his career as a writer he was overwhelmed by the force of the critical spirit, the demand for totality and the 'revolutionism without revolution' represented by the great Hungarian poet, Endre Ady. Ady's influence subsequently helped him to arrive at a unique synthesis in his study of German philosophy: his conservative epistemology joined forces with a left-wing ethic. And this in turn gave him a vantage-point outside all possible versions of 'power-protected inwardness' (Thomas Mann's expression) from which to assess Hungarian and European politics.

The First World War intensified the contempt he felt for all existing powers, institutions and dominant ideologies which were driving the world towards catastrophe amid transports of enthusiasm. In his eyes the world was caught up in a condition of 'absolute sinfulness'. Only the Russian Revolution held out a glimmer of hope. Lukács, who had been prepared by his previous reading of Marx for a change of attitude, finally glimpsed a new perspective in the midst of universal conflagration. And after a brief but intense inner struggle, he joined the Communist movement to which he remained faithful for the rest of his life.

In *Gelebtes Denken* his conversion is rightly given the central importance it deserves: 'My moving towards the Communists was the greatest turning-point in my life.' Everything which went before—including the famous writings whose influence survives to the present day—only interests him to the extent that it helped to prepare the way for that turning-point. From that time on he regards the books belonging to his idealist phase as the works of an ideologist of undoubted gifts who nevertheless exerted a pernicious influence in many respects and therefore deserves the most severe criticism. His subsequent development is something he understands as a progress within Marxism, marked partly by his ever-increasing grasp of theory and partly by the sometimes sincere, sometimes formal adjustments to practice. This progress logically culminates in the call for a Marxist reform or renaissance and in the production of his great systematic works, the *Aesthetics* and the *Ontology*. These books, which could not even have been contemplated during Stalin's lifetime, can now be seen to signal the start and the first highpoint of that labour of reform.

At the age of eighteen Lukács had bidden farewell to his ambitions as a writer, and in later years he occasionally refused—with conscious indifference—to accept even the most elementary rules of publishing and editing. Now in his final autobiographical fragment he succeeds in making visible the unity—embracing a huge lifespan—of his personality. One example among many concerns his early rebellion against his mother about which we can read the following: 'Guerrilla warfare with my mother: episodes of being locked in the dark room, when I was around eight. Father: set free without apologizing.' In the course of the recorded conversations Lukács added the following explanations:

'I was involved in guerrilla warfare with my mother. She was very strict with us. The house had a wood store, a room where it was always dark. One of my mother's favourite forms of punishment was to lock us up in it until we asked to be forgiven. My brother and sister always asked promptly for forgiveness, whereas I made a sharp distinction. If she locked me in at 10 a.m., I would say I was sorry at 10.05, after which all was in order. My father used to return home at half-past one. Whenever possible, my mother took care to see to it that there was no tension in the house when he arrived. Hence I would never apologize if I was locked in after 1 o'clock, because I knew that I would always be let out at 1.25 whether I had done so or not.'

The logic of this passage throws some light on the later mechanism of self-criticism. The child-guerrilla and the adult partisan were in agreement that self-criticism should only be the preferred route if Daddy was not due to come home on time. After 1956, when he couldn't be expelled from the party (because he had not been allowed to join it) and there was no danger of his being arrested, he weaned himself from the practice of self-criticism entirely. Lukács was very well aware of this aspect of his character. He makes this comment on his childhood rebellions: 'Resistance at first—then submission with the conviction: of no concern to me; if I want the grown-ups to leave me in peace: submission, with the feeling that the whole business is quite meaningless.' When he later tries to analyse why he had to recant the Blum Theses shortly after writing them in 1929, it is significant that he should defend his action in the following terms: 'Attempt to restrict the inevitable criticism to the Hungarian Party...Hence unconditional surrender on the Hungarian front (where anyway prospects of success were more or less nil).' The Blum theses outline the possibility of a democratic dictatorship of workers and peasants for the Hungarian Communist movement instead of simply a dictatorship of the proletariat. Lukács was forced to recant them in order to defend his party membership and even his life. The calculation he makes is the same as in the dark room. In both cases we catch a glimpse of the same sidelong glance.

* * * *

Even today, after so many books have appeared on the world of the Gulags, the few fragmentary sentences on the trials in the Soviet Union have a disturbing effect. 'Period of the great extermination of cadres. My position (parallel: Bloch). Good luck in the face of catastrophe (a) Bukharin-Radek 1930; (b) the Hungarian movement; (c) my apartment.' Hence Lukács perceives the main reason for his own personal survival in the fortunate coincidence of three circumstances. First, he had refused to meet Bukharin and Radek in 1930 when they were keen to establish contact with him. Had he met them in 1930, he believed, he would have been liquidated for it eight years later. He was always proud of his clairvoyance and had in fact no reason to be ashamed of it. He had always thought Radek an unscrupulous man and Bukharin's ideas he had sharply criticized in the mid-twenties, i.e. at a time when the latter was at the zenith of his power. So it was not simply opportunism that made him avoid a meeting with the two men. But a more damaging judgement on the age could scarcely be imagined than one which points out that such a meeting would logically and naturally have led to his death.

The second source of his good fortune lay in the fact that he was forced out of the Hungarian movement after the fiasco of the Blum Theses. Had he remained a member of the Hungarian Communist Party he would have been eliminated either by Béla Kun, its leader, or by the latter's enemies when Kun himself fell victim to the purges. Lukács had already indicated that Kun might have had some such intention after the collapse of the Hungarian Soviet Republic. He describes how Kun had left him and Ottó Korvin behind to organize illegally in Hungary under completely untenable conditions. Korvin, who had been People's Commissar for Internal Affairs, was the most hated member of the Republic among the supporters of the White Terror and was easily recognizable because of a physical deformity. Lukács too was a well-known and conspicuous figure. Both men had been opposed to Kun on many questions within the party from the outset. In *Gelebtes Denken* Lukács comments on the party's decision that he and Korvin should remain in Hungary with the words 'Suspicions about Kun'. The implication is clear. In conversation with his students Lukács went further than expressing his suspicions. He was completely convinced that Béla Kun had destined Korvin and himself for the role of martyrs. In Korvin's case he had actually succeeded. When one reflects that Kun himself fell victim to the movement, Lukács's comment becomes even more uncanny.

The third fortunate circumstance was his apartment. In the recorded interview Lukács remarks on this: 'In addition, and this is perhaps a very cynical observation, I had very inferior living quarters and they were less attractive to the NKVD.'

This sketch of the three fortunate circumstances responsible for his survival seems even more horrifying today than a routine list of disasters and tragic cases. However, looking back at the period Lukács discerns a glimmer of hope: the Seventh Congress of the Comintern, at which the Popular Front policy was proclaimed. 'Objectively, the beginning of the end of the time of crisis... Personally, not without difficulties (two arrests). Despite this my relationship with Gertrud at its most human and harmonious. No "beautifying", no "optimism". But feeling not just that I was approaching what I imagined to be my right path—Marxism as historical ontology—but also the ideological perspectives which would make it possible to make some of these tendencies a reality.'

Nowadays, the excessive objectivity with which Lukács reports on his own inner serenity while surveying the story of these terrors and their motives appears horrifying and grotesque. He could only do this because, while not actually approving of the Stalinist purges, he showed himself at least ready to accept them. The intrigues, denunciations and the deathly hunt for flats are dismissed as subjective side-effects. I have already pointed out that for Lukács and the other consistent representatives of the contemporary left the threat of Hitlerism ruled out any ideological and above all practical resistance from the outset. It goes without saying that practical opposition would have been hopeless in any case. In the recorded interviews Lukács gives a clue to the ideological subterfuges which enabled him to incorporate the trials into his worldview.

'It cannot be maintained that we did not disapprove of the trials tactically. Tactically we were neutral. The trial of Danton during the French Revolution had also involved many legal irregularities. And if Stalin used the same weapons against Trotsky as Robespierre had used against Danton, this cannot be judged according to current conditions since at the time the crucial question was on which side America would intervene in the war.' I asked, 'Do you think that the analogy between Robespierre and Danton and Stalin and Bukharin can still be upheld?' To this Lukács replied: 'No. But I do think that it was an excusable way for a Hungarian émigré living in Russia to have thought about it at the time.' We know from subsequent statements that he changed his mind about this and for what reason. Khrushchev's reasoning convinced him that the trials were *superfluous*, because the opposition had already been powerless at the time of the trials.

It is of course a known fact that in the crucial debate about the possibility of building socialism in one country, Lukács opted for Stalin's side of the argument as opposed to Trotsky's, and that he sided with Stalin on other issues in the 1920s. Despite this his later statements make rather curious reading today. After all, they furnish ideological justification for the most inhuman and, morally and politically, the most negative expressions of the Stalin era. When he attempts to distinguish the Stalin death camps from other death camps, he provides us with a fascinating illustration of the schizophrenia of the Communist intelligentsia. In his eyes Stalin's death camps were now a world-historical necessity, now surface pimples on the blooming face of the totality. Nevertheless we cannot withhold our sympathy from him entirely, since he steadfastly refuses to stylize and gloss over his past and instead confesses his monstrous illusions unflinchingly, even though the lessons of the past few decades, the dictates of public opinion and numerous personal examples, might have induced him to try to present events in a different light. On the other hand, his deeply rooted attitudes stand in harsh contrast to what he calls the 'reform of Marxism' and the 'Marxist renaissance'. Since his development does in fact contain no non-organic element, his aim is to salvage his entire life, his past and his future all at once. This is why he stands in need of a faith which will enable him to represent his entire development with all his mistakes and even his sins as meaningful and at the very least subjectively necessary.

* * * *

The picture that Lukács paints, both in the interviews we recorded and in *Gelebtes Denken*, of his dealings with the Hungarian uprising of 1956 and his relations with Imre Nagy is revealing both politically and morally. As was his wont, he characterized his behaviour according to the notion of a war on two fronts. 'So my position was clear: opposition to Rákosi, to any illusions of a particular, internal reform of his regime, and opposition also to bourgeois liberal reforms (which were widely advocated even in circles close to Imre Nagy).' In 1968 he adopted a similar view. Under the impact of events in Czechoslovakia he wrote a comprehensive analysis which he submitted to the Central Committee of the Hungarian Socialist Workers' Party. In that study, which has remained unpublished to this day, he made the following statement: 'If the alternative of bourgeois democracy were to gain the upper hand as the result of a socio-economic crisis in any state governed by Stalin's epigones, it would be possible—without being a prophet—to foretell the future with a high degree of accuracy. Within a short space of time, the CIA would have succeeded in creating a new Greece.' The quintessence of his opinion was summed up in the single sentence: 'The real alternatives are Stalinism or socialist democracy.'

Lukács's constantly repeated criticism of Imre Nagy is that he had no programme. Even in the context of Nagy's first period as Prime Minister (1953–1954) he wrote, 'Expected little of Imre Nagy. During his first, brief period of leadership—no contact with him (his lack of programme). This remained true even after the Twentieth Congress.' The same idea occurs also in connection with 1956. 'Nagy: no programme. Hence my position was purely ideological.' In the recorded interviews he added: 'Obviously he had a programme for reform in very general terms. But he had absolutely no idea how to implement it in particular spheres of government, what it involved in concrete terms, or what the specific rights and duties of individual Communists should be.' Lukács blamed the absence of a programme for the events that steamrollered the government, eventually forcing it to withdraw from the Warsaw Pact. Together with Zoltán Szántó he voted against this withdrawal in the six-man Party Executive. The others supported the government's decision. When asked whether he opposed the withdrawal from the Warsaw Pact on principle or for tactical reasons, Lukács replied: 'Initially, of course, I was opposed in principle. I was quite simply in favour of Hungary's membership of the Warsaw Pact. But I also took the view that we ought not to give the Russians an excuse to intervene in Hungarian affairs.' Actually Lukács held the unique opinion that the Warsaw Pact would simultaneously protect Hungary from both a capitalist and a Soviet intervention.

Hence Lukács's disappointment stemmed not only from Nagy's failure to formulate a programme, but also from disagreements over their respective programmes. The pressure of the popular movement, as well as an internal party tug-of-war, pushed Nagy after inner struggles into declaring his support for Hungarian neutrality. Lukács could not agree to this without infringing the inner laws governing his own life and a process of development extending over decades. This, rather than the absence of a detailed programme, is why he described his own position as 'purely ideological'. In the course of the interviews he added the following: 'The fact is that I think of 1956 as a great spontaneous movement. It was a spontaneous movement which stood in need of a certain ideology. I declared my willingness to contribute towards formulating this in a series of lectures.'

But if he did find himself so far away from Nagy's position, why was he prepared to play a leading role during the events of 1956? In *Gelebtes Denken* he has this to say: '...he had the power (or the popular support) to keep the spontaneous (and highly heterogeneous) movement running along socialist lines. Hence my membership, indeed my acceptance of a ministry, in order to help.' Therefore he sees their differences as differences within socialism even though there was no reconciling their views until 'late in November', that is to say, when they were both interned in Romania. The reasons for this reconciliation were perhaps moral rather than political. After all, the significance of the moral element in human relationships is often enhanced by the common experience of imprisonments and the burden of external pressures. In the interviews Lukács comments: 'My interrogators said to me that they knew I was no follower of Imre Nagy and so there was no reason why I should not testify against him. I told them that as soon as the two of us, Imre Nagy and myself, were free to walk around Budapest, I would be happy to make public my opinion of all of Nagy's activities. But I was not free to express an opinion about my fellow-prisoners.'

* * * *

At a time in Hungary when Georg Lukács has been effectively nationalized and turned into an acceptable figure, it may well be that the most interesting passages of *Gelebtes Denken* and the recorded interviews are those dealing with his situation and his ideas after his return from internment in Romania. The last period of his life, between 1957 and 1971, divides into two distinct phases. Up to his re-admittance into the party in 1967, he was regarded albeit to a decreasing extent as a public enemy who was 'easy meat for the sectarians', as he put it in *Gelebtes Denken*. He continues: 'I stick to my guns. In publications abroad (not possible in Hungary).' Around 1964 he wrote to János Kádár declaring that since his *Aesthetics* could not appear in Hungary it would be published first in West Germany, without approval if need be. In the interviews Lukács recounts his attitude: 'The result was that I received a summons. What was the name of the guy in the Politburo? Szirmai. I was summoned by Szirmai and told that they would gladly give me an exit visa if I wanted it. I said to him, "Look, all the power is in your hands. You can do with me whatever you want. If a policeman puts his hand on my shoulder when I leave this room, I shall be a prisoner unable to do anything. But you do not have the power to compliment me out of Hungary just when it suits you."'

Since the struggle between the state and an intelligentsia that insists on the right to its own opinion is not defined unambiguously in law, the situation varies according to the balance of political forces at any given time, as well as the ideology and character of the conflicting parties. In the Stalin era Lukács was 'absolutely cynical', as he himself once put it, in resorting automatically to the method of self-criticism. He changed both his field of action and his nationality in accordance with the immediate demands of the situation. That is to say, he accepted the need for a continual series of tactical retreats in order to safeguard his own life and his activity in the party.

When Stalinism was forced in its turn into a number of tactical retreats after 1956, at a time when the ageing Lukács was deemed invulnerable thanks to his international reputation, he occasionally allowed himself to go onto the offensive. In the process he set an example to other intellectuals struggling for freedom of speech in socialist states. In an interview he stated that he published as much abroad as he managed to smuggle out. When I asked him whether his right to do so was ever challenged, he replied: 'No one ever questioned it. After peace was re-established I discussed the matter with Aczél. What I said to him was, "Listen, as long as you forbid me to publish abroad I shall continue to smuggle my works out without a qualm. I do not acknowledge your right to prevent the publication of my books in German. If you give me a guarantee that my writings can be published abroad, I shall relinquish my right to smuggle with the greatest pleasure."'

The expression 'the right to smuggle' throws a harsh light on the uncertainties of the legal position. Morally the situation is unambiguous. The supreme duty of a writer towards himself and his ideas is to defend his writings with all the weapons at his disposal. Writers who renounce their rights resemble those radical demonstrators who stop at the crossroads just because the lights are red. However, the legal position is less clear. Both oppressor and oppressed have a moral code, but only the oppressor has a legal system. Despite this the state cannot, or can only partly, consolidate its domination of intellectual life by juridical means, since the oppressor's interest in controlling civil rights cannot be codified completely for reasons of ideology, propaganda or foreign policy. Hence in the existing socialist societies a series of half-hearted and contradictory laws are in effect supplemented by common law. Because of threatened but rarely codified sanctions, it is not *customary* to smuggle manuscripts abroad. For that reason smuggling manuscripts is a *crime*. Perhaps the most important achievement of Georg Lukács in the last phase of his life was to have broken with the common law on this issue.

'After peace was re-established' the war was carried on by other methods and in a different tone. The sensitive points in the relations between Lukács and the state authorities continued to give trouble. One such sensitive point was that of his students. As a born educator Lukács always felt the need to be surrounded by his students. The following note, taken from the period immediately following his return home in 1945, is symptomatic: 'Very important: contacts and conversations. My first students. Discover myself through teaching (Gertrud's influence). Character: seminar-like. Official opinions not decisive at that period. Hence, gradually: a highly promising young generation.'

As early as the debate of 1949 Lukács had to be protected against the damaging influence of his students. After 1967 this was to be repeated. The aim was to convince him once and for all that his true pupils were not those he thought of as such, but the spokesmen for the official cultural policy who constantly appealed to his authority and invoked his name to authenticate continuously changing ideological needs. 'I told Aczél,' he once said, 'that my fate would be similar to that of Krupskaya, whom Stalin once threatened to sack as Lenin's widow and replace with someone else.' In a sense this joke became reality after Lukács's death. The majority of his students were expelled from cultural life and some of them even opted to live abroad. At present the field is dominated by those of them with whom he had had a nominal relationship at best. These 'students' ensure Lukács's devaluation in the eyes of the public. Nowadays there is hardly a public statement or authoritative article on cultural affairs without its quota of citations from Lukács. The fast expanding army of his 'students' swarms round him like flies around meat.

There are many features of Lukács's life and works that justify this abuse of his name. Quotations can be found in his writings to fit all sorts of occasions. Conservative ideas predominate in his political and aesthetic *system*. One need 'only' discard his *method of thought* and he can be transformed into an acceptable thinker without difficulty. For it was his method of thought that made such an intolerable revolutionary of him. An illuminating instance of this is provided by the last ideological battle of his lifetime. It involved the question of continuity and discontinuity. In *Gelebtes Denken* there is only a brief reference to this: 'Polemic against continuity.' The interview with Lukács published in *New Left Review* in 1971 deals with this question in some detail. Lukács argues that according to De Tocqueville and Taine the French Revolution does not represent a discontinuity in French history at all, because it merely continues the centralizing tradition of the French state which runs from Louis XIV through Napoleon and on to the Second Empire. On such a view the Revolution is no more than a link in the chain of events. Lenin, on the other hand, always stressed the discontinuous elements in history. For example, he regarded the New Economic Policy as a total change of course from War Communism. Lenin's approach was reversed by Stalin, who represented every tactical change of direction as the logical consequence of the previous line, as if each change were the still more perfect continuation of earlier successes. Since Stalinism still survives we find ourselves confronted by this question: 'Should continuity with the past be emphasized within a perspective of reforms, or on the contrary should the way forward be a sharp rupture with Stalinism? I believe that a complete rupture is necessary. That is why the question of discontinuity in history has such importance for us.'

The spokesmen of the party were right to deploy against Lukács their programme of continuity, that is to say, their conviction that the evolution of Stalinism into its opposite should take place in a continuous manner. Lukács's insistence on discontinuity was incompatible with a reformist critique of existing economic and political conditions in the socialist states, and threatened revolutionary consequences. However, his demand for a complete rupture cannot be reconciled with another of his own formulae: 'the foundation: not opposition, but reform.' That is to say, his view of the world, his solidarity with actually existing socialism, i.e. with the system in which he created his universe, is often inconsistent with his method of thought, which entails the constant overthrow of that system. This contradiction is a recurrent theme in a number of his important works. He often fails to accept the conclusions his method makes possible. That is why his work is so impatiently rejected by so many different people, instead of being developed and extended. For the same reasons his books are exposed to a variety of misinterpretations, particularly since the author is no longer there to correct them.

Towards the end of his autobiographical sketch Georg Lukács formulated what he regarded as the most pressing task for posterity. In this passage his words assume an almost exaggerated solemnity and a programmatic passion. Obviously he affirms the need for reforms as quickly as possible. But the harshness of the tone and the remorseless clarity of his words exclude any bland or optimistic interpretation, let alone any reconciliation with existing reality. 'Both great systems in crisis. *Authentic* Marxism the only solution. Hence in the socialist states Marxist ideology must provide a critique of the existing state of affairs and help to promote reforms which are becoming increasingly urgent.'

That was Georg Lukács's final word.

1

Childhood And Early Career

Interviewer: I think it will be best if we proceed chronologically. I should like to use *Gelebtes Denken* as a starting point.

Lukács: In my own view my development advanced step by step and so I would agree that a chronological approach is the best since all the events in my life are closely linked. So the only logical place to begin is in fact at the start of the process.

Int: The first two sentences about your childhood run as follows: *'Of pure Jewish family. For that very reason: the ideologies of Judaism had no influence whatever on my spiritual development.'* I don't understand why you say 'for that very reason'.

G.L.: The Leopoldstadt families were completely indifferent to all religious matters. Religion only interested us as a matter of family convention, since it played a certain role at weddings and other ceremonies. I do not know whether I have already told the story about my father from the early days of the Zionist movement. He said that when the Jewish state was established he would like to be made consul in Budapest. In a word, we all regarded the Jewish faith with complete indifference.

Int: Do I understand from this that you lived in Leopoldstadt? Where exactly?

G.L.: I did not actually live in Leopoldstadt, but in the Andrassy Street district. At Andrassy St. 107 and, later, at Nagy János St. 11.

Int: So the term 'Leopoldstadt' stands really for a social group?

G.L.: The area around Andrassy Street used to lie on the edge of Leopoldstadt. It was where the Leopoldstadt upper crust lived.

Int: There is a reference here to another anecdote: 'Story about Nanny.'

G.L.: The story points to something important. I completely rejected everything to do with the rules of conventional behaviour. In my view this even included contact with uncles and aunts. My mother claims that as a child

I always said, '*I never say hello to strange visitors. I didn't invite them*'. Convention starts as soon as you accept that visitors have to be greeted. Despite this I have evidence that I could be reasonable even when I was still a child, provided adults found the right way to approach me. We had an old Nanny who used to look after us when we played. I once asked her, where some toy or other had disappeared to. She answered: 'Georg, it is where you left it.' I was deeply impressed by this reply, since up till then I had only heard nonsense from grown-ups. For example, I had to say 'Your servant' (*Küss die Hand*) to Aunt Irma. The fact that the toy was where I had left it was entirely rational, that was something I could accept. And in actual fact I do not recall being a very untidy child. It was a model of rationality I could use to counter the insistence on conventional behaviour. Another aspect of convention was its hypocrisy. Our parents took us children on a tour of Europe. We went to Paris and London and wherever we went, they took us to picture galleries. I thought this the height of hypocrisy since galleries contained absolutely nothing of interest to me. On the other hand, I knew that London boasts an excellent zoo and so I thought that was where we ought to go. I resented it terribly when my brother meekly assented to the gallery and displayed no desire to go to the zoo.

Int: How did you come finally to accept the need to greet visitors?

G.L.: I became fed up with the great row that inevitably accompanied every visitor and decided that it cost me nothing to greet them. Why shouldn't I say 'Your servant' to Aunt Irma? That was protocol, of course, but why should I quarrel with my parents because of it?

Int: And I suppose you reacted in the same way when your mother locked you up in the wood store?

G.L.: I was involved in guerrilla warfare with my mother. She was very strict with us. The house had a wood store, a room where it was always dark. One of my mother's favourite forms of punishment was to lock us up in it until we asked to be forgiven. My brother and sister always asked promptly for forgiveness whereas I made a sharp distinction. If she locked me in at 10 a.m., I would say I was sorry at 10.05, after which all was in order. My father used to return home at half-past one. Whenever possible, my mother took care to see to it that there was no tension in the house when he arrived. Hence I would never apologize if I was locked in after 1 o'clock, because I knew that I would always be let out at 1.25 whether I had done so or not.

Int: You tell another story about learning to read which is also very revealing.

G.L.: Yes, that is an amusing story. My brother was a year older than I and he was receiving private tuition in reading. I used to sit down at the table opposite him and I also learnt to read from looking at the book upside down. What is more I learnt to read more quickly that way than my elder brother. After that I was not allowed to join the lessons and it was not until more than a year later that I was permitted to learn to read normally.

Int: Have you any memories of your early reading?

G.L.: I was first influenced by a book when I was nine years old. It was the Hungarian prose translation of the *Iliad*. It made a powerful impression on me because I identified with Hector and not Achilles. At the same time I also read *The Last of the Mohicans*. Both books had a great importance for me. The reason was connected with the fact that my father, although a very decent, respectable man, believed, as a bank director, that success was the true criterion of right action. I learnt from these two books that success is no true criterion and that it is the failures who are in the right. This emerged even more clearly in *The Last of the Mohicans* than in the *Iliad* because the Indians who had been conquered and oppressed were manifestly in the right, and not the Europeans. Then it was a stroke of luck for me that we learnt English first, and not French as was customary in Budapest at the time. My father was a great Anglophile and so we read books like *Tales from Shakespeare* which impressed me deeply. We also read Mark Twain's novels *Tom Sawyer* and *Huckleberry Finn*. These books enabled me to recognize the existence of ideals in life. What appeared in negative form from my early reading now assumed positive shape. I gleaned an idea about how a human being should live. My childhood ideal was that human beings should live like Tom Sawyer. Later on I was influenced also by Auerbach's novel about Spinoza, particularly the story of Spinoza's struggle against religion and religious ethics.[1]

Int: There is a further reference to your childhood. When talking about your schooldays, you mentioned that you assumed that your classmates were somehow superior to your brother and the boys you knew socially. You then note, 'Hope of the poor—despite the scepticism induced by my reading.'

G.L.: My scepticism was directed at the legend that poor boys were good scholars and outstanding people. This myth was purveyed on every page of De Amicis' book, which was much read by children at the time.[2] The only efforts I made at the Gymnasium sprang from my wish to enjoy the benefits of being regarded as a good pupil by the teachers without my classmates thinking me a swot. These two ideas had somehow to be reconciled. I recall a trivial episode that took place when I was in the Fifth Form. One of the boys had gone up to the front to speak to the teacher about his marks or something of the sort, and when he returned to his place he hit me in the stomach, without being noticed by the teacher. I retaliated with a punch in the back. This was seen by the teacher, who made a song and dance about it. I told him that I had been punched first. I must confess that I still feel ashamed of this today. The fact that I always observe the proprieties in public life is partly explained by the terrible shame I felt on that occasion as a fifth-former. I believe that the experience of such feelings of shame can be a positive force in life.

Int: Childhood friends?

G.L.: As a child I had no friends at all. And even at school there was no one for years on end to whom I felt particularly close. To a certain extent I was on good terms with my elder brother's tutors. Of course these tutors, especially if they were women, were treated as inferior beings in wealthy bourgeois families. Hence I used to take sides with the governess against my brother. The whole relationship was very typical of Leopoldstadt at the time. The children were forced to obey the governesses, but deep down they despised them, regarding them as educated servants. At the time we had nothing but French and English governesses. I always identified with my brother's governesses. I had no need to apply myself. I was tremendously fortunate in being able to learn with great facility. I had normally finished all my homework by half past three or a quarter to four in the afternoon. While I was at the Gymnasium I remember that my brother was normally my mother's favourite. There is an amusing story connected with that too. Because he was favoured he was expected also to be the good pupil, the pride of the family. When he first went to a public Gymnasium as a fifth-former and then into the Sixth Form, things turned out to be the reverse of what was believed. My mother's theory was that I was very diligent and my brother lazy, and this was why I was a good pupil and he a bad one. In reality, however, I finished all my homework by 3.30 or 3.45 every day and then went cycling, while my brother would still be at his books when I returned home at seven o'clock.

Int: Did the Jewish problem have any impact on your development at secondary school?

G.L.: No, neither favourable nor unfavourable.

Int: Might it not have had an impact in the sense that it made things difficult for you even though you were unaware of it at the time?

G.L.: At the Protestant Gymnasium I attended, children from Leopoldstadt played the role of the aristocracy. So I was regarded there as a Leopoldstadt aristocrat, not as a Jew. Hence the problems of the Jews never came to the surface. I always realized that I was a Jew, but it never had a significant influence on my development.

Int: I put the question because I recently heard that Gyula Illyés once said he felt a great respect for Comrade Lukács because the Jewish longing for vengeance had never played a part in his development into a revolutionary.

G.L.: That was because I never felt myself to be a Jew. I accepted my Jewishness as a fact of birth and that was the end of the matter.

Int: Nevertheless, it is possible to distinguish between the way a person regards a matter and the way it is viewed by others.

G.L.: Of course, distinctions were drawn between Jews and non-Jews in Hungary at that time. I was lucky enough to win the Krisztina Lukács Prize. Until the envelope was opened no one had any idea who might have won the competition. As a result I was immediately accepted by Beöthy and Alexander and the members of their clique. For the next generation, as soon as the dictatorship began, the whole issue became much more difficult. Before the dictatorship it was not a serious problem.

Int: Perhaps we can now turn to the early years of your career.[3]

G.L.:* To give an account of my so-called literary career I would have to begin when I was around fifteen years of age. Like ever child I read voraciously. Even before then there were books that made a lasting impression on me, but it was not until I was fifteen that I first entertained the idea that I might myself become a writer.

This process was set in motion by two factors. The first was foreign. As a liberal reader of the *Neue Freie Presse*, my father happened to have in his private collection a copy of Max Nordau's *Degeneration*. I read the book and came to understand what real decadence meant in the work of Ibsen, Tolstoy, Baudelaire, Swinburne and others. Fortunately Nordau provided literal quotations of the poems of Baudelaire, Swinburne, and so on. I was carried away completely and of course became a staunch supporter of Ibsen and Tolstoy who were despised by my family. I acquired their work in the little Reclam editions and so by the age of fifteen I arrived at what was for the time an extremely avant garde Western position. As a youth I dreamt of writing plays in the spirit of Ibsen and Hauptmann. The second, local factor was the result of a coincidence. It so happened that my sister went to the same school as the sister of Marcell Benedek. They visited us and so I met Marcell Benedek himself. I shall not report the details of our encounter since he has told that story in his own autobiography. At all events my literary activities were greatly stimulated by this friendship and also indirectly by the personality of Elek Benedek whose influence upon me was not precisely literary, but rather of an ethical nature. I must say that Elek Benedek's own writings never spoke to me at all, not even at the time. But I was impressed by his puritanical way of always standing up for his own opinions, even where these brought him into conflict with his own society in which success, even when gained through compromises or even worse, remained the only standard of human values. Neither then nor compromises or even worse, remained the only standard of human values. Neither then nor later did I have any interest in the substance of his ideas, but the fact of his commitment to them meant that in my youth Elek Benedek as a moral person exercised a profound influence on my way of thinking. A further element in the process was the fact that I was a regular reader of *Hét* (The Week).

As a result of all these things I started to write plays in the manner of Hauptmann and Ibsen. Thank God, all trace of them has now disappeared. I'm sure they were appallingly bad. When I was about eighteen I burned all my manuscripts. From then on I had a secret criterion for the limits of literature: anything I could write myself was necessarily bad. Literature began where I felt that something had been written which I could not emulate. I made some use of this secret criterion and it was of benefit to me in that it led to my writing four or five very bad plays. A further consequence was that writing led me to interest myself in the literary criticism of the time. Alfred Kerr's impressionistic style influenced me greatly. Through family connections I received commissions while I was still in the Sixth Form to write reviews of plays for *Magyar Szalon* (The Hungarian Salon), a paper with an extremely small circulation. The main point of the exercise was that the editor wanted to make sure that he received a ticket for the première. He would attend the first night and give me the ticket for the second performance. In this way I came to write reviews once a month in the style of Alfred Kerr.

Int: Anonymously?

G.L.: No. These reviews were all signed. They are all listed in the Oltványi Bibliography. This phase of my literary development came to a climax when my youthful arrogance led me at the age of eighteen to oppose the unanimous view of the Hungarian critics of the time. The National Theatre had put on some plays by Sándor Bródy, his cycle *Idylls of the Kings*, which proved a resounding flop. Bródy was condemned as unpatriotic and he was accused of having falsified Hungarian history. I was greatly taken with these plays and I made no bones about conveying my enthusiasm. The result was that Sándor Bródy tried to get in touch with me by means of a common acquaintance. I think he was disappointed when he discovered that the only critic who had praised him was still a schoolboy.

*Int:** Ady too defended the *Idylls of the King* from Oradea.

*G.L.:** That is quite possible, but I had no idea of that at the time. At all events the Budapest critics were generally negative. Bródy swallowed his disappointment and suggested that I should contribute occasional articles to *Jövendö* (The Future) which he was about to launch. I did so and, still in the style of Alfred Kerr, I published one article on Hauptmann and another on Herman Bang.[4] This was the actual beginning of my literary career, but it was soon interrupted because I fell out with Bródy. He wanted me to write something on Merezhkowsky's book on Leonardo da Vinci, about which he was very enthusiastic. It was a book I disliked intensely. When one is young, one is not always very diplomatic. We quarrelled and I gave up writing for *Jövendö*. I have no doubt that we might have become reconciled since Bródy was not a man to bear grudges. If I had gone to see him after a few weeks, he would have welcomed me back. But in the meantime a change took place which brought to a close the phase which had lasted from my fifteenth to my eighteenth year—if indeed it may be thought proper to use such words to describe a period of juvenile dilettantism.

At university I made the acquaintance of László Bánóczi and this had an effect comparable to the moral change brought about earlier by the personality of Elek Benedek. I now found myself strongly influenced by Bánóczi's circle. An explanation for my susceptibility may lie in the fact that the Protestant Gymnasium had abysmal intellectual standards. I was searching for a path of my own, even though my work as a critic was as incompetent as my writing. The Bánóczi family taught me that it was necessary to study theory and history in a scholarly and serious but unmechanical manner. László Bánóczi's father, József, was an old gentleman with a refined sensibility, who had now become resigned. He was a not particularly talented yet intelligent man who, rather like Anatole France, responded to dilettantism of any kind with an epicurean irony. I now came to the conclusion that the whole of literature was worthless and that the impressionist style I had copied from Kerr was mere froth. So I did not return to Bródy after our quarrel mainly because I had resolved to study. From then on I did not write or publish anything for around four years. This apprenticeship went hand-in-hand with other activity which I do not wish to describe in detail, since it is public knowledge. This was the founding of the Thalia Society, together with Bánóczi, Marcell Benedek and Sándor Hevesi. This was one of the most important aspects of my apprenticeship, since, even though I never became a producer, I learnt a tremendous amount about dramatic techniques and forms from seeing how the texts were brought to life on the stage. I had very good personal relations with all those young actors like Dobi, János Doktor and Rózsi Forgács. We would meet every evening in Café Baross and Pethes would always preside over our gatherings. We called him the Prince and deferred to his authority in all questions affecting the theatre. In a word, there now began a comprehensive period of study, with the thorough reading of theoretical works. The result was that my impressionistic criticism was replaced by an approach based on German philosophy with a tendency towards aesthetics. It was at this time that I first studied Kant and then contemporary philosophers like Dilthey and Simmel.

Int: The name of Pethes comes up in your autobiographical sketch as a man you regarded as a leader.

G.L.: Well, leader is not a good word. We called him Prince. His judgement on all theatrical matters was infallible. If he said that the right hand had to be raised and the left should not be allowed to drop, you can be sure that he was absolutely right. We certainly believed in his infallibility. We admired him without reservation and in the Thalia phase he was undoubtedly our model.

Int: You came to know each other at the time when the Thalia society was being established?

G.L.: Pethes, Ódry and other actors were on friendly terms with Sándor Hevesi. We asked him to found the Thalia and act as manager. This gave rise to a coffeehouse society in which Pethes, who never acted in the Thalia, played the role of uncrowned king.

Int: Did he actively support it?

G.L.: With advice, certainly. It must be stressed that he was an actor who worked in a highly conscious manner, emphasizing the conscious, assertive side of acting. This encouraged an atmosphere in which matters could be thrashed out and he could play the dominant part.

Int: Comrade Lukács, what were your activities apart from organization?

G.L.: Apart from organization I had no activities. I experienced two disappointments in my brief career there. First, I realized that I was no writer, and then I discovered that I would never be a producer. I realized that I had a very good grasp of the relation between dramatic action and ideas, but was quite untalented when it came to perceiving that the decision whether an actor should raise his right hand or his left might be crucial.

Int: And what was Bánoczi's function?

G.L.: Bánoczi was a very shrewd organizer, and he kept the Thalia going for a long time after it had really failed. By that time we had really all lost interest in the project, because we were only preoccupied with literature and acting. Our time was filled with productions of *The Master Builder* or Hebbel's *Maria Magdalena* and so we had neither time nor energy for anything else.

Int: Did Marcell Benedek prove to be gifted?

G.L.: Marcell Benedek was a very good-humoured and splendid person who did not really have any particular talent. He was a man of letters.

Int: An aesthete?

G.L.: An aesthete. That is the right word.

Int: Were you involved in deciding on the programme?

G.L.: Yes, indeed. For instance, it was I who persuaded the others to put on Hebbel's *Maria Magdalena*.

Int: Were you involved as translator?

G.L.: No.

Int: But, Comrade Lukács, surely you translated *The Wild Duck*?

G.L.: Yes, I did translate that.

Int: And *The Wild Duck* was put on in your translation?

G.L.: Yes, in the Thalia.

Int: Did you translate anything else?

G.L.: No.

Int: As a writer, did you only attempt plays?

G.L.: Yes, only plays. There may have been a few fragments of novels, but for the most part it was plays.

Int: And did you never attempt poetry?

G.L.: Never.

Int: In your autobiographical sketch you mention the name of Leo Popper as one of your early friends.

G.L.: Leo Popper was perhaps the most gifted person I have ever encountered. He had an infallible intuition for quality. In most people a sense of quality comes into conflict with theoretical understanding. There is a tendency to diverge. But in his case no such division was present. This made him very unusual in the history of criticism.

Int: In your reference to your friendship in your biographical sketch, you mention that you will return to the subject since it was of such great importance in your development. Could you tell me more about your friendship, when you became acquainted and so on.

G.L.: David Popper, Leo's father, taught my sister the 'cello and the Poppers often came to our house. It was at this time that my friendship with Leo grew, and it did so because of the respect and even reverence—I feel that is the only way to put it—that I felt for his powers of discrimination, something which, particularly then, was very undeveloped in myself. I have since, of course, become much more experienced in these matters. Nevertheless it was from him that I realized that in art a sense of discrimination is the most important thing of all.

Int: When did you first meet?

G.L.: While we were still at school.

Int: Did you ever work on anything together?

G.L.: We did not collaborate because my interests were chiefly literary and he was working on the plastic arts. But under his influence I did write a number of things on artistic topics.

Int: Did he not translate any work of yours from Hungarian into German?

G.L.: No, he never did anything like that. He did indeed write German better than Hungarian, but he also wrote articles in Hungarian.

Int: Who translated *Soul and Form* into German?

G.L.: I wrote it myself, in both German and Hungarian. The original was in Hungarian, and then between 1910 and 1911 I translated it into German.

Int: In the biographical sketch there is a suggestion that you were in a state of despair about having received the Krisztina Lukács Prize for *The Development of Modern Drama*, and that Leo Popper rescued you from it. What was the reason for this crisis and how did he help you overcome it?

G.L.: I took the view that society was not competent to judge the matter. Consequently, the award of the prize to me implied that there was something wrong with the book. I searched the text to discover where I had gone wrong, but could find nothing. It was here that Leo came to my assistance...

Int: You mean that he was able to tell you what was wrong with the book?

G.L.: No, he told me what was good about it.

Int: This was also the context in which he tried to persuade you to join the Tisza Party. But you just laughed off the idea.

G.L.: When I won the Krisztina Lukács Prize I became quite well known for a time. My father, who was a supporter of the Tisza Party, wanted me to represent it in Parliament. It was this I found funny.

Int: Did you have political ambition at the time?

G.L.: I wanted to change things, that is to say, my ambition was to bring about changes in the old Hungarian feudal system. But there was no question of turning these wishes into political activity because there was no movement along those lines in Budapest at the time.

Int: And your family?

G.L.: I was completely estranged from my family, or at least from a part of it. I did not have any relationship with the family at all.... My mother was a shrewd woman who soon saw what was happening. She fell seriously ill and died of cancer of the breast. Under pressure from other members of the family I wrote her a letter. When she received it she said, 'I must be very ill for Dr Georg to write me a letter.'

Int: What became of your brother?

G.L.: My brother died under the fascists.

Int: What had he done previously?

G.L.: He had a middling position in a bank and when he was conscripted for labour service, instead of taking the call-up as a warning and making his escape, he said that he had not done anything blameworthy and that he was quite innocent. So he complied with the summons, went off to labour service and never came back.

Int: How did you resume your literary activities after the four-year interruption?

G.L.:* In 1906 I again started to publish. The outstanding event of note—it might almost be called my third literary discovery—coincided with the first appearance of *Szerda* (Wednesday). I submitted a short article to Ignotus. He was extremely impressed by it and gave it to *Szerda* where it was published. It was agreed with Ignotus that I would send him theatre reviews from Berlin where I was planning to go in the winter. Nothing came of this plan since *Szerda* went bankrupt. Nevertheless, my first conversation with Ignotus is of interest because of the warmth and friendliness he showed and because of the praise he lavished on my article. However, at the very end of our conversation he said with an unexpected seriousness: 'The fact is I think you are very talented. So I shall tell you something you should remember your whole life long. Your article is extraordinarily clever and perceptive and, as you shall see, we shall publish it. But for everything you have written in it, it would also have been possible to have maintained the exact opposite.' With this pronouncement Ignotus dismissed me. Of course this did not provide a basis for close contact with my third discoverer. I must add that up to a certain point Ignotus continued to support me and that I was only able to write regularly for *Nyugat* (The West) because he took up the cudgels on my behalf against Osvát. I do not think that my work would have appeared in *Nyugat* without Ignotus or that I could have published anything like as often as I did. As a young man I felt absolutely no gratitude. I did derive advantage from his patronage, but I had no time at all for his impressionism. It was quite obvious that my polemic against impressionism in my article 'Az utak elváltak', The Ways Have Parted,[5] which I wrote after the Kernstok Exhibition, was chiefly directed against Ignotus, even though he was not mentioned by name. But this was the route by which I arrived more or less at the threshold of literature.

Int: The name of Irma Seidler crops up in your biographical sketch. You dedicated *Soul and Form* to her.

G.L.: Irma Seidler was related to the Polányi family and I had an extremely important encounter with her in 1907. Whether it should be called love or not is another question, but she had a tremendously powerful influence on my development between 1907 and 1911. In that year she committed suicide. After that I published my essay *On Poverty in Spirit*.[6] This contains the account of her death and the expression of my sense of guilt.

Int: Where did your university studies take place?

G.L.: I began with the Arts Faculty in Budapest. I spent a term studying in Berlin and later spent another shorter period there. But before 1911 I did not spend much time abroad.

Int: When you first went abroad, did you join the circle around Max Weber right from the start?

G.L.: My aim was to become a German literary historian. I went abroad in the naive belief that literary historians actually have an influence on the course of events. I'd like to mention an anecdote on this point since it was of great importance to my life subsequently. At that very time there happened to be a debate raging about the colour of Lotte's eyes in Goethe's *Werther*. It was argued that in *Werther* Lotte's eyes were blue, while in real life they had been black. Someone had written a major essay on this point. I saw the whole affair as the living example of what Hatvany calls *The Knowledge of what is not worth knowing*.

Int: This obviously disillusioned you profoundly.

G.L.: The disillusionment was not all that great since I was already beyond the early stages of disillusionment. It was rather the end of a phase in the course of which I abandoned literary history entirely.

Int: And this led to a new orientation?

G.L.: Yes, it led me to philosophy. I came under the influence of Simmel and, later, Max Weber.

Int: How would you describe the positive aspects of their influence?

G.L.: I would sum it up by saying that it was Simmel who made an issue of the social character of art and this gave me a point of view, a basis for the discussion of literature that went well beyond Simmel's own. It is his philosophy that underpins my book on drama.

Int: And the essence of Weber's influence?

G.L.: Weber's influence came later and was more profound. Simmel had his frivolous side. Weber, on the other hand, wanted to create a comprehensive theory of literature without any of Simmel's frivolity. I ought perhaps to mention the fact, because it plays a part in my good relationship with Weber, that I once remarked to him that according to Kant the essence of aesthetics lay in the aesthetic judgement. My view was that aesthetic judgements did not possess such priority, but that priority belonged with being. 'Works of art exist. How are they possible?' This was the question I put to Max Weber and it made a deep impression on him. It is the fundamenatal problem of my *Heidelberg Aesthetics*.

Int: In your later judgement of Simmel and Weber, particularly in *The Destruction of Reason*, you condemn both of them unequivocally.

G.L.: Except that in moral terms I always felt positive about Weber, whereas I did not feel uncritical towards Simmel's frivolity and this led to our estrangement. In the case of Weber no such estrangement took place.

Int: Was it also at this time that your friendship with Bloch began?

G.L.: Yes.

Int: In Heidelberg you also made the acquaintance of Lask. Did this become a close friendship?

G.L.: It was a beautiful friendship. But there can be no question of Lask having influenced me. Bloch had a tremendous influence on me: in particular, he convinced me through his example that it was possible to philosophize in the traditional manner. Up until then I had been wasting my time with the Neo-Kantianism of the period. But now, in Bloch I encountered the phenomenon of a man who could do philosophy as if the whole of modern philosophy did not exist, and who showed that it was possible to do philosophy like Aristotle or Hegel.

Int: Why did Bloch visit Budapest?

G.L.: Bloch was Simmel's pupil and through Simmel he had got to know Emma Ritoók. Incidentally, the story is perhaps not without interest—Bloch had a very poor impression of me at first. He said I was not a serious person, and so on. Emma Ritoók naturally told me of this and my reply was, 'It is not essential that a great or an important philosopher should also have a good knowledge of people.' My reaction to his criticism impressed Bloch greatly. From then on we formed a very close friendship.

Int: How long did it last?

G.L.: As long as Bloch stayed in Heidelberg, let us say from 1909 to 1911.[7] We then parted because Bloch retreated to Switzerland before the war while I stayed at home.

Int: This was the period when you built up your literary career in Hungary.

G.L.:* My real literary activity begins partly with my work on drama and partly with my writing on *Nyugat*. On this point I must mention an event that I did not really understand at the time and only now is it really clear to me what a decisive influence it had on my whole literary development, and even on my life apart from literature. It was in 1906. This was the year when

Endre Ady's *Uj versek* (New Poems) were published. The *New Poems* had an absolutely overwhelming impact on me; to put it bluntly, this was the first work in Hungarian literature which enabled me to find my way back to Hungary and which I thought of as a part of myself. This is something quite separate from my current view of Hungarian literature, the result of many years' subsequent experience. At that time, I must confess, classical Hungarian literature was something to which I had no access. I was influenced only by world literature, in the first instance by German philosophy. The impact of German philosophy lasted my whole life. And this state of affairs was not basically changed by the shattering effect of Ady's poetry upon me. In fact it neither cancelled out the effect of German philosophy nor led me back to Hungary. It could be said rather that in my mind Hungary itself simply meant Ady's poetry. Nevertheless, something had taken place whose meaning I only understood later: namely, the realization that the history of German thought contained a fair measure of conservatism. This was true not just of Kant, whom I already knew, but also of Hegel (three or four years later I was starting to grope my way from Kant to Hegel), as well as the modern Germans I was reading. I know that I shall be accused of anachronism if I cite a later poem by Ady, but in his works I was aware right from the start of that sense of 'Ugocsa non coronat',[8] of that feeling of 'I shall not let myself be ordered around' that always seemed to me to be the background music to Hegel's *Phenomenology* and *Logic*. This gave rise to the idea, without precedent in the literature of the day, that someone could be both a Hegelian and a representative of the humanities while taking up a left-wing and within limits even a revolutionary stance. I am not talking here about the tremendous impact on me of Ady's poetic and literary qualities. But it must be said that my encounter with Ady's poems, quite apart from their literary significance, was one of the turning points of my life. This was no chance discovery, no mere youthful enthusiasm. There is perhaps no need to say it, but I have remained attached to Ady's work my whole life long. This is not just a projection, for I was the first person in Hungary to write, some three or four years later, on Ady's personal links with the revolution. I said that Ady was a revolutionary who regarded the revolution as indispensable for his own self-realization. If I now date this vague first impression at around 1906, I shall not be making myself guilty of any great anachronism. But I must of course emphasize that at the time I had not the slightest notion of the importance of the matter. I simply felt an unbounded enthusiasm for Ady's poems.

As I have said already, my literary activity proper began at this time. Between 1906 and 1907 I was in Berlin where I wrote the first version of my book on drama. I submitted it to the Kisfaludy Society and was awarded the Krisztina Lukács Prize for it. Also in 1907 I sent my article on Novalis to *Nyugat* where it appeared early in 1908, if I am not mistaken. I shall not go into detail about this since the books are well known.[9] I would only like to say something about the way I saw my position within the literary and artistic life of Hungary at that time, since there are no reliable accounts of this in the literary histories. I must start by making a reservation since, if I begin with personal relationships, it turns out that, at the point where these would have been important for me, there were none. I am thinking here of Ady. I met him on one occasion, but I cannot remember exactly when it was. The only thing I am sure of is that it must have been after the autumn of 1908, because that was when my review of *Holnap* (Dawn) appeared, the first piece I ever wrote about Ady. So without being able to place it precisely, I would put this meeting in winter 1908 or spring 1909. It came about through a close friend, the painter Deszö Czigány, who had also painted a portrait of Ady with whom he was on good terms. He took me with him once to the Három Holló restaurant (The Three Ravens). I have to say that absolutely nothing came of this meeting. It was an evening when The Three Ravens was full of Ady's friends from the gentry, and I was quite unable to take part in the conversation. I must add, because it is important from another point of view, that I did not feel any sense of disappointment. My lifelong attitude to important men has been that of Goethe's Philine:[10] 'And if I do love you, what concern is that of yours?' So it is no accident that I had no relationship of any kind with my other most important contemporary, namely Bartók. In his case the circumstances might have seemed much more favourable, for Bartók was one of the teachers at the Academy of Music where my sister was studying the cello and she attended his classes in music theory. Bartók was also in constant contact with our family in other ways. After 1919, for example, he lived in my father's villa on the Blocksberg. But at the time I found it impossible to express what I felt about music and so was extremely reserved in Bartók's presence. Not until the dictatorship did we begin to have anything of a relationship. This was when Bartók, Kodály and Dohnányi formed the music directorate. As People's Commissar I came into frequent contact with them, but of course that is not the same as a personal relationship. I only mention this to make the point that such matters are not necessarily decisive in the last analysis. I should also mention that I had only fleeting contact with Ervin Szabó, the third of my contemporaries in Budapest whom I admired most. I did not keep my distance from him to the same degree as with Bartók and Ady, and he was the only one of the Hungarian thinkers of the day to whom I am seriously indebted. But even so, our contacts with each other were somewhat desultory. Since we are on the subject, I can add that it was through him that I found out about French syndicalism, which at the time I regarded as the only oppositional socialist movement that could be taken seriously.

I should add, lest I have given a false impression that might become even more distorted when I describe my relations with *Nyugat* that it would be wrong to suggest that I was anything of a lone wolf. For example I was on excellent terms with the people engaged in the fine arts. Very early on I wrote an article on Gauguin in *Huszadik Század* (The Twentieth Century) and another on Kernstok and other members of the *Nyolcak* (The Eight) who had an exhibition at the time. And quite apart from that, I had been close friends not only with Deszö Czigány, but also, since early childhood, with Márk Vedres, even though he was much older than I. Furthermore, I was on good terms with the older generation of painters, with Károly Ferenczy, Adolf Fényes, József Rippl-Rónai, and also with Márffy, Tihanyi and later on with Nemes-Lampért, Béni Ferenczy, Noémi Ferenczy. In short I was in constant touch with a large circle of people in the fine arts. In contrast to that I had no personal relationships with the leading members of either *Huszadik Század* or *Nyugat*. As far as Osvát was concerned, it was love-hate at first sight. From the moment we first met we could not stand each other. He believed and openly asserted that I was a very bad writer. In this he was of one mind with János Horváth. This was in fact a widely held view and one against which I made no protest. Today I regard the style of *Soul and Form* as extraordinarily mannered and unacceptable by the light of my later standards. Not that I would defer to Osvát's judgement on this point; our views of what is good diverged too sharply. But we must not allow the discussion of such matters to be conducted on such an irrational plane! I became aware very quickly why I did not like Osvát. He belonged to a particular type of Hungarian critic, exemplified before by Zoltán Ambrus and, to a certain extent, by Jenö Péterfy. These critics imported the latest western trends, especially those from Paris (this is particularly striking in the case of Ambrus), and transferred them to Hungarian conservatism which, down to Ferenc Herczeg and Ferenc Molnár, was tolerant of every development, however mediocre. I felt a profound contempt for this aristocratic conservatism and I despised it in Osvát. How right I was to do so became apparent on my return to Hungary after 1945, when Osvát's collected essays were published. These contain only one piece of really sharp criticism, that against Ibsen. On the other hand, he is full of admiration for the very worst writers, from Ferenc Herczeg down to István Szomaházy. I know this contradicts the Osvát legend, but fortunately we have a text to hand which provides posterity with printed evidence of Osvát's genius as a critic.

*Int:** Comrade Lukács, you once told a story about what Osvát said of Hegel...

*G.L.:** Yes, I went to what is now the Hotel Duna, and used to be the Café Bristol, in connection with my articles. Osvát used to be there in the mornings. When I arrived with a pile of books from the University library under my arm—in those days briefcases were not yet fashionable—Osvát examined them as usual to see what I was reading. It so happened that I had a number of volumes of Hegel with me. 'Hegel is a bad writer,' he observed, snapping the book shut. Incidentally, our great myth-maker, Oszkár Gellért, spread the story that Osvát had repeated this to him at the time and added that Hegel was a bad writer, but that Engels was a good one. Here you can see how careful one has to be with such legends. It is not possible for Osvát to have repeated to Gellért in the evening what he had said to me in the Café Bristol in the morning. I was much too unimportant a writer for *Nyugat* for that. The anecdote is an unjustifiable projection of my present intellectual position to the year 1909. Moreover, it is simply untrue that Osvát thought Engels a good writer: he never read so much as a line of Engels in his life. Oszkár Gellért has simply created a legend that converts Osvát into a pre-Bolshevik Marxist. Of course, not a word of it is true. On the topic of my relations with the *Nyugat* circle, it is noteworthy that at that time I knew Osvát, Fenyö and Ignotus from the editorial discussions, but that I never met or got to know Schöpflin, for example, or Zsigmond Móricz, even though I had written about his first book. I did not personally know Kosztolányi, about whom I also wrote, nor Karinthy or Gyula Krudy: in short, I did not even meet the core group of *Nyugat*. I repeat that the reason for this was not any reserve on my part. This was why I mentioned my acquaintances among the practising artists whom I had no contact with at the level of organization, but whom I saw regularly in the Café Japan and other such places. But I never went to meetings of the *Nyugat* circle. My first meeting with Mihály Babits also took place much later, in 1916. Ervin Szabó had invited Babits, Béla Balázs, Andor Gábor and myself to a meeting to discuss how to mobilize writers against the war. Not long afterwards, in 1916 or 1917, on Mannheim's initiative, we dined together with Babits, and afterwards I went for a stroll with him, but we never became close. Of the entire *Nyugat* circle, I only had personal contact with Margit Kaffka, Anna Lesznai and Béla Balázs. I cannot tell you much about Margit Kaffka. We were on good terms, but not very intimate ones.

I'm not sure if you know that she had come to Pest as a teacher and was only able to free herself of her obligations sometime later. In this my father played a significant role because of his position on the City Council. I mean that we helped her to come to Pest. She also came to see me when she was on a visit to Berlin. So that is how close we were. I had a genuine, indeed a lifelong, friendship with Anna Lesznai. I think you know that we saw a lot of each other in 1965 and 1966, when she was living in Budapest. And I was very pleased to have witnessed the birth of her novel. In her youth she was known only for her poetry. I was very happy to have been able to tell her how outstanding I found her novel. What I told her was that I thought the first volume a masterpiece and the second a good novel. I am very pleased that our friendship lasted a lifetime.

2

War and Revolution

Int: Let us move on to the outbreak of war in 1914.

G.L.: All I can say about the war is that I was sharply opposed to it from the outset, and that I was very impatient of anyone among my personal acquaintances who inclined in any way to a favourable view of the war. I felt like this even where, as in the case of Béla Balázs, there was no direct support for the war. His reaction was: 'Go and suffer too!' Privately, though not in public, I told him what I thought of this attitude in no uncertain terms and I particularly expressed my disapproval of the end of his book. This contains a discussion between him and Anna Lesznai in the course of which he paints a glowing picture of the Austro-Hungarian Monarchy as a sort of Switzerland of diverse nationalities. I thought this mindless flattery, since I took an extremely bleak view of conditions at home. I do not know whether I have already made clear my position on the war, but I would like to do so now. My attitude was: 'The German and Austrian armies may well defeat the Russians and this will mean the overthrow of the Romanovs. That is perfectly in order. It is also possible that the German and Austrian forces will be defeated by the British and the French and that will spell the downfall of the Hapsburgs and Hohenzollerns. That too is quite in order. But who will defend us then against the western democracies?'[1] This question turned out to pose the actual problem. And you can see from this fact that my hostility to positivism was partly politically motivated. For all my condemnation of conditions in Hungary, this did not mean that I was prepared to accept English Parliamentarianism as an alternative ideal. But at the time I perceived nothing with which to replace the existing order. From that point of view the Revolution of 1917 was a great experience since it made it clear that things could be otherwise. Whatever view one took of this 'otherwise', it made a decisive difference to all our lives or at least to the lives of a considerable proportion of our generation.

Int: In connection with your attitude towards the war you once mentioned a letter of Simmel's.

G.L.: The Simmel letter is only interesting because I strongly suspect that people tend to stylize their past to make it accord with what they wish they had said or done. So I had been wondering with a certain suspicion, or rather with critical doubt, whether it was true that I had been opposed to the war from the very outset. It then occurred to me that I had once had a talk with Marianne Weber, Max Weber's wife—I cannot recall the precise date—in which she had praised the moral value of the deeds of heroism performed in the war. My response to this was to say that the more heroic the deeds, the worse it was. I then happened to come across a book published in honour of Simmel. It included a selection of his letters, including one to Marianne dated August 1914, in which he writes that if Lukács was not able to comprehend the greatness of the war, the position was hopeless, since the war could only be understood intuitively and it would be pointless to discuss it with him. So this proves that my conversations with her may have taken place at the beginning of August. Marianne had told Simmel about it and this was his reply. This confirms my feeling that my memory did not deceive me and that I had been against the war as early as the beginning of August. One has to be very cautious in such matters, for as you know, poor old Déry got into difficulties in the Rajk affair because he forgot an article he had written at the time.[2]

Int: Simmel was right in believing that the greatness of the war could only be grasped intuitively.

G.L.: I agree with him there, but I was only interested in the matter because of the objective proof it provided that the conversation really did take place in the first few days after the outbreak of the war.

Int: Comrade Lukács, were you in Berlin at the time?

G.L.: No. I went to Heidelberg in 1912 and lived there until the end of the war, when I returned to Pest.

Int: When precisely?

G.L.: Yes, when was it? I went to Pest in Autumn 1917 and then I was back in Heidelberg in Summer 1918. In August of that year I went back to Pest with the idea of returning to Heidelberg in the coming spring but of course that did not happen.

Int: How did you manage to avoid the army?

G.L.: That was due to the circumstance that the son of a bank director did not have to perform his military service if he did not wish to. Of course, we all had to go along to the barracks. I was told there that I would have to appear before a medical commission. The medical investigation established that I was suffering from severe neurasthenia.

Int: A disease to which you have been less prone than any other in your whole life.

G.L.: This severe neurasthenia became my own special illness. I must add that it was diagnosed by Korányi. Corruption in Hungary must be regarded as much more extensive and more serious than is usually believed, for Korányi was not approachable by just anyone. However, he could be approached by my father and as a result I served as an auxiliary during the war.

Int: Until the end of the war?

G.L.: No, only until my former school friend Iván Rakovszky, who subsequently became Minister of the Interior, paid a visit to my father. I must tell you the story, because it is rather amusing, not least because of the people involved. Rakovszky came to see my father in order to try to obtain a post as director in the Credit Bank. Since that was his aim, the discussions naturally had to proceed via Uncle Josi and of course someone raised the question about what Georg was doing. My father took the opportunity to complain that I was going to have to be in Pest as an auxiliary and what a bad time I would have of it. Whereupon Rakovszky replied that Uncle Josi should not worry, nothing was going to happen, he should tell Georg to visit him in Parliament and they could talk the matter over. And this is what we did. Four weeks later I was exempted and had no further dealings with the army. For his part, Rakovszky was given the post with the Credit Bank.

Int: So it was a happy end for all concerned.

G.L.: It is an event that should not be omitted from any account of my early life. The fact that I was the son of the director of the Credit Bank had no literary influence as such, and yet events such as these impinge on one's life in a very material way. Who knows in what Russian camp I might have perished, had I not had these connections.

Int: How were you able to keep your distance from the war while you were in Heidelberg? In your biographical fragment you note: 'Heidelberg: assistance from Jaspers (very much against his better judgement)...'

G.L.: Jaspers gave me a medical certificate. Since he was a supporter of the war, this went against his own convictions.

Int: So why did he sign it? Were you friends?

G.L.: We were on fairly friendly terms and I believe that I owed his assistance to a witty repartee, one which proved its worth subsequently. He had asked me whether I was taking no part in the war because I feared for my life. I answered: 'Of course, I'm afraid. If my call-up papers were to arrive at the end of the war, I assure you that I should not ask you for a medical certificate then.' This reply evidently helped to sway him.

Int: He didn't join the army either, or did he?

G.L.: He was a sick man. He was not called up.

Int: In the context of the war years you also refer to your first wife, Jelena Grabenko.

G.L.: She was a Russian and had once been a member of the Social Revolutionary movement, although she had long since parted company with them. During the war—these are personal matters of no interest—we lived apart: that is to say, she was living with a friend, and since she was Russian and had no income I supported her. In 1918 she parted from her friend, I don't know why, and came to Pest. But by that time our marriage had long since collapsed.

Int: Where did she actually live during the war?

G.L.: Jelena Grabenko? At first in Heidelberg and afterwards in Bavaria.

Int: She is often mentioned in Hungarian literature, for instance by Béni Ferenczi or in Sinkó's novel...

G.L.: She was a highly intelligent person, quite apart from the fact that she was an extremely talented painter. When she came to Budapest and met Kun, she gained the impression that he resembled Vautrin.[3] I think this a very perceptive and accurate comment and thought so at the time. This one remark makes it obvious that she must have been a very shrewd woman. In Budapest she became friendly with the younger generation—with the Béni Ferenczy circle, with Révai, with Sinkó and others. She lived there in the House of the Soviets and they all met at lunch and dinner and other times. She belonged to that circle without ever joining the Communist Party. All this continued in Vienna where she maintained good relations with Révai, for example.

Int: So she emigrated too?

G.L.: Yes, she did.

Int: And did you meet in Heidelberg?

G.L.: No, at an Italian seaside resort. She had been friendly with the Balázs's in Paris. She was visiting them and so we met.

Int: What is your present opinion of the main work you wrote during the war, *The Theory of the Novel*?

G.L.: *The Theory of the Novel* defines the whole age as the age of absolute sinfulness, to use Fichte's phrase. A particular feature of the book is its methodology, which is based on the school of intellectual history. But I think it is the only book produced in that tradition which is not right-wing in its orientation. Morally, I regard the whole age as reprehensible and art as commendable insofar as it opposes the age. It is at this point that Russian Realism becomes important since Tolstoy and Dostoevsky have shown us how literature can be used to condemn an entire system root and branch. In their works there is no suggestion that capitalism has this or that defect; in their eyes that whole system is inhuman as it stands.

Int: Is this what prevented you from looking to the victory of the English for any improvements?

G.L.: The fact is that I always regarded bourgeois democracy with scepticism. Anatole France remarks somewhere that rich and poor alike are forbidden to sleep under bridges. I always distrusted this notion of equality. But this did not lead me to any concrete political viewpoint. I only became aware that such a viewpoint was a real possibility when Liebknecht's action (in voting against the war in the Reichstag) made this obvious.

Int: At the time it must have seemed a startling innovation to have established a connection between the novel and history.

G.L.: The book undoubtedly contains a number of true observations. As a whole, however, it is based on the premiss that Tolstoy and Dostoevsky form the pinnacle of the revolutionary novel in world literature, and this is of course wrong. At all events, even though the book remains within the framework of bourgeois literature, it does investigate the theory of the revolutionary novel. At the time such a thing was unprecedented. The prevailing theory of the novel was conservative both artistically and ideologically. My theory was not revolutionary in a socialist sense, but it was when measured against the literary criticism of the day. In the final analysis *The Theory of the Novel* was the sequel to the essay on Ady, extending the ideas advanced there to a whole genre and generalizing them by application to the works of world literature.

Int: Comrade Lukács, are you depressed by the contemporary reception of *The Theory of the Novel*, or are you pleased by it? I am asking because you have said elsewhere that you do not regard the book as a constituent part of your life's work.

G.L.: That is a very complex question because we are still living in a transitional epoch and a transitional work like *The Theory of the Novel* must be evaluated as such.

Int: I have the feeling that the question is only partly resolved by treating the book as a transitional phenomenon. If a work like *The Theory of the Novel* can survive and exert an influence for over fifty years, it obviously does more than simply give shape to transitional values.

G.L.: Look, Fichte's 'age of absolute sinfulness' means that Europe broke out of the pseudo-consolidation in which people had lived down to 1914 and collapsed to the point where it finds itself now. In that sense we are fully justified in speaking of an age of absolute sinfulness. That is the negative side. But what is absent from this view is what Lenin inferred from it—namely, the need to change the whole of society from bottom to top. This dimension was absent from *The Theory of the Novel*.

Int: It is interesting that you wrote the book in 1914, but that it could not be published until after the war.

G.L.: That is not quite true. *The Theory of the Novel* appeared during the war in the *Zeitschrift für Ästhetik und Allgemeine Kunstwissenschaft*. It was only in book form that it appeared after the war.

Int: When you no longer agreed with what you had written.

G.L.: At the time the unity of *principle* took precedence over the unity of particular beliefs.

Int: Have you never considered publishing the Heidelberg MS, the fragment on aesthetics?

G.L.: No.

Int: Did the work remain a fragment?

G.L.: It remained completely fragmentary. A chapter appeared in the *Zeitschrift für Ästhetik und Allgemeine Kunstwissenschaft* or in *Logos*. I can't remember which. But I soon abandoned the *Heidelberg Aesthetics* because in 1917 I began to involve myself in ethical questions and lost interest in problems of aesthetics.

Int: Is it true that the chapter that appeared has not been included in the complete edition of your works which is coming out at the present time?

G.L.: It is present in the *Early Works*—that is, the one chapter.

Int: Does the manuscript no longer exist as a whole?

G.L.: A part has survived, but I do not know where it is or who has it.[4]

Int: In your autobiographical sketch for this period you make mention of the Budapest Circle. This is evidently a reference to the so-called Sunday Club. Who belonged to this?

G.L.:* The Sunday Club consisted of a number of friends around Béla Balázs and myself. We formed a group during the World War. I spent 1915 and 1916 as an auxiliary soldier in Budapest and that was when the Club came into being. Béla Balázs and Anna Lesznai were members: they were joined by all sorts of people, such as Emma Ritoók, a very old friend of Balázs, and then a host of younger theoreticians, such as Béla Fogarasi.

Int:* And Révai?

G.L.:* No, not Révai.

Int:* Anna Lesznai mentions Révai.

G.L.:* Máli is mistaken. In reality the first person to join was Lajos Fülep, with whom I had been on good terms earlier on. Then there was Frederik Antal who subsequently wrote about Italian painting and Hogarth; the young Karl Mannheim and Arnold Hauser were also members, and so on. Towards 1918 we were joined by a number of younger people, including Gergely, who later become Anna's husband, and above all there was the most talented person of them all, Charles de Tolnai. But Révai, who, if I am correctly informed, was a schoolfriend of theirs, was not a member of the group.

*Int:** And Margit Kaffka?

*G.L.:** For a while Kaffka came to our meetings too, but then she married Balázs's brother, Ervin Bauer. These two hated each other as only brothers can sometimes hate, and so she stopped coming.

*Int:** Do you think of the Club as a motley group, ideologically speaking?

*G.L.:** Ady's view of the war was the basic premiss of the Club. But the opposition to the war had many different inflections. I myself soon became absolutely opposed to the war. Mannheim or Hauser did not go so far.

*Int:** What form did the discussions take in the Sunday Club?

*G.L.:** They ranged over a whole series of confused and also mutually incompatible varieties of liberalism. It would be quite wrong to claim that there was a unified doctrine. For example, the general mood in the Club leaned towards the western democracies à la Mihály Károlyi. I think I was the only one to take a different view. As I have written elsewhere, 'Very well, Austria-Hungary and Germany may well defeat Russia and this will mean the overthrow of the Romanovs. That is perfectly in order. It is also possible that Germany and Austria will be defeated by the western states, and that will spell the downfall of the Hapsburgs and the Hohenzollerns. That too is quite in order. But who will defend us then against the western democracies?' Of course, in the Sunday Club this seemed an outrageous paradox. As far as I was concerned the answer to my question came from the Russian Revolution in 1917, that third possibility I had been looking for. What we believed in common was that it was necessary to refuse any concession to the Hungarian reactionaries, and we were therefore in favour of an alliance with *Huszadik Század* (The Twentieth Century). Ideologically, of course, we were vigorously opposed to their freethinking positivism, but this alliance led to the *Free School of the Humanities*, which began its activities in 1917. Talks were given by Lajos Fülep, Béla Balázs, Emma Ritoók and also Mannheim. I gave lectures as well. This institution, moreover, did not officially take up a hostile attitude towards the group around Jászi. Ervin Szabó, for example, sympathized with the establishment of the school and did not at all think of it as a reaction to Jászi's group. Of course, our radicalism should not be over-estimated: it was not radical in the modern, let alone a Bolshevik sense. I myself had to overcome a number of crises before the member of the Sunday Club could turn into a communist. It is absolutely untrue that the Sunday Club was a Bolshevik society, as was later claimed by the counter-revolution, by Emma Ritoók, for example. It is typical of the wide range of opinions within the Sunday Club that I was the only one to begin defending a Hegelian-Marxist position. Apart from myself only Frederik Antal had any Marxist leanings. Lajos Fülep took up a position based on the humanities, while Emma Ritoók was basically conservative. Anna Lesznai cannot really be classified in this way. It is not possible to turn the Sunday Club retrospectively into a Bolshevik or even a pre-Bolshevik grouping.

Int:* Could you also say a few words about your relationship to the *Huszadik Század* group.

G.L.:* I heard about it from Bánóczi while I was still a student, in the early years of the century. Perhaps you know that Margit Bánóczi later married Somló. But the whole circle was in touch with the Bánóczis. Through other contacts I also met Ervin Szabó quite early on. At the time it was the sort of group one belonged to as a matter of course. I can illustrate this. In 1905 or 1906 the Jászi group in the Social Sciences Society tried to oust the friends of Pál Wolfner and Andrássy.

Int:* That was in 1906?

G.L.:* I only remember that I was on holiday in the Tatras and had the greatest difficulty in obtaining enough money to travel from the Tatras to the general meeting in order to support the Jászi faction against the Pál Wolfner and Andrássy camp. I only mention this to show that from the outset I supported certain of the social aspirations of *Huszadik Század*. But I was utterly opposed to Jászi's brand of philosophical positivism. I should add that I always regarded Jászi as muddled and as a very untalented person as far as theory was concerned. On the other hand, I had a high opinion of Gyula Pikler and also thought well of Bódog Somló's capacities as a scholar. I was also on fairly good terms personally with Somló, as well as Ede Harkányi, who died so young. So there were a number of slender threads linking me to the members of the Social Sciences Society, although I always rejected the Anglo-French positivism that animated the group. I met Jászi from time to time. We talked together, but I did not like him particularly and I do not think that he much cared for me. I never had the sort of difficulties I had with Osvát. I do not recollect that Jászi ever failed to publish anything I had submitted to him. On the contrary, it was Jászi who published the Ady article that Osvát had rejected. The only person I really respected in the group was Ervin Szabó. He was the only one who really had any influence on my development. If you were to ask me what I had read by Jászi, I would have to say I have forgotten it all. Nothing is left of it at all. Many people said, even Ady said it, that they could see Jászi as their leader. I never saw him as my leader.

*Int:** Perhaps Jászi's strong point was his morality?

*G.L.:** Strange as it may sound, when I compare the profound significance which Elek Benedek's morality had for me, I realize that I was much less impressed by Jászi. His morality was not wholly free of sentimentality, and that grated on me. For example, Kristoffy and his friends were supported by the Jászi faction. Hence I thought it completely natural later on for Darányi to dismiss Jászi from the Ministry. I was quite unable to share the moral indignation of the Jászi faction and of Jászi himself. For who on earth could have expected democratic sentiments from Ignác Darányi? I was also realistic enough at the time to grasp that fact. Moreover, I have an unpleasant memory of Jászi from the time of the dictatorship.[5] I do not know whether it is typical of his personality in general, but it does him no credit to have visited me after the dictatorship began with the proposal that the Social Sciences Society should vote the active communist theorists onto the committee. By this he meant Elek Bolgár, Fogarasi and myself. I said to him, 'Look here, we have been active in public for many years. If you have not voted us onto the committee before, there is no reason to do so now we are ministers or whatever.' Jászi then asked me what should happen to *Huszadik Század*. I answered, 'Let it continue to appear! As long as you are not openly propagating counter-revolution', those were my actual words, 'nothing will happen to you.' It is a fairy story that Jászi was persecuted and that this was why he fled the country. Even Anna Lesznai's account does not fit the facts. No one had any intention of arresting Jászi. He emigrated because he feared, justifiably, that the dictatorship would be overthrown and that the counter-revolutionary movement would not just persecute the members of the dictatorship, but that it would go beyond that. In that respect he was absolutely right. But under the dictatorship he could have stayed just where he was.

*Int:** Can you say anything about your relations with the Galileo Circle?

*G.L.:** I had no very close contact with the Galileo Circle. I knew Karl Polányi well and I occasionally attended meetings of the Circle. It is possible that I even lectured there. I can no longer remember. At all events, there was no real contact. It was not until 1919 that I met the most radical members of the Circle, those around Korvin. They had earlier formed an illegal group, and since I was a bourgeois writer, they are unlikely to have desired any contact with me. When I joined the Communist Party, I met both Korvin and some of the younger members, such as Duczynska, Csillag and others. I was on very good terms with Csillag, but I was never very close to the Galileo Circle.

Int: Did you not develop a closer relationship with the Galileo Circle when it radicalized itself to a certain degree?

G.L.: My first real relationship, apart from friendships, was with the Communist Party. Before that I was not to be found either with the Radical Party or with the Social Democrats. I hadn't the faintest idea what took place in those parties.

Int: Polányi writes in his memoirs that at the Ady Memorial celebrations, he gave a militant anti-militarist speech while Comrade Lukács gave a militant Bolshevik speech.

G.L.: I can no longer check what Polányi thought on 6 February 1919, nor what I myself thought at the time. As a literary historian you are reading too much into what happened in the course of my development. You must remember that at the time I was extremely uninterested in what was happening around me. I had been a lifelong admirer of Ady and when Polányi asked me to make a speech I naturally agreed. But that this was of any significance for my general development, or that I had this or that in mind—all that belongs to the exaggerations of literary history.

Int: Let us return to the main theme. You said earlier that you gave up aesthetics because you had begun to be interested in ethical problems. What works resulted from this interest?

G.L.: At that time it did not result in any written works. My interest in ethics led me to the revolution.

Int: All the same, essays on ethical questions did appear—'Tactics and Ethics', for example.[6]

G.L.: That was a later article. It was written in 1919.

Int: But did it not arise from those interests?

G.L.: Of course. This is where I raise the question, the ethical conflict, of how it is possible to act unethically and yet rightly.

Int: The Hebbel problem...Judith's dilemma...

G.L.: 'If You (God) place a sin between me and my deed, who am I to quarrel with You about it, and to escape from what You impose!'[7]

Int: A marvellous sentence. But unfortunately, like all clever or beautiful sentences, it is open to abuse.

G.L.: There is no such thing as a sentence which is not open to abuse.

Int: Your activities as a thinker began with aesthetics. Then came your interest in ethics. This was followed by politics. From 1919 politics was your prime concern.

G.L.: In my opinion it should not be forgotten that my interest in politics always had ethical implications. 'What is to be done?' was always the main question in my mind, and it is a question which links the ethical and the political domain.

Int: What was your position during Károlyi's Autumn Rose Revolution?[8]

G.L.: It is important not to misrepresent the actual course of events in retrospect. I belonged to that broad stratum of the intelligentsia—the Germans call them fellow-travellers—who thought the entire situation untenable. A characteristic episode took place when I was present at a shooting incident at the chain bridge. There were about four or five hundred people there; I was one of them. The only thing I recollect from the whole episode was of myself standing on Vörösmarty Square with the very likeable wife of László Dienes, a chemist and a highly intelligent woman. We set off together and ran beneath the arcades along the bank of the Danube. I played no significant role in this demonstration. The same is true of my actions throughout the October revolution. I did indeed support the revolution, but I played no active part in it, for apart from the little Sunday Club I had absolutely no connections. I only became active after the revolution had triumphed, when the problems that arose from the emergence of the Communists started to become interesting. I must confess, and there is documentary evidence to back it up, that I only joined the Communist Party after certain hesitations. That is a peculiar thing, but this is often how things happen in reality. Although I was quite clear in my mind about the positive role of force in history and although I had never felt at all critical of the Jacobins, it turned out, when the problem of force became pressing and the need arose to decide whether I would further it by my own activities, that theory does not necessarily coincide with practice. And it was only after an inner conflict had run its course in November that I felt able to join the Communist Party in the middle of December.

Int: Was it at this time that you wrote 'Tactics and Ethics'?

G.L.: Yes, it was. The essay appeared in January. It was an inner balancing of accounts which made it possible for me to join the Communist Party.

Int: But I imagine that your inner ideological debate was not concluded by your entry?

G.L.: Despite the hostility to the war and to positivism which I have already mentioned, I had not had any previous contact with the movement and had not arrived at any concrete political position. I did not realize that there was a concrete political form of resistance until Liebknecht's actions in Germany made it apparent. Now, it should never be forgotten—and this is not a question of fact, but a universally valid proposition, whatever may be thought about Lenin's theory and practice, about which so many wrong and misleading things are said nowadays—that it is Lenin's exclusive achievement to have rescued the honour of the International by proclaiming that the opportunity provided by the war should be seized by the working class in order to overthrow capitalism. It is only because of Lenin that we were able to discover this truth. Admittedly, the discovery could not be made without crises. I would not deny that I too was exposed to a period of uncertainty. It only lasted a few weeks, but it was present nevertheless. Fortunately we have a fairly accurate documentary reminder of the period in Ervin Sinkó's novel, *The Optimists*. In this he describes something which we should not allow ourselves to forget, and that is the confused ideological relationship which the intelligentsia developed to communism at the time. It is evidence of the depths of confusion that I was one of the people who could see matters most clearly. This is not meant as self-praise, I only wish to give an idea of the general mood. Even among people like myself who had read Marx, the understanding of Marxism was extremely superficial. No one had any experience of the movement or of revolution and I should add, even though it goes against orthodox beliefs, that the political maturity of people who came to us from Moscow was terribly overestimated.

Int: Was the party already divided into those orientated towards Moscow and those who weren't?

G.L.: No. Everything was very chaotic at the time. We were delighted with every arrival from Moscow, imagining that they could give us valuable information about what things were like 'over there' and explain the theoretical significance of everything that had happened. I tried everything I knew and received assistance through my personal contacts, with my old friend Ernö Seidler, for example. But I must say that what the people from Moscow told us was not very intelligent.

Int: Did these discussions take place among yourselves?

G.L.: They partly took place in the Sunday Club, and then I gave a big lecture at the Academy of the Communist Party. As far as I can recall, my subject was in fact the problem of force. The discussions and dialogues—Sinkó gives a very accurate account of them—also went on unceasingly in Visegrádi Street.[9] I was not the only one who could not see my way clearly. The position was very complicated. On the one hand, we were convinced that this was the only way out of the situation as it existed, not just in Hungary, but for the whole of mankind. On the other hand, we had not the faintest idea about the theoretical grounding or the specific stages of this solution. Modern historians of the party cannot imagine that there are matters on which party officials are completely ignorant. Hence this situation does not exist for them. They represent matters as if what happened was that Kun and his supporters arrived in Budapest with their Leninist teachings and distributed them to everyone else via the relevant channels. They talk as if, after a certain time had elapsed, there were people around with first-class knowledge and others with only second-class knowledge, and so on. I confess to you that it was not until I had emigrated to Vienna that I began to gain an insight into Lenin's genuine theoretical importance. Neither from Kun nor from Szamuely nor from any of the others who returned from Russia was it possible to learn anything worthwhile on the subject.

Int: Could you not read anything by Lenin at the time?

G.L.: At that stage nothing but *State and Revolution* was available in translation. Of course, I must add that, well written as *State and Revolution* was, the uninitiated and the reader unfamiliar with Marx would have been unable to understand it. For such a reader would conclude that he was confronted with a scholarly exposition of Marx. After all, *State and Revolution* deals with all of Marx's discussions of this topic. And this is what might create such an impression. I must confess that it was not until later that I understood the profound theoretical importance of the book. As for myself, I can only say that I joined the party completely unprepared and that in this respect I also failed to learn anything in the party. My real, enforced years of apprenticeship began under the dictatorship and after its collapse, when a number of Communists set about studying and trying to appropriate the teachings of Marxism as understood by Communists.

Int: Comrade Lukács, did you never belong to any other group which then merged with the Communist Party?

G.L.: No.

Int: Then how do you explain the fact that you became a people's commissar so soon? Was it your reputation?

G.L.: It was partly because in this respect Kun and Szamuely were practical men. After all, I was, if not a great writer, at least a so-called famous one. They thought this a positive merit, and I am convinced that without my public reputation I would not have been allowed to give my first lecture as part of the great lecture series. The second reason was perhaps that, after Béla Kun's arrest in February, a second Central Committee had been set up and *Vörös Ujsag* (Red News) appeared under its direction. We had succeeded in gaining a certain reputation among the left Social Democrats, with the Landler faction and those close to it. They were taken by surprise when *Vörös*

Ujsag continued to appear after the arrest of the entire top leadership of the Communist Party and when it proved, in both their eyes and those of the public, to be better than it had been before. I cannot judge that myself, but I recall an anecdote about my father with whom I never discussed such matters. He was also president or whatever of the federation of capitalist and private enterprise employees, an organization with a sort of interest in social welfare, and in that context he met someone who to his great surprise said to him, 'Herr Direktor, it really is fantastic; since your son has been editing *Vörös Usjag*, it has improved tremendously.'

Int: Comrade Lukács, were you on the editorial board or were you actually editor-in-chief of the paper?

G.L.: The paper was edited by a board. The man with the official title of editor was Ferenc Rákos, but he did not count. Alpári, Bolgár, Révai and I were the de facto editors. If I was generally seen as the editor, this was presumably connected with the fact that mine was the best-known name in the group.

Int: How did your organizational contacts with the Communist Party begin?

G.L.: I had long been close friends with Ernö Seidler, who was in the leadership of the Communist Party. He had arrived in Budapest before Kun and his supporters and we had had long discussions on these matters. I have already mentioned that I sympathized with the Russian Revolution from the very beginning and I also agreed with the proclamation of the Soviet Republic in Hungary. But in the last analysis, I had grown up in a world of bourgeois prejudice. Hence the slogan of the dictatorship of the proletariat provoked a kind of ideological crisis in me. The product of this crisis was an article in *Szabadgondolat* (Free Thought) in which I expressed my opposition to the dictatorship. After the resolution of this crisis in November 1918, Seidler took me with him for talks with Kun and Szamuely.

Int: By that time the Communist Party had been established.

G.L.: The Communist Party was set up in the middle of November, so I was not among its founding members.

Int: Is it true that you joined the leadership after the first set of leaders had been arrested?

G.L.: Yes, that is correct. When I joined the party Kun and Szamuely wanted me to take a place on the editorial board of the theoretical journal. I accepted that, and if my memory serves me, an article of mine appeared in the *Internationale*. When Kun and his associates were arrested, a number of comrades began to take soundings about who might succeed them in the leadership. Someone—I no longer recall who—brought me together with the illegal

Central Committee. It should be pointed out—I do not believe this has been documented—that there were two currents in the party at the time. The first, which had suffered a setback with the arrest of Kun and his supporters, was in something of a panic and feared that an extreme reactionary movement would seize power in Hungary. Their position was that we ought to reorganize ourselves into a sort of Ervin Szabó Circle and continue to work at the level of theory and ideology. The second group, to which I belonged, believed that the work of the original leadership should be continued, illegally if need be, legally if at all possible.

Int: Who belonged to the first group?

G.L.: I can no longer remember.

Int: And the second?

G.L.: Tibor Szamuely, for example, had gone underground and strongly supported the second group. I could not give an exhaustive list of the members of the two groups, nor is it important that I do, for it was an internal debate without consequences for the outside world. The Communist Party survived, and the augmented leadership resumed the previous policies, with a single, minor modification in which I may claim to have had a share. Kun had maintained good personal relations with Landler, hoping to bring Landler's left-wing Social Democrat group closer to the party by means of a shrewd campaign of persuasion and argument. Some of us in the leadership argued that the Landler group would now hover between two positions and that if we criticized their vacillation, this would accelerate their shift towards the Communist Party. We thought it was not true that this would simply deepen the gulf separating us. I should note that when I spoke with Landler about this during the dictatorship, he admitted that the Communist Party's sharp criticism of his vacillations had indeed had an impact on his subsequent position.

Int: Was the leadership during the dictatorship in agreement about such vital issues as land reform?

G.L.: On the question of land reform we were unfortunately all in agreement. This was partly under the influence of the Social Democrats and partly because some of us thought that land distribution was only a transitional step which could be dispensed with since capitalist development was more advanced in Hungary than in Russia. If we transformed the large estates into farming co-operatives, we would skip the stage of bourgeois revolution and advance directly to socialism. This was a pitfall none of us avoided. As for myself, I think it remarkable that whereas in the realm of culture I firmly held that real revolutionary change had to support itself on revolutionary bourgeois elements, on the land question, since I was no politician and had not concerned myself in detail with the nature of the problem, I simply accepted the standpoint of the party. I do not want to gloss things over: there is no doubt that I did not oppose the view of the party, even though as a political commissar in the army I had often seen how the peasantry distrusted us because of our failure to distribute the land.

Int: Were there any issues on which the party leadership was divided during the dictatorship?

G.L.: There were disagreements on minor matters, because Kun, who was a fairly shrewd tactician, maintained very good relations with Weltner and Böhm[10] and more or less discussed everything with them in advance. Some of us thought that there was a danger of party tactics being too narrowly confined within limits set by Weltner and his associates. There was opposition on this point, and even Tibor Szamuely felt sympathetic to it. Ottó Korvin, Gyula Lengyel, László Rudas and Elek Bolgár were the main critics, and I was on their side. This intellectual opposition tried, as we put it at the time, to drag Béla Kun a little to the left, towards the Communists. Despite this, the opposition was still very far from setting up as a clearly defined faction or grouping.

Int: But weren't you in favour of merging the two workers' parties?

G.L.: Since power lay in our hands, we tended in general to put too much weight on unification. In my case this was strengthened by a personal factor. The vestiges of Ervin Szabó's syndicalism still lived on in me. I hoped, therefore, that a union of the parties would lead to a breakthrough for the syndicalist doctrine that the organs leading the proletariat into the revolution would be more highly developed than the parties. My essay, 'Party and Class',[11] must be seen as the last expression of the syndicalism I inherited from Ervin Szabó, rather than, say, as an important stage in my own development, for the realities of the dictatorship soon showed me that that point of view was untenable.

Int: Do you still believe today that Kun's relations with the Social Democrats were too close?

G.L.: It was essential for Kun to maintain links with the Social Democrats within certain limits. On the other hand, we were dissatisfied because the dictatorship had failed to take the giant strides we had expected in its progress towards that earthly paradise which we thought of as communism. When I say earthly paradise, this must be understood in a very sectarian, ascetic sense. There was absolutely no thought in our minds of a land flowing with milk and honey. What we wanted was to revolutionize the crucial problems of life.

This mood was very prominent in the dictatorship and emerged clearly on specific issues on which, in my opinion, the opposition was in the right. One such issue was the Clemenceau Note, which caught napping even our great statesman Kun. He believed Clemenceau's assurance that Romanian troops would withdraw if we pulled our troops back from the Czech border. Béla Kun was simply tricked by Clemenceau, and we in the opposition were smarter than Kun, since we knew it was just a trick and that we should gain nothing from accepting the terms of the Note. But that does not mean that there are any grounds for speaking of a faction in the leadership.

Int: Could you say something about your activities as people's commissar?

G.L.: There is little that can be said about that. At the time we all felt a bitter hatred for capitalism and all its forms. We wanted to destroy it at all costs and as quickly as possible. This unquestionably had an influence on the cultural policy of the party. Experiments were made which were fundamentally correct, but naive in their execution, designed to eliminate the commodity character of the artist and works of art and to remove them from the market-place. The purpose of the so-called Artists' and Writers' Registries was to make the artist materially independent of the sale or non-sale of his works. It is obvious, and it became obvious to us soon after the dictatorship, that our approach was naive, and it would be ludicrous to defend this as a communist measure. On the other hand, our policy had the very positive effect of placing the control of art and literature in the hands of the artists themselves, by means of the literary and artistic directorates we set up. This can be best seen in the case of music, where authentic artists were put in leading positions. The Directorate of Music, consisting of Bartók, Kodály and Dohnányi, practised a dictatorship which enabled the Bartók-Kodály tendency to gain a dominant position. But they also carried out a reform of opera, as can be seen from the fact that the dictatorship witnessed a great première: the first Hungarian performance of Verdi's *Otello*. There was a similar, if not quite so impressive situation in the plastic arts. A leading role was played there by people like Béni Ferenczy, Noémi Ferenczy and Nemes Lampérth. They were joined by some very talented young historians of art, such as Kálmán Pogány, János Wilde and Frederik Antal, who later made a name for himself. With their assistance they carried out the socialization of works of art in private hands, so that in the summer of 1919 an exhibition could be held which ranked alongside anything in the world. This had been confirmed by a true expert like Dvořak, who said it was a model of what an exhibition should be. Politically, Dvořak was a conservative, but he was nevertheless pleased to see the pictures taken away from the collectors and put into museums. In a much more attenuated form the same trends could be seen at work in literature. There is one further matter which provides an insight into our cultural policy. In the period immediately preceding the dictatorship, a radical movement had emerged among the teachers, particularly at Gymnasium level. The People's Commissariat for Education managed to throw out all the ministerial old guard above the rank of secretary, and to replace them and all leading members of university departments with leaders of the radical teachers' union. I may add in parentheses that I managed to overcome Kunfi's resistance on this point because I had the stronger nerves. Towards 3 a.m. Kunfi's nerves gave way and he gave his agreement. All this involved a real change, so that we tried to work out a serious programme right from the start. I should add that his programme was put into effect by the revolution in 1945. Eight years compulsory schooling, the four Gymnasium classes to be followed by university, all of these things were already present in the reform programme of the dictatorship.

Int: What were your relations with writers like at the time?

G.L.: They had their own Writers' Directorate...

Int: Did Kassák belong to it?

G.L.: Kassák was a member, even Déry. From Osvát to Déry to Kassák, more or less every shade of opinion was represented.

Int: Was Babits also in it?

G.L.: Of course. He was even given a chair.

Int: Did you have no objections to that?

G.L.: There are all those stories about our supposed use of compulsion. But who can force anyone to accept a chair? What is less pleasant is when Kassák writes in his memoirs that I once tried to force him to go to the front at the point of a revolver. That is all nonsense, because if Kassák had gone to the front as a political commissar and turned up in my territory, I would have sent him back home. I would certainly not have sent him to the front. That would have conflicted with my principles, since I thought that for a Communist or a non-party man to go to the front was a very great honour. To send someone to the front at gun-point would have been quite alien to me. Besides, Kassák would have exposed himself to the greatest difficulties at the front. When I went there—and this I can vouch for—it was crawling with ultra-left communists. I sent them all home without exception. I had no need of them. I chose my subordinates from among the decent Communist workers in the army. But Kassák is not the only one to have spread lies about what happened. There is also Mihály Babits, who claims that in 1919, when Kun and his friends were under arrest, Béla Balázs and myself approached him and asked him to join the party. That is absolutely ridiculous and without any foundation in fact.

Int: As a people's commissar, were you in possession of a gun?

G.L.: I had acquired a pocket pistol long before the dictatorship and I used to take it with me on my travels. During the dictatorship itself I only used it once, and then in an amusing situation with great success. There were some anarchists in Budapest and we got on with them like cats and dogs. On one occasion they had requisitioned too many houses in the 8th district, and since some young workers lodged a complaint with me about it, I threw them out and let the workers in. So, one fine day an anarchist delegation arrived and pushed their way past my secretary in the anteroom. They gained entry just like present-day Germans and began to shout. One shouted that Comrade Lukács ought to be shot for what Comrade Lukács had been doing. On hearing this I reached into my pocket, pulled out the revolver and placed it on the table: 'Go ahead!' There was dead silence in the room. Five minutes later the anarchists sat down and we discussed the whole business peaceably. To that extent I can claim to have been a great success under the dictatorship.

Int: Was there no disagreement with Kassák?

G.L.: Kassák probably did not like me any better than I liked him. I had my reasons for this. I had never had any great respect for his poetry, but when I joined the party, Kassák was already flitting around as one in the know and I accepted him without reservation as a Communist writer. Then, in February, after Kun and the rest of the first committee had been arrested, an article suddenly appeared in Kassák's paper asserting that it was a slander to call them communists and that Kassák himself was a supporter of the permanent revolution and independent of all parties and human factions. This was a matter on which I had already formed my own opinion. Then, on 21 March, Kassák again became the official court poet of communism, and that proved too much for my radical bourgeois stomach. Since then I have always despised Kassák and regarded him as an unpleasant fellow. His ambition had always been to be appointed official poet to the Commune, but I did not believe the Commune had any need of an official poet. Representatives of every shade of opinion that can be tolerated under communism should write freely, and if one ideology prevails over the others, well and good. I always took the side of Kassák and his friends when the Social Democrats and the trade-union bureaucrats launched a campaign to destroy them. I did not allow them to be gagged. But equally, I would not allow them to be granted official recognition. Incidentally, attempts to strengthen one's own position by gaining official recognition from the Communists were not confined to Kassák and his friends. The Social Democrats and Jászi and his friends made constant efforts to achieve the same goal. I think that I have already mentioned such an episode involving Jászi, and similar stories could be told in connection with Kunfi. When the Social Democrats took over *Uj Idök* (New Times), Kunfi proposed that I should join the editorial board. I refused, saying that since they had taken it over, they should run it as they wanted, without any interference from me. I had a similar view with regard to Kassák and his friends.

Int: Did your friendship with Balázs survive during the Commune?

G.L.: Yes, though there is no truth in the stories that Balázs enjoyed a privileged position. He worked in the People's Commissariat and spent a short time at the front.

Int: These stories have obviously received sustenance from the general belief that you seriously overestimated him in your book *Balázs Béla és akiknek nem kell* (Béla Balázs and his enemies).

G.L.:* In his case anti-capitalism was socially even less justified than in mine, although a version of romantic anti-capitalism was present in him too. And the *tertium datur* that I defended, both against the free thought of the type found in *Huszadik Század* and against Ottokár Prohászka, could be found in him too, in his poems and plays. I cannot judge whether I overvalued them at the time, but if it is now argued that I praised him too highly, this partly reflects the fact that in my opinion his lyric poetry before 1918 is under-estimated. At that time Béla Balázs was a much more important poet than is recognized today. It is typical of the distortions that can occur that, for example, Gyula Juhász has been turned into a great poet. I would go even further: it is my personal opinion that even Árpád Tóth was a better poet after 1919 than he was before 1918. And likewise the *Jónás könyve* (The Book of Jonah) is immeasurably superior to Babits's early work. If we therefore want to make an adequate assessment of these people, we have to widen our view and see how they developed after 1919

This brings us to the really problematic point about Béla Balázs. The enthusiasm and dedication with which he joined the revolution of 1919 and remained loyal to it afterwards, is truly impressive. But to a certain extent that was also his misfortune. For the point about communism is that it is a little like the saying, *qui mange du pape en meurt*. You cannot just sample Marxism. Either you must be converted to it—and I know that is no easy matter, since it cost me twelve years before I took the decisive step—or else it is perfectly possible to view the world from a left-wing bourgeois position. In Balázs's case what finally resulted was a baleful mixture composed of a superficial Marxism and his earlier poetic attitudes. In my opinion he has not—as a poet—since written anything worth mentioning—apart from some very beautiful poems in the *Férfi-ének* (Male Voice Choir). From that point on Béla Balázs became a writer who had lost his way, and it is no accident that we quarrelled in the twenties. I'm glad that I have mentioned the case of Anna Lesznai, because it makes it clear that my judgement is not coloured by any communist sectarianism. There can be no doubt that Anna Lesznai's poetry was always much further from communism than Béla Balázs's. Nevertheless, I always accepted her poetry for what it was, even during my communist phase and even though I knew that it was alien to my social convictions. The reason why I could never accept the non-organic amalgam that Balázs had produced was not that its communism was superficial, but that it was non-organic. For that quality also affects his achievement as a poet. Hence my relationship to Balázs really only extends to the *Nyugat* phase, and my collection of essays about him was not the start of our collaboration but the end.

Int: Were there other writers who approached the People's Commissariat with official requests?

G.L.: Almost every writer came to the People's Commissariat. Kosztolányi, for example, wanted a collective to translate *Capital*.

Int: It would not have been at all bad for Kosztolányi to have translated *Capital*.

G.L.: It would not have been bad as far as the Hungarian language was concerned. But you should not forget that the profound contempt in which I was held by the Hungarian writers had much more to do with Hegel than with Marx. It is typical of the state of public opinion before the dictatorship—and here I am referring not to a writer but to Polányi—that Polányi once read out a passage from Hegel's *Phenomenology of Mind* in a seminar at which I was present, caricaturing it by his manner of reading. He read out a long sentence which was followed by uproarious laughter, and then another long sentence that provoked a similar reaction. In short, I have grave doubts whether Kosztolányi would have succeeded in rendering Marx's stylistic debt to Hegel into Hungarian.

Int: I must say that when I tried to make use of quotations from *Capital*, it turned out that even in the translation by Rudas and Tamás Nagy hardly a sentence will pass muster. The translation does not even succeed in conveying Marx's meaning in every case.

G.L.: That may well be.

Int: Kosztolányi's text would at least have made good popular reading.

G.L.: But I have grave doubts whether much would have remained of Marx's original meaning.

Int: Comrade Lukács, in addition to your educational tasks, did you also have any military duties?

G.L.: Yes, but it was only an episode, even though it lasted for six weeks.

Int: To what post were you assigned?

G.L.: I was political commissar attached to the Fifth Division. When the Czech-Romanian offensive was launched in April, the Council of People's Commissars resolved, if my memory serves me right, that half the people's commissars should join the larger army units as political leaders. So Vágó and Pogány became Corps commanders, and Landler later became Commander-in-Chief. These were military, not political commands. But the communists joined a whole series of units as political commissars. I volunteered for this job and was sent to Tiszafüred, where we found ourselves on the defensive. The defence of Tiszafüred had been grossly mismanaged because the Budapest Red Army units ran away without firing a shot. The two other battalions, who would have been willing to defend Tiszafüred, were thus unable to maintain their positions, so that the Romanians penetrated their lines and Tiszafüred fell. I set about restoring order as energetically as I could. That is to say, when we crossed the river to Poroszló, I set up a court-martial and had eight men belonging to the battalion that had run away in panic shot in the market-place. By these means I more or less managed to restore order. Later, I was Political Commissar for the whole of the Fifth Division. Together we advanced to Rimaszombat against the Czechs, and I was present when we took the town. I was then ordered back to Budapest. That was the end of my activities with the Red Army.

Int: Who had been in charge of the People's Commissariat in the meantime?

G.L.: The departmental heads. Whenever a day's lull was expected in the fighting, I would commandeer an engine and a third-class carriage. I took the special train to Budapest in the evening and returned the following afternoon.

Int: It is as well that we live in a small country. In Russia that would have been harder. What influence did you have on military developments?

G.L.: Militarily, it was only possible for me to intervene in the most obvious situations. I had devised a good method for this. Our highly counter-revolutionary Chief of General Staff used to explode with rage whenever I applied it. I used to say to him, 'Look here, you are a soldier. You have your own soldier's language, just as I have my own philosopher's language. But I understand nothing of military matters. If you want to tell me that this or that battalion has to be moved from one place to another, you must not go into detail about this grouping or that concentration and all sorts of other matters understood only by specialists. I do not have the faintest idea about these things, so you must explain matters in such a way that I, as a layman, will comprehend why you are doing things one way and not another.' He was a man of short stature, the Divisional Chief of Staff, a former captain or major. He was furious with me, of course, because he was actually engaged in sabotage and you really cannot explain that away in layman's language. I knew from Clausewitz that a serious military strategy could be put into ordinary language, but the sabotage could of course not be explained.

Int: Comrade Lukács, I think that a long time ago, even before 1956, you told the story that you always visited the kitchens at the front.

G.L.: On my regular trips, I would stop the car two or three kilometres from the front, conceal it behind a convenient bush and appear unexpectedly among the troops. I always make a bee-line for the kitchen and made them give me whatever they were cooking. The cooks were always terrified of me: since they could never be sure when I would turn up in the kitchen, they were never able to cover things up.

Int: At divisional level that is the practical consequence of materialism; you have to start in the kitchen.

G.L.: Two things were uppermost in the minds of the men. One was the kitchen, the other was the mail. I did not think myself an outstanding military organizer, but on these two points I made sure that everything worked properly throughout the division. The soldiers were given decent food and their letters arrived every day.

Int: Did you have any contact with the higher military command, with Stromfeld and Böhm?

G.L.: In general we simply carried out the orders we received. There was only one occasion when I sabotaged an order and that was at the time of the great Romanian offensive before the first of May. Our division was holding the Tiszafüred-Eger line. The only other significant Hungarian force was in Szolnok and in between there was an undefended bridge over the Theiss at Kisköre. I called on the army commanders either to organize the defence of the bridge or, if they were unable to do that, to blow it up, since otherwise the Czechs could just walk in between us and Szolnok and that would be the end of us. Stromfeld was unwilling to do either for all sorts of military reasons, so I had the bridge blown up without his approval.

Int: Were you punished as a result?

G.L.: No. With hindsight Stromfeld agreed that I had been in the right—militarily speaking.

Int: Did you know him well?

G.L.: No. We became friendly later, by which time he had already joined the Communist Party.

Int: Does your friendship with Gábor Gaál also date back to your time at the front?

G.L.: Yes. I had asked the Ministry of Defence for an officer of the reserve who was also a member of the Communist Party and whom I could use as an adjutant. Gábor Gaál was recommended to me. I went with him to the front and we spent six weeks, or however long it was, in each other's company. So I know him from that time. I was very impressed by him and we became friends.

Int: Did this friendship survive later on?

G.L.: We remained on friendly terms in Vienna. Then Gábor Gaál left Vienna and at the time personal correspondence did not really exist, so that we became, if not estranged, that is not the right word, then just separated from each other. For years I only knew from the press what he was doing. I knew that he took over all my articles that appeared in the German, Hungarian and Russian papers. I believe that he published a good deal of what I wrote.

Int: Did you not send anything to him direct?

G.L.: I did not send my work to anyone direct. I handed it in at the appropriate party office, which then took charge of publication. Where the articles appeared I could no longer tell you.

Int: I believe that after the fall of Béla Kun's dictatorship, you and Korvin were ordered to stay in Budapest.

G.L.: That is so.

Int: What were your instructions?

G.L.: We were supposed to organize the Communist Party. When the Romanians arrived, I was at the front with the task of introducing as much order as possible into the Fifth Division. I had not had much success, and later that evening I arrived by car and asked the comrades who were present for advice from the party. The party's opinion was that Korvin and myself should remain in the country to keep the illegal movement in being and to act as its leaders. I was supposed to take over the ideological leadership and Korvin the organization. Even at the time I had my doubts about whether Korvin and I were the most suitable people for the task, for if any communists were well known then we were the ones who qualified. In Korvin's case there was also the question of his appearance, since he had a hunchback.

Int: So did you regard this mission as the result of animosity towards you?

G.L.: That is not something that can be proved. Four or five communist leaders sat down together and discussed the matter in party headquarters with Kun, and when I arrived from the front the decision had already been taken.

Int: '*Suspicions about Kun*'—what is the meaning of this note in your autobiographical sketch?

G.L.: Look, my relations with Kun had deteriorated quite sharply even during the dictatorship. My first wife's opinion gives a good indication of the bad feeling between us. I have already quoted it. When she first saw Kun, she had the impression that he resembled Vautrin. I thought then, and I still do, that this was a very perceptive and accurate remark. Even then there were constant disagreements and tensions between us, although they related only to moral issues in the communist movement. So I took a very cynical view of the mission. What I said at the time was that Korvin and myself were being prepared for martyrdom.

Int: Did Korvin also have disagreements with Kun?

G.L.: Yes. Korvin's sharp insistence on class struggle often caused him to clash with Kun's compromises. When Korvin ventured a mild disagreement with the attitudes of certain centrist Social Democrats, Weltner and his friends naturally leaped to the defence of the Social Democrats, whereas Kun failed to support Korvin.

Int: What happened after Korvin was caught?

G.L.: Korvin was caught after about a week and since he had very naturally and reasonably not given me the names and addresses of his friends and fellow-workers, I found myself completely isolated. In the circumstances there was no point in my staying in Budapest. A further factor was that after a denunciation by someone outside, the flat where I was in hiding was searched by some soldiers under the command of an officer. The flat belonged to Olga Máthé, the widow of Béla Zalai. I was very lucky not to have been caught.

Int: It is almost unimaginable that anyone can escape in a house search.

G.L.: It is much simpler than people imagine. I should add that it was partly due to my own precautions. Olga Máthé was a photographer, a very courageous woman. Her flat consisted of a small room where she lived with her daughter, a large dining-room and a studio which led into the loft. There was a chaise longue in the studio and that is where I slept. We quarrelled every day because she wanted to make up the bed for me. I resisted this since I planned to slip up to the loft if the doorbell rang during the night. I knew my way around the loft very well and I had already worked out in advance that I could hide behind a huge chest that was standing there. I had great difficulty in convincing Olga Máthé that if there were no bedclothes on the chaise longue, it would not occur to anyone that someone might be hiding there. One morning, at around three o'clock, there was in fact a ring at the doorbell, and the flat was searched. I listened to what was happening from behind my chest. Since the person who denounced her had claimed that Olga Máthé had received a visit from Béla Kun and taken a picture of him, and not that she was hiding anybody, they did not bother to look any further. I had gone to see her in the afternoon without any luggage, and of course people are always going into photographers. The concierge took me up in the lift, but there was nothing remarkable in a man going up to see Olga Máthé, since five or even ten people would do just that every day. So no one suspected that anyone might be hiding there. Of course, I could not stay in the flat after that, since I could not risk another search. After a discussion with my comrades it was decided that I should go to Vienna to strengthen the emigration. I did so in late August or early September. Budapest had by then been occupied by Mackensen's army and their officers travelled back and forth between Budapest and Vienna. During the dictatorship the Whites were taken out of the country to Vienna and after the dictatorship Reds were also conveyed there for good money. My family bribed a lieutenant-colonel from Mackensen's army to let me leave the country as his chauffeur. But since I could not drive, we bandaged my arm as if I had had an accident en route, and the officer drove instead. The matter was purely a business arrangement.

Int: How long did you remain in Vienna?

G.L.: I suppose I remained there from late-August or early-September, when I left the country, until the Second Party Congress, that is to say, until 1930–31.

Int: Is that when you started to live together with your wife Gertrud?

G.L.: We started to live together while we were in exile. Of course, we had known each other before that. I had known her for a long time, but we did not become close until after my lecture on ethics in 1918. Our conversations about that lecture revealed that we had so much in common, both morally and spiritually, that the closeness we established then has never ceased to play a crucial, indeed a dominant part in my life. I had never before met a woman with whom I could have such an intimate relationship.

Int: What did you live on in Vienna?

G.L.: I wrote, sold my possessions—I still owned all sorts of things. Somehow or other we managed to live.

Int: Was there no party salary at that time?

G.L.: At the start I could be said to have barely scraped by. Then, for three years, I edited the Russian Embassy trade journal for a hundred dollars a month. We could live well on that. In 1928 my father died and, after all sorts of complicated manoeuvres, I finally managed to get hold of the inheritance. We lived on that until my departure for Russia.

Int: Did you not earn anything from your writings during this period?

G.L.: I wrote, but at the time a Communist writer or a theoretical writer could not possibly live from his royalties, even though there were bestsellers even then.

Int: Were you left in peace by the Austrian authorities?

G.L.: It varied considerably. At first I was treated as an important figure, since the police did not yet know whether we were murderers on the run or future ministers. I personally was lucky to be acquainted with some Social Democratic theoreticians I had known in Heidelberg. And if the police did happen to treat me roughly, as was once the case, I went to see one of them to lodge a complaint. My friend informed Renner, who then telephoned the Chief of Police and told him that that was not good enough. After that everyone was extremely friendly to us for the next six months. Even with the swing towards the reaction they could not touch us, because the Hungarian extradition treaty applied to the Social Democrats as well as to us. If they had decided to extradite us, they would have been forced to hand back Böhm, Kunfi and the others as well. Hence we were left in peace in the shade of Böhm and his colleagues. Subsequently the situation grew progressively worse. However, I did not become involved in the Austrian Communist movement, only the Hungarian one. And that was so conspiratorial that it was impossible to prove anything against me.

Int: I have seen a letter written to Chancellor Seipel by Thomas Mann.[1]

G.L.: Yes. When Kun was arrested in Vienna in 1928, they wanted to expel me, so friends of mine wrote to Thomas Mann and he sent a letter protesting against the expulsion.

Int: So, up to 1928 you did not receive any financial support from Hungary?

G.L.: Fortunately we had few prejudices. We were already living together, but we decided not to marry, because, as the widow of a civil servant, Gertrud received a pension and money for the children and there was absolutely no reason why we should give up that money. Then in 1923 it looked as if I would be offered a professorial chair in Jena. This meant that we would have to get married since an unmarried man could not go to Jena with a woman and children. So we married in Vienna. When the Jena plan fell through a few weeks later, Gertrud showed what courage she had—it was really very beautiful and brave of her. She pretended the wedding had not taken place and shortly afterwards renewed her widow's passport at the Hungarian Embassy, so that officially we were not married until 1933, in Russia.

Int: Why did the chair in Jena fall through?

G.L.: Getrud lived with her elder sister in Hütteldorf, and I was given a room there too. We lived together throughout the whole period. In Berlin we even arranged things so that Getrud took a flat and I rented a furnished room in the same flat.

Int: Did the fact that you were not married lead to difficulties with the Austrian authorities?

G.L.: No. There were no difficulties of any kind, because we had a perfectly respectable household. It was nothing out of the ordinary for a houseowner to hand over a floor of the house to her sister and for her sister's children to live there too. Nor was there anything unusual in Gertrud renting out a room to someone.

Int: Did you also meet Attila József in Vienna?

G.L.: Yes.

Int: Did you only know him slightly?

G.L.: Yes. He only spent a short time in Vienna. If my memory does not deceive me, I met him through Anna Lesznai. I had a high opinion of him from the outset, and I have never concealed my high regard for him in the party.

Int: There is also a document, a letter from Attila József to Jolán József....

G.L.: About how enthusiastic I was about his poems. Yes, there is an Attila József letter about that. It was written in Vienna at that time.

Int: Did you know then about Attila József's quarrel within the Party and his subsequent expulsion?

G.L.: You must remember that up to 1930 I was an active member of the Party and so was informed about everything. In 1929, after the Blum Theses, I left the Hungarian movement. By the time the dispute with Attila József took place I had ceased to have any contact with the Hungarian movement.

Int: Did you then join the German Party?

G.L.: No. Up to 1930 I was a member of the Austrian Party and in Russia I joined the Soviet Party. From 1931 to 1933 I was a member of the German Party and when we decided to go back to Russia, there was a general decision to the effect that German émigrés should remain in the German Party and not be taken into the Russian Party. For this reason I remained in the German Party until 1945.

Int: In the intervening period were you not a member of the editorial board of a Hungarian periodical?

G.L.: That is correct. I was on the board of *Uj Hang* (The New Voice). The Germans did not show much interest in that since they knew I was a Hungarian and that was why I was involved.

Int: Does that mean that you were not even a member of the Hungarian Party up to the time of the Blum Theses?

G.L.: Officially I was a member of the Austrian Party. Any Hungarian Communist living in Austria had to be an Austrian Party member, because the Hungarian Party was banned.

Int: So officially you were a member of the Austrian Party, but in terms of organization you belonged to the Hungarian Party?

G.L.: That is right.

Int: And am I correct in thinking that you met Attila József in the company of Anna Lesznai?

G.L.: We also met on other occasions. I simply came to know him through Anna Lesznai. Another person who came to see me on his way from Paris to Hungary, was Illyés. I also had a lengthy conversation with him. Lajos Nagy also visited me in Vienna, and I had a long conversation with him as well. So, even though I did not do any writing myself, I did maintain relations with Hungarian writers.

Int: And with the non-Communist emigration?

G.L.: I have already mentioned that I was on bad terms with Kassák. I developed a good relationship with Sándor Bartha, when he and his friends began to move towards the left.

Int: How did the internal party dispute come about in the emigration?

G.L.: There were a number of contributory factors. Right at the start one part of the émigrés gathered around Landler and another around Kun—quite a finely balanced situation. It must have been about December 1919, when Landler came out of the internment camp in Karlstein, that I had a conversation with him in which he more or less offered me an alliance against Kun. I can only report that I was not willing to commit myself. I told him that his friends, József Pogány and others, were not a whit better than Kun's. I did not want to be associated with Pogány any more than with Béla Vágó. To give you an idea of the situation I should mention that, as you perhaps know, Pogány later went over to Kun's side. There was also a divergence of opinion of another kind, one which was favoured by the fact that the leaders of the emigration in Vienna were condemned to inactivity at the time, but that they still needed to reorganize and to orientate themselves in a particular direction.

In this context the question of Béla Kun's methods became very important, for they reveal, as I can now see, how terribly little Kun had in common with Lenin, even though he met him once or twice. Basically he had been brought up in Zinoviev's school. He was a typical Zinoviev disciple and set about creating a party and a reputation by demogogy, violence and, if need be, bribery. In fact, the first quarrel broke out over a matter involving bribery: the so-called gold scandal. The situation was that Kun was in Moscow in the summer of 1920 and one day—it happened, for reasons I can no longer recall, that I had personal contacts at the Soviet Embassy—somebody pointed out to me that a parcel had arrived at Vágó's address which had a weight out of all proportion to its size. I told Landler of this. We all began to suspect that Kun was sending money to his supporters, that he was making sure that five or six leading comrades received perquisites from Moscow. I could not list all the evidence now, but we also had reason to suspect that Rudas was one of the recipients. So I decided to try and intimidate Rudas, which was not too difficult, since he was one of the greatest cowards imaginable. It so happened that we were renting furnished rooms in the same apartment, and I put him in a panic about the terrible consequences that might arise, how he might be expelled from the party, and so on. In short, Rudas was completely taken in and confessed, if my memory serves me, that five kilos of gold coin had arrived and been distributed by Vágó in accordance with a list sent by Kun. Rudas also showed me his share. Together with Landler we persuaded Rudas to return the money to Vágó with the explanation that as an honest Communist he could not become involved in such matters. This put a formal stop to the business for the time, but it gave rise to bitter feuding between Vágó and Rudas which led to an explosion one day at a party meeting. In the midst of an argument they each reproached the other with the story of the gold, so that a committee of inquiry was set up which resulted in Vágó's expulsion. The whole matter had to be brought to the attention of the Comintern. That was done in Spring 1921, and the Hungarian delegation to the Third Congress was instructed to raise the question in some form or other. It came up on the agenda of the Comintern. The facts that would have proved embarrassing to Kun were hushed up by a committee of inquiry. The Comintern established a Central Committee which contained four Kun supporters and three Landlerites—Landler himself, Hirosik and myself. Kun's most important representative in this Central Committee was József Pogány, who tried to make Hungarian politics with Zinovievite radicalism and all sorts of pseudo-activities. Kun's old connections with Zinoviev were very influential in the growth of factionalism. The issue on which we diverged was the role of the emigration itself. Kun, who on this point was in agreement with Zinoviev, ascribed great importance to the emigration. There was even talk of moving the émigrés back across the frontier in large numbers. Landler took a very sceptical view of such a proposal, arguing that the real movement would have to originate in Hungary and that the émigrés could not do anything but assist it from abroad by virtue of their more advanced ideological development. In the eyes of the Landler camp the émigrés were always subordinate to the indigenous movement.

Int: What form did the basic conflict take?

G.L.: It broke out on the very important question of union dues. You probably know that in the old Social Democratic Party these also contained the party dues, so that in effect everyone who joined a union also made a contribution to the Social Democratic Party. Kun and his colleagues now declared that it was wrong in principle to have a system which automatically made members of a union into members of the Social Democratic Party. They demanded that in future the Communists should repudiate this agreement and refuse to pay the Social Democratic Party contribution. As an intelligent man, Landler at once opposed this idea on the grounds that it would place the illegal Communists in Hungary in an impossible position. They could give one of two reasons for refusing to pay their contribution to the Social Democrats: if they said they were Communists, they would be put in gaol; while if they simply opted out, their position in the party would become impossible. We defended the view that if the Hungarian Communists wanted to work legally within the workers' movement, they would have to pay this entry fee. When Pogány tried to force his sectarian and ill-considered measure through at all costs and with every means at his disposal, Landler, Hirosik and I walked out of the Central Committee meeting. We announced our resignation from the Committee and explained the problem to the Vienna Party. Those were the circumstances of the split in the party. When Kun and his associates demanded that the decision should be published in the paper, the Landler faction broke away and established its own rival paper a little later.

Int: So did the Landler faction have its own leadership and organization?

G.L.: Of course.

Int: It is very interesting that the factions came into being over such an important, but also practical issue...

G.L.: Landler was different from Kun—and this is what made me become his loyal supporter—in that he had no programme which he could have used to appear before the world as the leader of the Communists. He simply concerned himself with the practical possibilities of reviving the Hungarian movement. That made a great impression on me, and from then on I supported him enthusiastically.

Int: How did Kun obtain the gold in the first place? There is a story—Kosztolányi alludes to it in the opening pages of his novel *Anna Édes*—that when Kun flew over Hungary...

G.L.: No, no, all those fairy stories came into being much later. They had obtained the gold during the Russian Revolution through requisitioning—that is to say, Kun's supporters, or a number of them, had requisitioned the gold somewhere or other and then just stolen it. In short two and a half kilos of gold were simply there for his private use. I am convinced that the Russian partisans also stole. Partisans who hand over everything they have taken don't exist anywhere in the world.

Int: Was any part played in the internal quarrels of the Hungarian Party by

History and Class Consciousness, which appeared at that time and had such an impact internationally?

G.L.: Well, yes, to the extent that Zinoviev and Kun used the debate about the book to damage my position in the Party. But no one cared about it in the Hungarian movement, so that *History and Class Consciousness* had no serious consequences for me in the Hungarian context. Of course, there were some effects since Rudas wrote an article attacking it. This gave his criticism a factional flavour. All Kun's supporters felt bound to attack the book. There is a nice story from that time. At a Hungarian meeting in Moscow Rudas and his colleagues launched a sharp attack on *History and Class Consciousness* and accused Comrade Lukács of being an idealist. A steel worker from Vienna who belonged to Landler's group then stood up and said that of course Comrade Lukács was an idealist, he did not just think about his physical wellbeing like Comrade Rudas. That was the level of the debate. It is not worth preserving it for posterity.

Int: Did the Kun group have its centre in Moscow and the Landler group in Vienna?

G.L.: The Landler group really only existed in Vienna. Later after the Viennese emigration split up, Jenö Hamburger settled in Moscow, and Gyula Lengyel in Berlin, so that centres sprang up there too. But the stronghold of the Kun party was in Moscow.

Int: Comrade Lukács, how far were your life and your work influenced by these internal conflicts?

G.L.: What I think is important is that we were all messianic sectarians. We believed that the world revolution was imminent. The Hungarian work was determined by Landler's realism on actual Hungarian questions. This produced a dualism. Internationally we were messianic sectarians, in Hungarian affairs we were practitioners of *Realpolitik*. This dualism finally resolved itself in favour of realism with the Blum Theses.

Int: Did the Kun party have purely messianic notions?

G.L.: That is a complicated question, but the fact is that the messianic element actually began with Kun. It was a messianic sectarianism. It is in this context that people like Roland-Holst belong. In Moscow, in the Comintern, the bureaucratic sectarianism that originated with Zinoviev was generally embodied in the Kun party. For example, there was a plan to transport en bloc to Hungary all the prisoners-of-war who were then living scattered all over Russia, so that they could provide a base for the illegal Party. That was idiotic, of course, since every soldier returning from Moscow had to reckon with the strictest possible police surveillance. It was a stupid bureaucratic idea, based on the premise that a mass party could be brought into being at a stroke, instead of step by step.

Int: How far was the International involved in such plans?

G.L.: In the International Kun was, as we used to say, Zinoviev's shammas, and Zinoviev supported Kun in everything.

Int: And how was it possible for the Landler group to carry out its work?

G.L.: It was possible only thanks to the awkward fact that the Landler group had right on its side. In the Comintern at the time this played a certain role. The result was that on matters of principle the Landler group always won, but that Kun and his supporters always had a majority on the Central Committee. That was how Zinoviev's policy functioned in that area.

Int: Comrade Lukács, in connection with *History and Class Consciousness* I would like to put to you a question which is still relevant today. How do you react to the fact that this book still has such an international impact at the present time?

G.L.: The book has a certain value because in it questions are raised which Marxism evaded at the time. It is generally acknowledged that the problem of alienation was raised for the first time there and that the book makes the attempt to integrate Lenin's theory of revolution organically into the overall framework of Marxism. The fundamental ontological error of the book is that I only recognize existence in society as true existence, and that since the dialectics of nature is repudiated, there is a complete absence of that universality which Marxism gains from its derivation of the organic from inorganic nature and of society from the organic realm through the category of labour. It should be added that the messianic sectarianism we have been discussing is very prominent in the overall social and political framework.

Int: Is it this aspect to which the book owes its renewed impact in recent years?

G.L.: Yes, I think so. But its impact is partly to be explained by the fact that there is hardly anything that might be called a philosophical Marxist literature. For all its defects *History and Class Consciousness* is even today better and more intelligent than many of the things that bourgeois writers scrawl about Marx.

Int: I have noticed that *History and Class Consciousness* has been read by very many students in France since the events of May 1968. One of the student leaders even referred to it in a statement as one of his three favourite books. *History and Class Consciousness* corresponds to a state of mind in which the will to revolution coexists with the rejection of concrete political forces.

G.L.: Since the analysis of class consciousness contains idealist elements and since the ontological materialism of Marxism is therefore less in evidence than in my later works, the book is of course more accessible to bourgeois readers.

Int: Tell me about how you came to write the Blum Theses.[3] Why were they called Blum Theses?

G.L.: Blum was my pseudonym in the movement at the time.

Int: What was the background to the Theses?

G.L.: During the preparations for the Second Party Congress, I was asked to formulate the political and social strategy of the party. The result was the Blum Theses. As you know, Kun rejected the theses out of hand at the time. I do not know if I have already told you that highly amusing story about Manuilsky, which makes very clear at what level of theory the Comintern was then operating. I was in Budapest on an illegal mission when a meeting of the Executive Committee was called in Berlin in which Révai took part—he is the source of my information. At this meeting Manuilsky gave the opening speech and began by saying how much he wanted to praise the achievements of the Hungarian Party. The Comintern had in passing raised the question of a democratic dictatorship, and hardly had it done so, than the Hungarian Party was ready with a serious resolution to that effect. The following morning, Manuilsky announced that it was terrible to see such liquidationist, revisionist tendencies as the Blum Theses gaining currency! In the interim he had obviously received a telegram from Moscow.

Int: One gains the impression that government by telegram has a great tradition.

G.L.: Quite so. People always start from the completely abstract assumption that the Hungarian leaders at the time were all disciples of Lenin, whereas the fact is that Lenin did not have a single disciple in Hungary. Kun and his colleagues were all followers of Zinoviev, and in Zinoviev's International it was already possible to discern tendencies that were later adopted by Stalin. The tactics that emerge from this Manuilsky episode were confined exclusively to the Zinoviev and Kun school. It is ludicrous to think of Kun as a disciple of Lenin. Lenin had an extremely poor opinion of Kun and did not take a great interest in him. To be quite impartial, I should add that Lenin also had a very poor opinion of me. These things must not be glossed over. Whereas he regarded Kun as a disciple of Zinoviev, he simply thought of me as an ultra-leftist.

Int: Did Lenin have any particular respect for anyone in the Hungarian Party?

G.L.: Not to my knowledge.

Int: Did the disagreements that began to emerge in the Soviet Party after Lenin's death have any marked effect on the Hungarian Party?

G.L.: Not really. Since Kun was on Zinoviev's side, they merely led to the growth of a certain feeling of sympathy for Stalin in the Hungarian Party—a sympathy I myself shared.

Int: At that time Stalin and Zinoviev were united in their opposition to Trotsky. Is that right?

G.L.: Yes. But the disagreement between Stalin and Zinoviev had already begun to emerge, and I must confess that my anti-Kun attitude led me to sympathize with Stalin's antagonism towards Zinoviev.

Int: Did Trotsky not have any important supporters in the Hungarian Party?

G.L.: Trotskyism was insignificant in the Hungarian Party. There was no Trotskyist faction.

Int: Was the fate of the Blum Theses affected by the conflict between the Soviet Party and the Zinoviev-led International.

G.L.: I do not think so. I believe that Révai described the situation very accurately in a letter to Kun, when he said that he did not agree with the Blum Theses, but that they were a precise expression of that Landler policy which had led to the foundation of the HSWP[4] after the rejection of Kun's trade union theses. According to Révai the Blum Theses had to be thought of as the theoretical résumé of that policy.

Int: And why was Révai not in agreement with the Blum Theses? Did he not belong to the Landler faction?

G.L.: He was one of Landler's supporters, but Landler died in 1928. It could be said that the Blum Theses spelt the demise of the Landler faction. The theoreticians of the faction—Révai and others—did not agree with the idea that the Hungarian movement should actively support the Hungarian Socialist Workers Party. They became converted to Kun's line, which wanted to create a movement from above, directly from Moscow. This led to Révai and Hay, a very gifted young man, leaving the Landler faction.

Int: Had Révai given any earlier indications that he was on the point of leaving the Landler faction?

G.L.: With men like Révai it is always difficult to say exactly where and when the breach begins.

Int: Did you cease to have any contact with Révai in Moscow after this?

G.L.: Our relationship did not come to an end, but it was completely transformed.

Int: So was this the start of the Révai tragedy?

G.L.: Révai took up a very extreme position. Don't forget that there was only one critic who objected to *History and Class Consciousness* on the grounds that it was insufficiently radical—and that was Révai. His essay can be found in the Grünberg *Archive*. At the same time the conviction seems gradually to have grown in Révai that he had been chosen by providence to become the great Hungarian statesman who simply had to be part of the Hungarian leadership whatever the circumstances. For this reason he believed that he had to be prepared for any sacrifice, however great. This is the essence of his tragedy.

Int: Then I was perhaps not very wide off the mark when I said that here is where his tragedy started. As soon as he had gone over to the view that it was essential to build up an émigré party under outside control, he had really discovered his later role as a man standing outside and above with all the strings in his hand.

G.L.: That is absolutely correct.

Int: Had you started to have a personal relationship with Révai while you were still in Hungary?

G.L.: Yes, even before the dictatorship, and particularly after Kun's arrest, when the Second Central Committee was set up. Both Révai and myself were members of the editorial board of *Vörös Ujsag* (Red News) and so we always worked together. Hence, during the dictatorship we had a lot of personal contact with each other.

Int: Is there any truth in the anecdote in Ervin Sinkó's novel that your friendship began when Révai initiated a discussion on a point of theory and was 'converted' by Comrade Lukács?

G.L.: Yes, he said something or other, I no longer remember what. I only know that I replied, 'Look here, this is not my opinion, this is what Marx says in *A Contribution to the Critique of Political Economy*.' Révai came to see me the next day and said, 'You were right.'

Int: Can we go back to the break-up of the Landler faction?

G.L.: After the Landler faction broke up, a number of first-rate people went over to Kun, because within the Hungarian Party a group was starting to form around Sándor Szerényi. This move towards Kun gave rise to a transitional period which ended with the Seventh Comintern Congress and the policies arising from it. These developments fully confirmed the views I had advanced in the Blum Theses.

Int: What was the position adopted by Sándor Szerényi?

G.L.: He was hostile to Kun and took a point of view based purely on the situation in Hungary and completely untenable for that reason.

Int: Was his group to be taken seriously?

G.L.: Yes, indeed. It had come to power after the Third Congress and used its power for all sorts of purposes. Révai, for example, believed, and said as much to Gertrud, that he would rather be Horthy's prisoner than Szerényi's subordinate. And in fact he went to Hungary where he was caught and spent around two-and-a-half years in gaol.

Int: Comrade Lukács, to what extent was your career affected by the situation after the Blum Theses?

G.L.: Up to the Blum Theses I had been an official in the Hungarian Party, so my activities were largely determined by this fact. After the Blum Theses, when I realized—and that is the essential point of the Theses—that the proletarian revolution and the bourgeois-democratic revolution, in so far as it was genuine, were not separated from each other by a Chinese Wall,[5] I found myself on terrain where I could move freely and where a space was created in which ethics might have reality. Allow me to make a confession. After I wrote the Blum Theses I realized, on the one hand, that I am no politician, because a politician would not have written the Blum Theses at that juncture, or would at least not have published them. On the other hand, while working on them I came to understand that the proletarian revolution is not an isolated occurrence, but the consummation of an historical process. In that sense the Blum Theses have a positive side. They opened up an ideological path which led towards democracy. In order to have a free hand in what was so obviously a crucial issue, I submitted completely to the Hungarian line. I did not want to give Béla Kun the opportunity to triumph by making the Blum Theses into an international issue. The upshot was that the whole matter was reduced to the level of a Hungarian question and the contents of my entire philosophy changed. I moved from the Hungarian line to a German or alternatively a Russian line.

Int: Would it be too much of an exaggeration to say that *The Young Hegel* represented a continuation of the Blum Theses?

G.L.: In my case everything is a continuation of something else. I do not think that there are any non-organic elements in my development.

Int: I only meant to say that your study of the revolutionary phase of capitalist society might be connected with the realization that there was no Chinese Wall between the proletarian and bourgeois revolutions.

G.L.: Yes, on this point you are absolutely right. I began to investigate the ideological side of the problem, a realm that later became the focal point of my work.

Int: You mentioned earlier that you went to Hungary illegally during this period.

G.L.: In 1929.

Int: What was the nature of your mission?

G.L.: I was to lead the movement. The members of the Foreign Affairs Committee took turns in going to Hungary for three months, so as to lead the movement in person. There was a general view in the emigration that only Kun and Landler should be exceptions to this rule. There were also people who wanted to treat me as an exception. But since Kun would have objected to this, I felt unable to accept the opinion of my friends. I believed that I could avoid being caught, if I was sufficiently careful and was lucky enough not to encounter an informer. I thought also that even if I were caught, there would be so many international protests that I would escape a death sentence.

Int: You spent three months in Hungary?

G.L.: Three months.

Int: Were the undercover lodgings and everything else arranged from Vienna?

G.L.: Everything was arranged in Vienna, but very badly. My lodgings, for instance, were very fine. They were situated in the city woods, but at the same time were no more than a stone's throw from the offices of *Nyugat* (The West). This was too much of a risk. I had a contact, my so-called cousin. I gave her the task of coming to see me in great excitement with a story that her mother was in a terrible state because of some intrigues in Szeged involving her uncle's will, and that I was the only person who could sort matters out. I told all this to my landlady and paid a month's rent in advance to be on the safe side. So we arranged that this cousin would call for me the next day and accompany me to the train for Szeged. Things did not go entirely smoothly, however, and I want to tell the story because I am proud of the way I managed to keep cool. In the evening my landlady came to tell me that her nephew, who had been living with her, had broken into her wardrobe and stolen some money. She went on to say that she had already notified the police. That was very interesting. A further humorous note was that she happened to be Schweinitzer's cousin and had already been to tell him what had happened.[6] My landlady then wanted to know whether I had noticed anything untoward about her nephew. So I said to her: 'What is the world coming to, Madame? I have come to live in your house, I did not inquire whether the maid was trustworthy or not. Therefore I had no qualms about leaving the keys to the cupboards in the door, as you can see.' I waved in the general direction of the cupboard. 'For if you say that someone is trustworthy, I trust them implicitly. And now you come and tell me I should have had my doubts about your nephew? What is the world coming to?' She complained a little more, but after that we were on the best of terms. I am proud of myself for having dealt with the situation so competently.

Int: You mentioned earlier that the Party wanted you to travel first class.

G.L.: That was sheer insanity. Not always, of course. People like Zoltán Szántó were able to travel undisturbed in a sleeping-car from Vienna without anything happening to them. But if I had travelled in a sleeping-car, I would have been on tenterhooks about whether I would meet an old schoolmate or someone of the sort who would instantly recognize me.

Int: So third class was better.

.L.: I went to Bratislava and from there I travelled home third class on the Berlin-Budapest Express.

Int: What did you achieve there?

G.L.: I had contacts with about eight people, the leaders of the various cells. I took part in the meetings of the local Central Committee and was in effect in charge of affairs for those three months.

Int: So your visit was useful.

G.L.: It had a certain utility. It was also beneficial to ensure that undercover activity was not made into a fetish. The fact was that in general, though not always with the comrades in Pest, it was possible to achieve total success if one went about things punctiliously. There was a very slight possibility, about a thousand to one, that someone I knew from before would turn up at the wrong moment. But there are more than a million people in Budapest and the probability of such an encounter was extremely slight. During my stay in Budapest there was a period when arrests were made on a large scale and I could not rely on the normal procedures. For example, I instructed Imre Sallai, who produced the newspaper, that I would hand over my manuscript at 10.05 a.m. on such and such a street corner. At 10.05 I met him on the corner and gave him a folder. He went to the right, I went to the left and no one had any suspicions. All sorts of technical problems occurred with such arrangements. If Sallai was late, the risk of being caught increased not just ten-fold, but far more than that. For if I strolled up and down and then was seen to pass something on to someone, the whole thing became very obvious. All such variations had to be reckoned with. There was a school of thought among undercover workers that you should not leave from or arrive at major railway stations, but only use smaller stations. In my own view smaller stations were highly dangerous. How many people boarded the Vienna Express from Gödöllö? Simply to wait on the platform at Gödöllö for the Vienna Express was enough to lay oneself open to suspicion. On the other hand, if you turned up at the East Station... I operated a system whereby I would show only a platform-ticket at the barrier to the train. Another comrade then brought my luggage through, boarded the train and stayed on it for a couple of minutes. After that, I would board it myself. No one paid any attention, because that sort of thing happens perhaps a hundred times at the East Station every time a train leaves. So long as everything is done as carefully as possible, the chances of being caught are minimal.

Int: Could you name any of the Communists you met in Hungary in 1929?

G.L.: Well, those people are no longer of any interest. Of those who are important today I could mention Sándor Szerényi. Or to take another example, a better one, there was István Friss who as a young man was editor of the illegal newspaper.

Int: In connection with the dictatorship of the proletariat we spoke of Kun's role in the creation of martyrs... Were these activities characteristic of the whole period?

G.L.: No, I am imputing to Kun something at which he never even hinted. However, I am personally convinced that some such thought lurked at the back of his mind.

Int: I have not read the volume of Julius Hay's autobiography that has come out,[7] but apparently he claims that Kun sent his political opponents to Hungary so that they would be caught and killed.

G.L.: It is not impossible. I do not want to make any moral judgements about Béla Kun, but from what I knew of his character... I believe I have already quoted my first wife's perceptive remark that he reminded her of Vautrin.

Int: Are there any dates or facts, or is it just a matter of surmises?

G.L.: These are matters that cannot be proved one way or the other. After all, I myself went to Budapest and came back safe and sound. So I do not think one can prove that he did anything so disgusting. What was disgusting was Kun himself, as a moral being. But as far as such accusations are concerned, it was I who made efforts to get back to Budapest.

Int: But the fact that you came back safe and sound does not actually prove anything in Kun's favour. After all, you had to change your lodgings on the very first day.

G.L.: There are such things as coincidences. The coincidence with my lodgings cannot be placed at his door, since it was the locals who had arranged it for me and they could not know about my close contacts with *Nyugat*.

Int: In a word, Hay's assertion may be true or it may be false.

G.L.: It cannot be regarded as proven. One thing is certain: namely, that Kun had a pretty casual way of dealing with so-called awkward people working undercover. But there is no evidence to indicate whether that was out of political conviction, negligence or even malice.

Int: I believe that Hay mentions this story in connection with Sallai.

G.L.: Such suspicions are only justifiable in Sallai's case, because under the dictatorship Sallai was Korvin's deputy. In consequence, it was quite certain that he would be hanged if he were caught. Obviously, the risk was too great to take. On the other hand, it is quite true that Sallai wanted very much to go back to Hungary. It is not the case that he was sent. The situation was such that if one of the leaders never went to Hungary, he would ultimately lose credibility in the Hungarian Party. In my view Kun and Landler were the only exceptions to this.

Int: While we are on the subject, what were your relations with Hay?

G.L.: Early on we were very friendly. I liked his first plays, *God, Emperor and Peasant* and *Having*, very much indeed. But after that Hay turned into a theatre man on the make and our friendship disappeared completely.

Int: Where did you first meet?

G.L.: In Moscow.

Int: Did you not have any friendly contact after 1945?

G.L.: After 1945 we did not have any contact at all. He had simply become a man on the make.

Int: I take it that his undoing was due to something that may not be tragic in the case of a philosopher or in certain other fields, but is a grave drawback for a writer, and this was that he had no mother tongue, no language of which he was really master. His German was doubtless better than his Hungarian, but not even in his early plays did he have an ear for the striking or pithy language you need for the stage.

G.L.: On the other hand his early plays do contain genuine conflicts. There is no doubt that *Having* does focus on a serious conflict. You must not forget the state of Hungarian drama in those days. That was a striking achievement.

Int: Even today that would be a striking achievement. Even today conflicts are thin on the ground in our theatre.

G.L.: In Hungarian plays there are no conflicts. Hay's works were a real turning-point in the Hungarian theatre.

Int: Where did you live after your illegal trip to Hungary?

G.L.: After the Blum Theses I went to Moscow for the Second Party Congress.

Int: When did you first visit Moscow?

G.L.: My first visit was at the time of the Third Congress of the Comintern in 1921, but that was only for the few weeks of the Congress itself. After the Second Party Congress, however, I stayed for over a year. From there I went on to Germany and returned to the Soviet Union after Hitler's seizure of power until the liberation.

Int: Where did you work during your first long stay in Moscow?

G.L.: I worked in the Marx-Engels Institute. We have already discussed the Hungarian Blum Theses. But there was then a very interesting development. If you look at the Stalin era now, of course you have to investigate the actual vestiges of Stalinism and deal with them much more rigorously than is normal at present. But on the other hand, it is sheer prejudice to imagine that everything Stalin did was wrong or anti-Marxist. I mention this in connection with the fact that in 1930, during my first extended stay in the Soviet Union, the so-called philosophical debate took place in which Stalin opposed Deborin and his school. Of course a number of the later features of Stalinism did manifest themselves in this debate, but for all that, Stalin defended an extremely important point of view which played a very positive role in my own development. For what he did was to launch an attack on the so-called Plekhanov orthodoxy which was so prominent in Russia at the time. He protested against the need to view Plekhanov as a great theoretician who provided the main mediating link with Marx. Stalin maintained that it was instead the Marx-Lenin tradition—and by implication the Stalin line as well—which had to be considered valid. If you only consider Stalin's chief purpose in this argument, then obviously you have a Stalinist way of thinking, but for me it still had one extremely important consequence: Stalin's criticism of Plekhanov gave me the idea of making a similar critique of Mehring. Both Plekhanov and Mehring had thought it necessary to supplement Marx's thought by extending it to areas of knowledge that go beyond social and economic questions. You will perhaps recollect that Mehring introduced Kantian aesthetics into Marx, and Plekhanov introduced what was essentially a positivist aesthetics. The way I interpreted Stalin's critique of the Plekhanov orthodoxy was to see it as a view which rejected the idea that Marxism was just one socio-economic theory among others. Instead Stalin saw it as a totalizing world-view. This implied that it must also contain a Marxist aesthetics which did not have to be borrowed from Kant or anyone else. These were ideas that were developed further by Lifshitz and myself. At the time I was working with Lifshitz in the Marx-Engels Institute. Our entire subsequent development was set in train by our work on this idea. You won't find much made of this in the histories of philosophy, but it remains a fact that we were the first to speak of a specific Marxist aesthetics, as opposed to this or that aesthetics which would complete the Marxist system. The notion that aesthetics forms an organic part of Marxism is to be found in the essay I wrote on the Sickingen debate between Marx and Lassalle, and in the case of Lifshitz, it is present in his early book on the young Marx.[8] In contrast to our other ideas this one has, interestingly enough, a very wide currency in the Soviet Union. And the reason for its popularity is that no one really knows that it was Lifshitz and I who introduced it.

Int: What is your general view of Lifshitz?

G.L.: My view of Lifshitz is that he was one of the most talented people of the period, above all in the realm of literature. He had a very clear understanding of the problem of realism, but he did not extend it to other cultural spheres. You should not forget that I wrote *The Young Hegel* in the thirties and that my views on Hegel ran counter to the whole official line, since in Zhdanov's eyes he was just one of the Romantic critics of the French Revolution. This is to say nothing of the beginnings of my work on *The Destruction of Reason*, which also dates back to that time. In that book I criticized the dogma that modern philosophy is concerned exclusively with the opposition between materialism and idealism. Accordingly I adopted a position which was critical of both rationalism and irrationalism, in either their materialist or idealist forms. All this means that thematically I had already gone far beyond what Lifshitz was doing. Poor old Lifshitz stayed behind in Russia. I don't mean that as a criticism, but after all, what could he achieve in Russia? His ideas became conservative through and through. I will not say that this put an end to our friendship, but the fact is that Lifshitz is still brooding over ideas that I have long since left behind me.

Int: There must have been more to it than that, since his name could hardly be mentioned in Hungary after 1945.

G.L.: Yes, but that was because of the Jewish question. Intellectually, he was always highly orthodox, particularly in his insistence that only materialist philosophy is compatible with realism in the arts.

Int: What are the works of modern literature about which you disagree with him? After all, Comrade Lukács, you too are on record as having rejected a large number of modern writers. I am thinking, for example, of the plays of Ionesco or Beckett. Which are the modern works that you would accept and Lifshitz reject?

G.L.: In modern drama there are undoubtedly traces of an incipient revival of the tragic. I have watched these developments with great care, because in my opinion it is important to point out that these things still exist today. Lifshitz entirely rejected such phenomena.

Int: In which particular writers do you see signs of this revival of the tragic?

G.L.: I see it, for instance, in Dürrenmatt's *Besuch der alten Dame* (The Visit). I feel very critical of his subsequent work, but his first play...

Int: Were there also disagreements between Lifshitz and yourself on the plastic arts?

G.L.: We disagreed to the extent that I regarded Cézanne and Van Gogh as pinnacles of modern art, whereas he placed the high points much further back in the past.

Int: Where in the past?

G.L.: In the Renaissance.

Int: That is indeed a long way back. Were there similar divergences of opinion in music?

G.L.: Music was not so important in those days: it only began to concern me when I found myself confronted with the problem of Bartók.

Int: Comrade Lukács, what was the motive behind your move to Berlin?

G.L.: That is very simple. I wanted to leave Moscow. After the Blum Theses, I called on Ryazanov and he summed up the situation very wittily. 'Ah ha,' he said, 'you have been Cominterned.'

Int: And what became of Ryazanov?

G.L.: Ryazanov was Director of the Marx-Engels Institute, a famous Marxist responsible for editing the great edition of the works of Marx and Engels. He was an eccentric man, but very highly cultivated and with a very profound knowledge of Marx. While I was in Moscow he had some difficulties with the authorities, as a result of which he was transferred to the provinces. In the period of the great trials he finally disappeared. Nothing is known about the details.

Int: And why did you settle in Berlin?

G.L.: I was only interested in Vienna as a centre of Hungarian activities. But I could not go to Vienna because the Hungarian Party—that is to say, Kun and his colleagues—would have objected. I opted for Berlin, then, with the idea, the quite correct idea, that I could do some serious work in the German Party. In the two or three years of my stay in Berlin I worked exclusively on German problems.

Int: Didn't Andor Gábor remain in Vienna?

G.L.: No, he had moved to Berlin in the Twenties.

Int: And Béla Balázs?

G.L.: Balázs also went to Berlin and then on to Moscow. But there had long since been a parting of the ways between us during the emigration.

Int: Why was that?

G.L.: We have already discussed it. Balázs was on the left politically. But he was undergoing an intellectual transformation, busily integrating his old ideas into official communism. This gave rise to a dualism which I could not accept either intellectually or artistically. With the exception of his first volume of verse, *Male Voice Choir*, the works he produced suffered from this dualism and gradually led to an estrangement between us. I should add, so that you can see that my attitude was not one of sectarianism, that I always advised Balázs against joining the Party. My opinion was that this question of ideology would not prove so troublesome in a man who remained a bourgeois writer in sympathy with the Communists. No one would have obliged such a man to commit himself to any Marxist doctrines and he might have remained a left-wing, bourgeois writer. But he wanted to join the Party at all costs.

Int: Do you also have such a scathing view of Balázs's contribution to film theory?

G.L.: Balázs was lucky that there was no Marxist theory of film, and so he could write about it as he thought fit and the dualism did not make its appearance. I do not know whether you have seen *Cinka Panna*, for which Kodály himself wrote the music after 1945? It was simply awful. On the one hand, Balázs could not be dissuaded from trying to establish himself as a Marxist scholar. So what he did was to turn Rákóczi and Bercsényi into opportunists and opposed them to László Ocskai, who was to be the representative of the plebeian democratic policy. That in itself was already the height of idiocy. But he then went even further and came up with the following plot: Bercsényi sends an emissary with a plan of action to Ocskai. The outstanding feature of this plan is that it is identical with Ocskai's original plan. But since it now comes to him as Bercsényi's own idea, he refuses to implement it. The whole film is full of such over-simplifications and I advised Balázs to burn the manuscripts when we were still in Moscow.

Int: How profound was the process of ideological change in the case of Andor Gábor?

G.L.: Andor Gábor had no difficulty in accepting the messianic sectarianism that arose after 1919 and expressed itself in Hungary in a passionate hatred of Horthy and his supporters, and in Vienna even dispensed with the sectarian features. But in the phase of transition towards Stalinism, Gábor felt a profound sense of disillusionment, and ultimately that is what finished the old man off. For I do not think there is anyone in the whole world who has read his later works—it is unfortunate that Gábor's wife should have thought fit to produce them in ten volumes. His Viennese poems are still worthy of mention, and his pamphlet-like articles from the *Becsi Magyar Ujság* (Viennese Hungarian News) were first rate. They are among the best Hungarian pamphlets. Unfortunately, it has to be said that apart from myself there is not a single Hungarian writer who survived the Stalin era intact. We have already spoken of Hay. So when Révai defended Exile literature at the Party Congress in Hungary, he was really quite in error on this point. The writers who had remained in Hungary were quite right in rejecting his point of view. Neither Balázs, nor Gábor, nor Julius Hay...

Int: To say nothing of Béla Illés.

G.L.: Béla Illés, Sándor Gergely...

Int: But Béla Illés managed to deteriorate, for his first book was not bad at all.

G.L.: The *Carpathian Rhapsody* is still worth reading as a book, but what he wrote after that is terrible.

Int: We can now turn to your stay in Berlin. When did you arrive there?

G.L.: In Summer 1931.

Int: Did you remain there until Hitler's seizure of power?

G.L.: Hitler came to power in January 1933 and I left for Moscow in March.

Int: You seem to have made a habit of staying in a place for two months after the counter-revolution had triumphed.

G.L.: I stayed in Berlin because the Party had the completely misguided idea that I ought to accomplish the transformation of the intellectual organizations into an undercover network. That was of course naive, for who had any idea at the time what an undercover organization under Hitler would look like?

Int: What did you do in Berlin? Did you write?

G.L.: I mainly wrote.

Int: Did you work for a newspaper or a journal?

G.L.: I did not actually have a contract, but I wrote regularly for the *Linkskurve* and other Communist papers.

Int: You wrote a relatively large number of essays for the *Linkskurve*. Did you write them all at this period, or had you sent them any articles from Vienna?

G.L.: No, they were all written in Berlin. They have now been reprinted. In Volume 4 of my Works.[9]

Int: Were you at all active in the German Writers Association?

G.L.: There was a large left-wing group in the German Writers Association, a number of whom were Communists. I was one of the leaders of this Communist group.

Int: Was it possible to declare openly that one was a Communist?

G.L.: Well, I could not conceal that I was a Communist; and nor could such people as Wittfogel or Becher, both of whom played an important role at the time. Everyone knew that they were Communists.

Int: Was your position not made more difficult because you were an émigré Communist and had no organizational links?

G.L.: Before Hitler came to power that did not cause any problems. I do not know whether others had the same experience, but I was a fairly well-known German writer, and not just in Communist circles. Having been written about by Thomas Mann and others, I belonged to the so-called writers' élite. So the fact that I was a Communist was overlooked.

Int: Is it true that this period, let us say until the end of your emigration in Germany in 1933, was the time in which the Marxist views you still hold today were initially formed?

G.L.: Well, some of my views do date back to this period, as can be very clearly seen in my critique of Willy Bredel's naturalism in *Linkskurve*. My attack on him came at a time when the official view of the German Communists was that Bredel was the great representative of proletarian literature. I have always denied the artistic merits of such Communist naturalism.

Int: Does your acquaintance with Brecht also date from this period?

G.L.: Yes.

Int: So much is being written in East Germany now about your relationship with him, so many slanders...

G.L.: At the time I thought Brecht a sectarian and there can be no doubt that his first plays, his *Lehrstücke* [didactic plays], are very strongly sectarian in character. In consequence I was always somewhat critical of Brechtian tendencies, and more recently my criticism has been increasingly sharp. The credit for this must be placed firmly at the door of Brecht's wife who, as can still be seen today, has always adopted whatever was the official line in order to promote Brecht's reputation as a writer. I can tell you a story to illustrate the point. My position in Germany then was that I had received official permission to continue my cultural activities as a writer. But I was told that I should refrain from interfering in politics. I then found myself under attack by Frau Brecht at a party meeting on the grounds that I ought to support this or that political position at the regional party assembly. I replied simply that I would be very grateful if she would go along to the police and repeat it all there, but not here.

Int: How did your relationship with Brecht develop in later years?

G.L.: There were undoubtedly differences of opinion during the debate on Expressionism, and it is quite evident that Brecht's sympathies lay closer to the Expressionists than to me. But during the war—I no longer recall the precise year—we once met in Moscow. He had been living for a time in Denmark and Finland and had then travelled across the Soviet Union to America. We met in a Moscow café and he said to me: 'The fact is that there are a host of people who want to set me against you at any price and I am quite sure that there are just as many eager to set you against me. We ought not to let ourselves become involved in such matters.' Our talk ended amusingly as we agreed to meet an hour after peace was concluded in such-and-such a café. So, we parted on friendly terms in Moscow even though I had criticized all sorts of things in the course of the Expressionism debate. I should add that, as a result of my deep involvement in Hungarian affairs, I was guilty of one serious literary omission in failing to write an essay about Brecht's last period even after I had become aware of its major importance. If I had done so, my opinion of his achievement would have been plain for all to see. Still, I always looked Brecht up when I went to Berlin and we often spent time together. I told him what I thought of his later works and we discussed the matter. I can honestly say that we became quite friendly, and this is confirmed by the fact that I was one of the people who was asked by his wife to make one of the speeches in Berlin immediately after his death. I happened to be staying at a German spa and was invited to go to Berlin to make the speech.

Int: If I may be a little critical, I think that there may be another side to your omission. For it may very well be the case that with the exception of *The Threepenny Opera*, Brecht's early plays will not survive...

G.L.: That is so.

Int: But his early poetry will prove to be of lasting value.

G.L.: To tell the truth, I have never really studied Brecht's lyric poetry in any detail. On the other hand, I have a very high opinion of his later plays. I talk about them in my *Aesthetics* and elsewhere. It was simply a mistake on my part, due to my heavy workload, that I did not write a single article for a German journal during the thirties explaining how much Brecht's later plays differed from the earlier ones.

Int: In the thirties? Don't you mean the forties?

G.L.: Yes, the forties.

Int: After all, in *Progress and Reaction in German Literature* you could not have had any knowledge of the later plays, since you wrote it in the thirties.

G.L.: That is right. I meant the forties. I simply made a mistake.[10]

Int: Do you know why Brecht did not stay in the Soviet Union as an émigré. Did he give you any explanation?

G.L.: The fact was—how shall I put it?—that Brecht always thought up the most extraordinary schemes for making sure, on the one hand, that a safe, kosher place was kept for him in the party and, on the other hand, that he always retained complete freedom for himself. It is characteristic of him that, before going to East Berlin, he took out Austrian citizenship and retained it to the end.

Int: To my knowledge he kept his money in a Scandinavian bank and sold the copyright of his works to the West German publishing house Suhrkamp. That is to say, he involved four different countries in ensuring the safety of himself and his works.

G.L.: In short—and his wife was very much the moving spirit in this—Brecht was an extremely cautious man who, when it came to safeguarding his freedom, did not think twice before accepting a good deal.

Int: What contact did you have with other writers in Berlin? With Anna Seghers, for example?

G.L.: I was on friendly terms with Anna Seghers until fairly recently. Our correspondence, too, was always very friendly. It was only when she succumbed to Ulbricht's latest literary fashion, in what was to my way of thinking a completely mindless and superfluous manner, that our friendship just died a natural death.

Int: Had she already started to write in Berlin?

G.L.: Yes, in the thirties, before Hitler came to power.

Int: I believe that she was married to a Hungarian.

G.L.: Yes, her husband was a Hungarian, but one of the unpleasant kind. I didn't think he was completely kosher—I mean, he always slavishly followed the Party line. In that respect I think he had an unfortunate influence on her.

Int: What about other writers like Bloch or Becher?

G.L.: I had some contact with Bloch. With Becher I had a good friendship. He was my most important link with German writers, since my former literary connections had come to a full stop. This was partly because they were no longer alive, partly because some of them, such as Thomas Mann, took an extremely diplomatic view of their relationship with me.

Int: What form did his diplomacy take?

G.L.: He would never say anything good about me without immediately qualifying it.

Int: Was this out of political prudence or out of a wish not to jeopardize his bourgeois prestige?

G.L.: I think that in Thomas Mann's eyes, I am not sure what the Hungarian word is, I was something of an uncanny figure. It is not impossible that this was so right from the start and that it had nothing to do with my communism. It was more a matter of both our characters. A very suspicious fact has emerged recently. An American professor wrote to me that he had been examining the manuscript of *Death in Venice* in the Thomas Mann Archive and had found literal extracts from *Soul and Form* without any quotation marks. Anyone who is familiar with Thomas Mann's early years knows full well that he never missed the first opportunity to make the acquaintance of a critic. In my case he never made any attempt. And at the time I was not even a Communist. In short, there must be some other reason which has remained unknown to me. This is why I think that in his eyes there was something uncanny about me.

Int: There may be confirmation of this in the literary tradition that the character of Naphta [in *The Magic Mountain*]...

G.L.: There is no doubt at all that I was the model for Naphta. But he was too intelligent not to have known that Naphta's opinions were very different from mine. On this topic too the letters contain a large number of highly diplomatic utterances. For instance, in his correspondence with a German literary historian of French origin, he begs him to say nothing about the Naphta question because I had hitherto made nothing but friendly remarks about his great novel, *The Magic Mountain*. What he meant was that I had obviously not noticed that Naphta was based on myself.

Int: As if it would have interested you, Comrade Lukács...

G.L.: I once gave an interview in the *Spiegel* in which I said that if Thomas Mann had asked me in Vienna whether he might use me as a model, I would have agreed, just as I would have done had he said he had left his cigar case at home and asked me for a cigar.

Int: There is another text which provides philological proof that Thomas Mann had you in mind when creating the character of Naphta. In Mann's letter to Chancellor Seipel there are passages which are almost identical with what Hans Castorp says about Naphta.

G.L.: It cannot be denied that Thomas Mann wanted to describe me in his portrayal of Naphta. But if I can recognize particular, well-known writers in his early stories and find this amusing and the portraits entertaining, why should I object when I receive the same treatment? Similarly, I would never inquire whether a person who has been depicted in a novel really bears any relation to his portrait, since this question is really without interest. What is important is whether the writer has succeeded in portraying the human type he had in mind. And in the same way I would not ask whether Naphta is a good likeness of myself. In Naphta Thomas Mann has obviously succeeded in his intention. Hence there is nothing wrong with Naphta at all.

Int: A writer either bases his characters on his acquaintances or else he aims at an abstraction in which the reader can recognize everyone or no one.

G.L.: If Thomas Mann had had to worry all the time that people might recognize me... I should add, of course, that the writer must sometimes deviate from his model because of the needs of the particular story. To give a very simple illustration of this: In August 1919 I left Budapest, and of course I was quite without money. I only had one suit when I left, and I continued wearing it throughout 1919 and 1920. It was also the suit in which I visited Thomas Mann, so that it was impossible for him to see me as an elegant man. He invented Naphta's elegance because it fitted his conception of the character. I should add that elegance has never been a characteristic of mine. There is a very nice remark by Max Liebermann, who once said he had painted someone so that he was more like himself in the picture than he was in reality. A writer needs a particular figure. Thomas Mann used me as the basis for his character, but he freely altered everything according to his needs. I do not imagine that he paid much attention to whether I was elegantly dressed or not.

Int: I am sure that his knowledge that you came from a wealthy family would have affected the way he portrayed the character.

G.L.: That is quite possible; nevertheless, I was not elegantly dressed when I visited Thomas Mann in May 1920.

Int: I believe you met again in 1955 during the celebrations on the 150th anniversary of Schiller's death.

G.L.: That too was very typical of Thomas Mann. In the course of the celebrations in Jena we were staying in the same hotel. The meals were organized in such a way that the bigwigs, the top bureaucrats, Ulbricht and the rest, all ate together in a separate room together with Becher and the bourgeois writer Thomas Mann, whereas I dined together with the middle classes in the hotel. It did not occur to Thomas Mann once to say to Becher, 'Surely we could invite Lukács to join us!'

Int: Nor did it occur to Becher.

G.L.: That is because Becher was another such diplomat as Thomas Mann.

Int: But this had serious consequences in his case. Whereas Thomas Mann's diplomacy did not affect his work, Becher's talent was destroyed by his attempts at diplomacy.

G.L.: As you see, I am very liberal in such matters. A good writer can be allowed almost anything. I once had an exchange of letters with Thomas Mann—unfortunately they were all destroyed in Vienna—which made me afraid that we might fall out altogether. I wrote to him while the Szántó trial was in progress, urging him to send a telegram to Horthy protesting against the trial. Thomas Mann replied with a long letter in which he told me that he had just attended a session of the PEN Club in Poland and that all these great ideological debates were truly marvellous, quite unlike politics in which he would not care to become involved. In reply I wrote an extremely rude letter accusing him of thinking that politics was wonderful when it came to lending ideological support to Pilsudski's semi-fascism at a PEN Congress. That really was something to get excited about. But when the problem was to rescue a decent Communist from death, then politics suddenly became a dirty business. I was convinced that this letter would put an end to any relationship between us. Instead I received a cable three days later, 'Have telegraphed Horthy.' I regret very much that this telegram is no longer in existence.

Int: But the letter might well be in the Thomas Mann Archive.

G.L.: No, the letter is not there either. I destroyed it.

Int: But what about the letter you wrote, Comrade Lukács?

G.L.: That may very well be there, but they are unlikely to be very proud of it.

Int: The copy of Mann's letter must also be there. As far as I know he always took a copy of everything you could think of, partly for posterity, so that the materials would be there for the opening of the Archive.

G.L.: It is possible that the letter is somewhere or other. Our view at the time was that we might wish to make use of Thomas Mann on other occasions, and indeed that we ought to use him when possible. Hence I had to take care that, if my house was searched, no letters from him would be discovered. That is why we destroyed them.

Int: Did your friendship with Ernst Fischer date back to your years in Vienna?

G.L.: No. It started in Moscow.

Int: For I believe that Ernst Fischer corresponded with Thomas Mann on similar matters.

G.L.: Ernst Fischer was from the outset a Communist who was in touch with neutral observers and sought to establish contacts with them.

Int: Let us go back to your departure for Moscow in 1933. Did you already have to travel illegally?

G.L.: All my journeys were illegal. I had no passport, since the Hungarians would not give me one. I had already travelled with a forged passport even when I was going back and forth between Vienna, Prague and Berlin. Before 1945 I never travelled anywhere in Europe with a legal passport.

Int: When you returned to Moscow did you resume work at the Marx-Engels Institute?

G.L.: No, I did not return to the Marx-Engels Institute. In the meantime a campaign had been launched against the RAPP[11] on Stalin's initiative which undoubtedly had its positive sides. Its aim, a laudable one in my opinion, was to undermine the position of Averbakh, the Trotskyist head of the RAPP. This was Stalin's only interest in the matter. But there were also others involved in the campaign, notably Yudin and above all Usevich. They attacked the bureaucratic RAPP aristocracy with its narrow-minded insistence on allowing only communist writers into the organization. They wished to replace it with a general association which every Russian writer would be entitled to join and which could then organize the affairs of Russian authors in general. I also took part in this campaign. To a certain extent the movement was split into two parts. The purely Stalinist wing was content with the isolation of Averbakh, who was eliminated in due course and killed during the great purges. The other wing founded the periodical *Literaturnii Kritik* with the aim of bringing about a democratic revolution in Russian literature. I was involved in this during the last phase of my stay in Russia.

Int: What scope did the journal have during the period when Stalinism was on the rise?

G.L.: It must not be forgotten that the practical influence of Stalinism made itself felt via the central Party apparatus. I do not know why, but it was undoubtedly the case that Stalin thought of the philosophers Mityin and Yudin as his men. They therefore played an important role on the Central Committee, and Yudin could make use of Usevich to negotiate concessions for *Literaturnii Kritik*. This was why I was spared at the period of the great trials; in fact, none of the activists on the board of *Literaturnii Kritik* fell victim during the purges. I was fortunate in that Usevich was my Moscow friend. She in turn was friendly with Yudin. In this way we worked as a team in the Central Committee, even though Fadeyev and others, who belonged to other factions, attacked us incessantly. Thanks to my proverbial good fortune, my arrest was prevented by a concatenation of events. On the one hand, we were protected by Yudin. On the other, I was no longer active in the Hungarian Party, and so no one in the Hungarian Party had any memory of me. The trials were held between 1936 and 1937. The debate about the Blum Theses had taken place around 1930. Anyone who had kept his distance from the Hungarian Party during the whole of the intervening period had been completely forgotten. Personal matters were not so fixed as they are today in an age of detailed records and so forth. In addition—and this is perhaps a cynical observation—I had very inferior living quarters that were less attractive to the NKVD.

Int: In this connection there is another passage in your autobiography which I do not understand: '*Good luck at a time of catastrophes, Bukharin-Radek 1930...*'

G.L.: When I returned to Moscow, Bukharin gave me a very friendly reception. He had been kind enough to arrange a contact for me, which I turned down. But for that fortunate circumstance, I would have been drawn into Stalin's purges.

Int: And what is the meaning of, '*Good luck, nevertheless, in 1941*'?

G.L.: In 1941 I was arrested after all.

Int: Is that what you call 'lucky'?

G.L.: What I mean by 'lucky' is that I was not arrested until 1941. By that time the executions had stopped.

Int: Comrade Lukács, throughout your memoirs there is a constant refrain, 'I was extremely lucky'. I cannot help thinking of Solzhenitsyn's Ivan Denisovich, who also had constant good fortune.

G.L.: I went through one of the greatest purges known to history. At the end of the campaign, when the factors motivating it had ceased to be important, I was arrested and held in detention for two months. That can only be described as good luck.

Int: Did you ever learn why you had been detained?

G.L.: When I was put in prison, I was told that I was being arrested as the Moscow representative of the Hungarian Political Police.

Int: What evidence was there for this charge?

G.L.: I haven't the faintest idea since no documents were produced. When I was arrested, they searched my flat and confiscated a file which contained my curriculum vitae and applications for various Party posts and other posts as well. All the questions put to me were connected with the information in that file. The level can be gauged from what my interrogator said to me on one occasion: 'I have read all these things and it is clear that at the time of the Third Congress you were an ultra-leftist, that is to say, a Trotskyist.' I replied that the only truth in his assertion was that I had indeed been an ultra-leftist at the time of the Third Congress, but at that time Trotsky himself had not been a Trotskyist but had supported Lenin. Then he asked me who had been Trotskyites at the time. I said that some of the Italian Communists and a section of the Polish Communists had been Trotskyists, as well as the Germans, Maslow, Ruth Fischer and Thälmann. When I mentioned Thälmann, he went red in the face and said I was lying. I said it was pointless for us to argue about what was a lie and what the truth. Instead I recommended that he look up the records of the Third Congress in their library: particularly Thälmann's speech, Lenin's reply and Trotsky's intervention. He didn't mention the matter again.

Int: Were your books confiscated?

G.L.: No. Nothing was taken.

Int: Did you have any books in your possession that could have been confiscated?

G.L.: No. I was told that my library had been confiscated, but Gertrud had made sure that they took nothing.

Int: Had you destroyed any books that could have compromised you?

G.L.: Yes. That was necessary, since it would have been very dangerous if they had discovered any Trotsky in my possession.

Int: Was it mainly Trotsky's works that you destroyed?

G.L.: Mainly Trotsky, Bukharin and such people who had fallen under the wheels. I should mention that it was Andor Gábor who forced me to destroy them. He appeared one day with his wife and a large bag, removed all the books I had by Trotsky and Bukharin and threw them into the river the same evening.

Int: It must have been very like the scene in Tibor Déry's *No Judgement* in which he describes how Andor Gábor warned him to take care and rewrite his book. Gábor must have been a very careful man.

G.L.: Gábor was a very remarkable man. He would have liked to protect everyone and showed great courage in this respect. For example, he was in regular correspondence with detainees, sent them food parcels, and so on. In general, Gábor was a man of rare integrity.

Int: How do you explain your relatively quick release?

G.L.: As I learned subsequently, Dimitrov intervened on my behalf.

Int: Did you know him personally?

G.L.: I knew him from Vienna, when he was there as a Bulgarian émigré. Dimitrov was constantly besieged by English and American journalists and since my English is good, even though my pronunciation is poor, I often had to translate for him and his people.

Int: Did you not have any contact with him in Moscow?

G.L.: We did not meet in Moscow. He was such a great man, and I such an unimportant one, that an ordinary meeting was out of the question.

Int: How did Dimitrov learn about your arrest?

G.L.: Very simply. Gertrud told Becher, and then Becher, Révai and Ernst Fischer went and told Dimitrov about it. Since Dimitrov thought well of me—for some reason or other he had done so since Vienna—he at once started a campaign on my behalf. Fortunately László Rudas had been arrested with me, so that the Hungarian Party joined him in his efforts. At the time Mátyás Rákosi was already preparing himself to become the future leader and was naturally on good terms with Rudas. When Dimitrov proposed a campaign to rescue Lukács and Rudas, Rákosi could hardly say, Yes to Rudas and No to Lukács. That would not have looked good.

Int: I did not know that Rudas was ever arrested. That means that there can hardly have been anyone who was not arrested.

G.L.: Only very few people were never arrested at all.

Int: Révai?

G.L.: Révai was never arrested.

Int: Nor was Béla Illés.

G.L.: That is correct. But Béla Illés was interned somewhere for a while. He was caught up in the anti-Kun wave.

Int: Does that mean that the other members of *Literaturnii Kritik*, Lifshitz and Usevich, were not affected by the purges?

G.L.: Usevich was spared throughout. She was a party member of very long-standing. As a young girl she had even been on the special train with Lenin. She had a great Party past.

Int: That was true of others too.

G.L.: But she never expressed any views outside literature. She was neither a Trotskyist nor a follower of Bukharin, and so was not affected by the purges. Incidentally, she came from a very old Bolshevik family. Her father, Felix Kon, had played a prominent part in the Polish Party, and she used to say with pride that there had never been a Polish uprising in which her family had not been involved. Simply on the basis of her pedigree she belonged to the Party elite.

Int: On its own that would have carried no weight with Stalin.

G.L.: Not on its own, but in philosophy she could rely on Mityin and Yudin, and in Stalin's presence Yudin always supported her. This was of immense service to her, especially since Stalin had no interest in literary problems in the narrower sense.

Int: Are Usevich's own works worthy of attention?

G.L.: Absolutely. But nothing by her has been translated.

Int: During the Stalinist repressions was it possible for the *Literaturnii Kritik* to defend opinions that deviated from the main Stalinist line?

G.L.: We attacked the orthodox Stalinist line on Naturalism. It should not be forgotten that Engels's letter about Balzac appeared for the first time then. We denied vigorously, without suffering any serious consequences, that ideology can be a criterion for the aesthetic achievement of a work of art—a line diametrically opposed to Stalinism. We argued that great literary works could emerge on the basis of a very bad ideology, as was the case with Balzac's royalism. This implied that a good ideology can coincide with very poor works of literature. Usevich then went on—I was not so involved in this as I knew no Russian—to attack the political poetry of the day, but she could do this without ending up in gaol.

Int: You were obviously alive to the fact that Stalin had diverged from Lenin's policy here. How far was your world-view subsequently affected by this realization?

G.L.: I think I can say that I ignored it completely. Except where literary issues were concerned, people did not interfere in our work for such reasons. That is to say, only Fadeyev really opposed us. He had been allowed to attack us. Then during a reorganization he achieved the suspension of *Literaturnii Kritik*. On the other hand, his powers did not extend to bringing about our arrest, even though that would not have been incompatible with his attitude. As for philosophy, this was the period when I started on my philosophical work and here I found myself to be in flat contradiction to Stalin's line. I wrote my book on Hegel in the second half of the thirties, at a time when Zhdanov had proclaimed Hegel to be the ideologist of feudal reaction to the French Revolution. No one is likely to claim that my Hegel book supports that interpretation. At a later stage Zhdanov together with Stalin depicted the entire history of philosophy as a long-running conflict between materialism and idealism. *The Destruction of Reason*, however, much of which was written during the war, focuses on a different polarity: namely, the struggle between rational and irrationalist philosophy. It is indeed true that the irrationalists were all idealists, but their rationalist opponents were idealists too. Hence the polarity which I depicted in *The Destruction of Reason* is wholly incompatible with the Zhdanovian theory.

Int: Did you write *The Destruction of Reason* during the war? I thought it was in the early fifties.

G.L.: I completed the book in the early fifties, but the greater part of the manuscript was finished during the war. It should be remembered that the polarity of materialism and idealism was seen as the sole theme of the history of philosophy well into the fifties. This emerged very clearly after the appearance of *The Destruction of Reason*, when I was attacked on the left for having neglected this supremely important problem.

Int: One of the fundamental propositions of *The Destruction of Reason* is that there are no innocent philosophies. Nietszche and earlier irrationalist philosophers are implicated in the rise of fascism. Comrade Lukács, could one not extend this line of argument and inquire whether Marxism was responsible for Stalinism?

G.L.: If I say to you that two times two is four and you as my orthodox follower insist that the answer is six, then I am not responsible for that.

Int: One could reply with equal justification that it is very unlikely that Nietzsche would have been personally attracted to Hitler and that he too cannot be held responsible for what was done with his ideas.

G.L.: The question is whether a theory is adopted or not. Insofar as I employ the conceptual apparatus which Engels developed for Balzac namely, his invocation of the disjuncture between art and ideology in order to explain something about Tolstoy—Engels himself becomes responsible for my interpretation of Tolstoy. If, on the contrary, I completely distort the character of Engels's argument, then Engels is not responsible. Historical responsibility can be reduced to the actual adoption of ideas. I deny, for example, that Engels's idea of the negation of the negation can be understood as a legitimate continuation of Hegel's negation of the negation. The latter is a purely logical category. In the Paris Manuscripts Marx says 'A non-objective being is a non-being.' In other words, a being that lacks materiality (*Gegenständlichkeit*) cannot exist. Being is identical with materiality. In contrast, Hegelian logic begins with a being without materiality, and the first part of Hegel's *Logic* is an attempt to convert non-materiality into materiality by including the categories of quantity and quality. This can only be done by logical casuistry. An instance of such casuistry, which in my view has occupied a central position in the ontological analysis of Marxism, is that our over-valuation of logic and epistemology has led us to imply that negation is also a form of being, even if only in a very figurative sense. So we not only talk about the negation of the negation, but we also encounter the idea that *omnis determinatio est negatio*, which was also taken over from Hegel.

Int: Doesn't that idea go back even beyond Hegel, to Spinoza?

G.L.: Yes. But in Spinoza the idea makes sense. In his philosophy it means that things are real if they are the inseparable parts of substance. As soon as they become autonomous objects their autonomy negates that substantial unity. Here, then, negation has a meaning even though we would be unable to apply it to anything without Spinoza's concept of substance. Hegel made an advance here when he defined otherness as negation. Of course, a certain element of negation is present in otherness. I can say that this is a table and not a chair. However, what makes the table a table is not that negative fact, but those positive features which are present in the table and make it something other than a chair. In my vulgar way I used to say that, if it is true that *omnis determinatio est negatio*, then you can argue that a lion is not shaving cream. Logically the sentence is impeccable, since a lion is in fact not shaving cream. But such propositions can be multiplied infinitely without any of them having a real meaning, because negation is a secondary matter in the definition of otherness. It arises in comparisons, but even there it is secondary because the mutual otherness of tables and chairs, for example, arises from positive factors, and the fact that a table is not a chair is a matter of minor importance which is actually insignificant in practical thought. On the other hand, negation becomes very important—apart from the fact that its true meaning has become rather faded—as soon as we wish to understand reality in purely logical terms. Negation in that sense would be involved in the statement, 'twice two is not five'. If I say, 'Dragons do not exist', that is a legitimate negation. The vast majority of negative propositions, however, are not genuine negations. If I assert that a lion is not shaving cream, that is not a genuine negation, but only the purely logical consequence of a subsidiary logical proposition.

Int: I understand. I think that even in the case of the dragon, we negate something that corresponds to nothing in reality.

G.L.: The negation consists precisely in the fact that the concept of being cannot be applied to a seven-headed dragon.

Int: So it is a positive assertion.

G.L.: If you can make a meaningful assertion about the crocodile and not about a seven-headed dragon, then the term 'not' obviously has a genuine meaning. But one thing is often overlooked in the extension of the meaning of negation: namely, that in practical life every negation entails a positive determination. If I assert that I am a republican, I imply that I am opposed to monarchy. That is not comparable to the assertion that there are no seven-headed dragons, for monarchies actually exist. Elimination and destruction are just as much a part of labour as labour itself. That is the specific character of human labour. If I make a stone axe, it is unavoidable that I eliminate pieces of stone from the future axe. This process of elimination is a negative activity, since I simply throw away those pieces of stone and do not concern myself with them further. In a word, my action contains an element of negativity. But this element is not identical with logical negation. In extreme cases, logical negation can only say that something should not be the case or that it is not the case. But when I remove fragments from a piece of stone in order to make a stone axe, this does not imply that something is not or should not be the case.

Int: The 'should' is dominant.

G.L.: The 'should' is dominant.

Int: The idea that something 'should not be the case' can best be expressed as the idea that 'this stone should not be round, but sharp'.

G.L.: The essence of the matter, however, is that 'it should be sharp', for alongside the assertion that 'it should not be round' I could also assert that 'it should not be elliptical', that 'it should not be a parabola' and a million other things, none of which contributes to the definition of a stone axe.

Int: Let me return to *The Destruction of Reason* and ask whether you do not think it a defect that you do not criticize in it the type of irrationalism characteristic of Stalinism? I am thinking, for example, of the cult of personality, which is undoubtedly a kind of irrationalism.

G.L.: Philosophically, Stalinism was dominated by a kind of hyper-rationalism. What you call irrationalism was in fact a type of hyper-rationalism. From Schelling onwards trends hostile to rationalism gained ground within German philosophy—including Kierkegaard. A value in the real world was ascribed to these trends. With Stalin rationalism acquired a form which bordered on the absurd, but it was still something other than irrationalism.

Int: But does it not in some sense form part of *The Destruction of Reason*?

G.L.: I have never doubted for a moment that Stalinism involved the destruction of reason. But I would not think it right to criticize Stalin, let us say, because we had discovered some parallel or other to Nietzsche. We would never arrive at a true understanding of Stalinism by those means. The essence of Stalinism, in my opinion, is that the workers' movement continues to assert the practical nature of Marxism in theory, but that in practice action is not governed by a deeper insight into reality. Instead, that deeper insight is twisted into a set of tactics. For both Marx and Lenin the basic direction of the development of society was a given. Within those parameters, however, certain strategic problems emerge at any particular time. And within those same parameters you find yourself confronted by various tactical options. Stalin reversed the order, regarding tactics as primary and deducing the theoretical generalizations from them. For example, in concluding the pact with Hitler, Stalin adopted a justifiable tactic. But he drew from it the completely mistaken theoretical consequence that the Second World War was like the First: Liebknecht's motto, 'The enemy is in our own country' was applied to the English and French opposition to Hitler, and that was clearly a misapprehension. Today, too, the difficulty with Russian policy is that the leadership never faces up to the question of what is crucial from the point of view of world history, confining themselves instead to immediate tactical issues. We need only think here of the conflict between Israel and Egypt. The Russians' big power politics leads them to infer that the Egyptians are socialists and the Israelis are not socialists. In truth, of course, neither country is socialist.

Int: Comrade Lukács, your understanding of this inversion of theory and tactics is perfectly valid, but I believe that the super-rationalism of which you spoke is in many ways indistinguishable from an ordinary irrationalism. Take, for example, the belief that the wisdom of world history can be personified, not just in the person of Stalin, but in the party's tactics at any given moment.

G.L.: Doubtless when the rational is transcended, the possibility of transformation into the irrational does exist, because the rational is always concerned with concrete things. If I over-emphasize the abstract features of what is concrete, I arrive at a point at which the rationality of what was previously rational ceases to be so.

Int: You made the same point in an earlier conversation in connection with the concept of necessity. The over-extension of the concept of necessity leads ultimately to theology.

G.L.: I believe—and my view seems to tally with the natural sciences—that necessity in its classical sense can only be found in mathematics. In reality you have to investigate the probability with which actual processes will take place. For example, if the probability that a machine will function accurately is .99, then I use it as if that probability were necessity. I ignore the .01, even though in theory we are dealing not with necessity, but with a probability of .99. Anyone can observe how in daily life we treat extremely high probabilities as if they were necessities. In the classical meaning of the word, I think it is correct to say that necessities do not occur in the real world.

Int: Was not the exaggeration of necessity the very thing that characterized Stalinism philosophically? For example, it was argued that the victory of the Revolution, or more precisely, the overthrow of Czarism plus expropriations would necessarily lead to socialism after such and such a time had elapsed. That is ultimately an exaggeration of necessity that verges on the irrational.

G.L.: In *The Destruction of Reason* I tried to define a specific form of irrationalism. In Stalinism the concept of necessity is over-extended to the point where it becomes senseless. It is true that this senselessness does verge on irrationalism, but I do not believe that it is essential to an understanding of Stalinism. It is a subsidiary motif.

Int: If you were to search for the philosophical roots of Stalinism, where would you look primarily?

G.L.: The most important distortion, without which Stalinism would not have been possible, is in the way that Engels, and after him a number of Social Democrats, interpreted the idea of social determinism from a standpoint of logical necessity, as opposed to the actual social context of which Marx speaks. What Marx actually says again and again is that x people in a particular society will always discover x ways in which to react to a given system of labour, and that the process which characterizes that society will be a synthesis of those possible reactions. That cannot really be a matter of necessity in the sense that 'twice two is four' is necessary.

Int: What other books did you write during your stay in the Soviet Union?

G.L.: I wrote the essays contained in *Studies in European Realism*. Then I published a book concerned with problems of theory, followed by a collection of essays on Goethe, Balzac, Tolstoy and so on. I didn't write any other books. I wrote a large number of articles, but the publication of *The Historical Novel*, for example, was not feasible in Russia, even though I did submit it to a publisher.

Int: Your book on Hegel did not appear either.

G.L.: Even though I was not arrested during the great purges, I was still something of a suspect person in the eyes of the publishers, suspect not in the sense that I might be an enemy, but in the sense that I did not conform to the Marxist line laid down by Fadeyev.

Int: Since you mention the purges again, Comrade Lukács, could you say how you regarded them ideologically?

G.L.: I thought the trials monstrous, but consoled myself by saying that we had taken up sides with Robespierre, even though the trial of Danton, from the legal point of view, was not much better than the trial of Bukharin. My other, decisive consolation was that the crucial task of the time—the destruction of Hitler—could not be expected from the West, but only from the Soviet Union. And Stalin was the only existing anti-Hitler force.

Int: Do you hold the same views about this today? And if so, to what extent? I am not referring to Stalin in general, but more specifically to the trials.

G.L.: I could not have done anything about the trials even if I had wished to. I did have one opportunity to go to America, but I did not wish to do so.

Int: My question was not concerned with your personal behaviour, but with whether your understanding of the trials has given way to a different view?

G.L.: What I now see, and did not understand at the time, is that for Stalin these trials were absolutely superfluous. He had completely eliminated the opposition with the Bukharin trial, so that there was no advantage to be gained from the great wave of arrests. After Bukharin's trial it would have been futile for anyone to venture to oppose Stalin. Nevertheless Stalin persevered with his policy of intimidation, and in this sense I think the trials were superfluous.

Int: In my view the Soviet Union was weakened by the trials rather than strengthened. I am thinking above all of the military trials.

G.L.: The process began with the military trials and I believe that Stalin held the amateurish opinion that one soldier could easily be replaced by another. He gave up this belief on the outbreak of war and released all the generals from gaol.

Int: Much has been written about the initial defeats on the Western front, and it is generally held that they took place because all the members of the General Staff with any military experience had been arrested.

G.L.: That is all of a piece with Stalin's mentality. Since he regarded the pact with the Germans as tactically necessary, he relied on it more than was justified.

Int: Were the émigrés in agreement with Stalin on this point?

G.L.: Not I.

Int: Did you always view the pact sceptically?

G.L.: I always regarded it sceptically.

Int: You once said that you found the trials acceptable because the German threat made it essential to unite all available forces, and because anyone who opposed the central government only weakened the Soviet Union. If my memory does not deceive me, you said that although you did not believe in the evidence produced during the trials, you did not disapprove of them ideologically or, more accurately, tactically.

G.L.: It cannot be maintained that we did not disapprove of the trials tactically. Tactically we were neutral. I repeat, if Stalin used the same weapons against Trotsky as Robespierre had used against Danton, this cannot be judged according to current conditions, since at the time the crucial question was on which side America would intervene in the war.

Int: Do you think that the analogy between Robespierre and Danton and Stalin and Bukharin can still be upheld?

G.L.: No. But I do think that it was an excusable way for a Hungarian émigré living in Russia to have thought about it at the time.

Int: If you were to criticize that analogy today, how would you proceed?

G.L.: I would begin with the obvious fact that Danton was never a traitor and never lost faith in the republic, as Robespierre claimed. The same could not so clearly have been said of the accused in the Stalin trials.

Int: They were forced to admit to being traitors. Even Bukharin had to confess to treason. That is a huge and terrible difference, but only in a moral sense.

G.L.: It is only a moral distinction. But I am not thinking here of Bukharin, because I consider him to have been a man of extraordinary integrity. I believe he was a bad Marxist, but that does not provide grounds for executing him. Zinoviev and the rest, however, did a great deal to help Stalin on his road to power. They were the victims of their own actions.

Int: What role did Trotsky and his followers play in all this?

G.L.: I barely knew the Trotskyists. I knew Trotsky himself from the Third Congress and did not like him at all. I read recently in the last volume of Gorky's letters that Lenin had once said that although Trotsky had great achievements to his credit in the Civil War and was on their side, he was not really one of them and had a bad streak reminiscent of Lassalle. I agree completely with this analogy.

Int: But in contrast to the associates of Zinoviev and Kamenev, it cannot be denied that Trotsky and his followers were genuine revolutionaries. Think of Joffe, for example, who committed suicide.

G.L.: Kamenev and Zinoviev changed into bureaucrats after the Revolution. This had not yet happened to Trotsky's immediate circle. But I did not distinguish too clearly between them, because I simply disliked Trotsky and the Trotskyists on account of this Lassallean streak.

Int: And Trotsky's writings?

G.L.: Trotsky was an extraordinarily brilliant and intelligent writer. As a politician or a political theorist, I think nothing of him at all.

Int: And as a historian? What do you think of his historical studies of the Revolutions of 1905 and 1917?

G.L.: I cannot judge them. At all events Trotskyism—and here I would include Zinoviev, Kamenev and Bukharin—could only be seen as a trend which would help to bias public opinion in England and America against the Soviet Union in the struggle against Hitler. It is significant that Bloch, who was in America, refused in much the same terms to identify with Trotskyism.

Int: Comrade Lukács, you seem to be saying that Trotsky did more damage to the Soviet Union in the eyes of American public opinion than did the trials? I have the feeling that the trials caused the greater damage.

G.L.: These things cannot simply be weighed against each other. There is no doubt that the trials caused damage. It is also beyond doubt that they did damage simply because they took place. I think we are talking about a complex issue here. What was at stake at the time was the whole question of the Stalinist leadership, of whether Stalinism had given rise to a worse dictatorship than was to be expected of Trotsky and his supporters. Of course, we answered this in the negative.

Int: But in the last analysis the question was not whether we should strive for a Stalinist or Trotskyist dictatorship. Trotsky might have been a bad politician and a bad ideologist up to the mid-twenties, but later, whether from necessity or for tactical reasons, he came to see all sorts of things differently, to learn from his own errors and...

G.L.: I do not doubt that Trotsky was an extremely decent man, a talented politician, an outstanding speaker and so on. All I am saying is that there was no chance of his becoming a serious rival to Stalin who would have been acknowledged as such in both West and East. You must not forget that Trotsky's ideas simply could not be reconciled with the Stalinist policy, which was the only one to hold out any hope of resisting Hitler. For the starting-point of real resistance was the Stalin Pact.

Int: Comrade Lukács, did you ever think it possible at the beginning of hostilities, at the time of the German advance, that the Germans might win?

G.L.: No, no. From the start I was confident that Russia, which had once annihilated a greater man than Hitler, Napoleon, would also annihilate Hitler.

Int: So you placed your trust in Russia?

G.L.: Yes.

Int: And the fact that the Allies finally joined in on that side...

G.L.: Which side the Allies would join was a momentous question at the time. For if England and America had joined Hitler, I do not know how the war might have ended. But as it was, with the Anglo-American-French attacks, the scales tilted in favour of Hitler's enemies.

Int: Did the members of the emigration generally share this faith in ultimate victory, or was defeatism the dominant mood in those circles?

G.L.: There was defeatism, and it was very powerful too.

Int: In Hungarian circles or generally?

G.L.: In Hungarian circles. But you could find it elsewhere as well—in Becher, for instance, who was a cowardly and impressionable person.

Int: When did you start to feel hostile towards Trotskyism?

G.L.: I was working at the Institute of Philosophy and my attitude was determined by the fact that Russian philosophy formed an unambiguous united front against Hitler. Only the Trotskyists were opposed. Hence I was opposed to the Trotskyists.

Int: To what exactly did the Trotskyists object?

G.L.: They objected to the United Front against Hitler.

Int: Very interesting. Was Trotsky himself involved in this opposition?

G.L.: I do not know.

Int: As I remember it, Trotsky launched an extremely fierce attack on Stalin before the Stalin-Hitler Pact, perhaps for tactical reasons. Trotsky prophesied that Stalin would even form an alliance with Hitler.

G.L.: The pact with Hitler was the precondition for Hitler's attack on France and England and hence for the unleashing of a European war in which these states, and perhaps also America, would become more or less reliable allies of the Soviet Union.

Int: Did the first phase of the war cause any bad feeling in the Soviet Union? I am thinking of the Polish invasion and the fighting in Finland and the Baltic states.

G.L.: All these events caused bad feeling. There were not two people, at least among the émigrés I knew, who were able to get up in the morning as supporters of Stalin and go to bed at night with the same convictions. On mature reflection, however, it become clear that Stalin's policies would bring about an alliance against Hitler. That was an intellectual insight and not the spontaneous reaction of the émigrés.

Int: I have just been reading Malraux's memoirs. Apparently Bukharin told him during a walk they had together in the early thirties that Stalin's policies would lead to the systematic expansion of his own dictatorial powers. Bukharin talked in quite a neutral manner and without any bitter criticism of Stalin and added that Stalin would undoubtedly have him, Bukharin, executed. According to Malraux's account it sounded like a simple factual statement. Was it at all possible to sense or even to know the likely course of events?

G.L.: It is very easy to imagine that Bukharin, who was an old Communist with long experience of internal struggles and who had known Stalin when Stalin was quite an insignificant person, might have been able to foresee such an outcome.

Int: Comrade Lukács, do you remember Ervin Sinkó's book, *The Novel of a Novel*?

G.L.: Yes.

Int: As a member of the movement Sinkó was not outstandingly intelligent. But it emerges from his book, which he of course wrote with the benefit of hindsight, on the basis of his diary, that when the book opens in 1934–35, the general mood in Moscow, in literary circles and among those in the movement, pointed in just one direction: that the dreadful chain of events would unfold inexorably. I do not know to what extent this reflects Sinkó's own subjective situation.

G.L.: Sinkó's subjective situation did have a certain bearing on his views here. But of course there was no one in Moscow in his right mind who did not perceive what was going on.

Int: Did you meet Sinkó in Moscow?

G.L.: No. When Sinkó arrived in Moscow, he came with a recommendation from Romain Rolland to Béla Kun and the Comintern. Since I was on very bad terms with both the Comintern and Kun, I did not wish to meet Sinkó. He phoned me and asked when we might meet and I told him that we couldn't. I was afraid that he would side with Kun and that together they would intrigue against me.

Int: In general such suspicions were entirely justified, but in the case of Sinkó...

G.L.: In the case of Sinkó it so happens that these suspicions were not justified, but I still do not regret my attitude. I had not replied to the criticism of the Blum Theses, but I defended myself by withdrawing from all Hungarian affairs. This meant that both for Sas—Sándor Szerényi—and his colleagues, and later for Kun, there was no longer any real reason to attack the Blum Theses. Hence when Kun was toppled after the Seventh Congress and I rejoined the Hungarians, no one thought to recall the Blum Theses to mind. They had been consigned to oblivion.

Int: Did you not even have contact with your Hungarian friends during that period?

G.L.: I was in touch with my old friends, of course, but there were very few of them in Moscow. Jenö Hamburger was there, and I was in touch with him. Every month he paid my contribution to the Hungarian Club. But my contact with him was entirely private and he had absolutely nothing to do with Hungarian affairs, particularly as this came at a time following the overthrow of Sas and his colleagues, when Kun succeeded in winning over to his side the best members of the Landler faction, including Révai. Since Gertrud was in Vienna when Révai was ordered to Budapest, they met on his last evening and Révai said to her—I am quoting almost verbatim—that his entire tour was very badly prepared and he was sure he would soon be caught. Despite that, he thought it would be better to be in prison in Budapest than to be involved in Hungarian politics under Sas and his associates.

Int: Where did you spend the war years?

G.L.: I spent a year in Tashkent and after that I was in Moscow.

Int: What did you do in Tashkent? Work?

G.L.: The Moscow writers were all ordered to go to Tashkent, and so we lived there as best we could. We were involved in all sorts of things, or not, as the case might be. I had a fairly comfortable time because Alexei Tolstoy visited Tashkent as delegate of the Writers' Union and he knew of me as a writer with a reputation abroad. Hence he included me in the elite. Incidentally, I only met him once for a few minutes, but this did not lead to further contact.

Int: Were there any other Hungarians in Tashkent apart from yourself?

G.L.: Yes, of course. In fact, there were an incredible number of Hungarians.

Int: There are an incredible number of Hungarians everywhere in the world. I have a final question, a personal one. Am I right in thinking that Ferenc Jánossy was also arrested?

G.L. Yes, but that was not in connection with myself.

Int: Had he already worked in the Soviet Union?

G.L.: He had been working in a firm for about ten years, and he made one mistake. On the outbreak of war a large part of the firm was evacuated to Western Siberia and only a small part of the workforce remained in Moscow. He was one of those who chose to stay. Had he gone to Siberia he would never have been arrested.

Int: How long did he remain in detention?

G.L.: For years. He was not freed until 1945. When the party celebrated my sixtieth birthday, Jenö Varga came to us and offered to intervene on Ferko's (i.e. Ferenc's) behalf. All I had to do was to write him a letter. It was at this time that I learnt I had been elected to the Hungarian Parliament. It was unthinkable for him to have remained in an internment camp while I was a member of parliament in Hungary. So I wrote the letter.

Int: What were the circumstances in which you returned to Hungary from the Soviet Union?

G.L.: The most notable feature of my return was that all my Moscow heresies were wiped from the record. It is very significant that an article appeared in a journal completely annulling the Blum Theses. That is to say, it was announced that the Second Congress had made an incorrect decision on the issue of democracy and dictatorship, and that the mistake had been put right by Stalin. The Blum Theses were not so much as mentioned; it was as if they had never existed. The point I want to make is that my existence or non-existence in Hungary has always been a highly problematic matter. In 1959, for example, on the anniversary of the dictatorship, the Petőfi Museum exhibited a plaque from 1919 on which my name had been covered over. It is obvious that anyone who behaved as I had in 1956 and 1957 could not have been a people's commissar in 1919. The only people fit to have been people's commissars in 1919 were those who acted correctly and in accordance with party policy in 1956 and 1957. It is important not to lose sight of that fact. So everything that has been written about me in the official party history is extremely problematic, to put it mildly. I am not referring here to the judgements made about me, for judgement is the prerogative of any historian. But the idea that someone could not have been a people's commissar in 1919 just because his behaviour in 1957 was not above reproach, is one of the peculiarities of the Hungarian Party.

Int: I do not think such attitudes are the prerogative of the Hungarian Party. Trotsky too was a person who in 1905 could not have been...

G.L.: Of course, that was a speciality of the Stalin era and Trotsky was the first to suffer from it.

Int: He had been chairman of the St Petersburg Workers' Soviet...

G.L.: And he could not have been, because an opponent of Stalin could not have been a revolutionary. The same situation on a smaller scale obtained here, because in Hungary everything is on a smaller scale.

Int: Let us go back to 1945. What they wanted at the beginning was to pretend the past had not happened.

G.L.: Exactly. The outstanding feature of the period between 1945 and 1948 was that I could do what I liked. The two workers' parties were competing for popular support, and the intelligentsia naturally played a crucial role. Hence from 1945 until 1948 or 1949 I was allowed complete freedom. The Rudas debate broke out just after the union of the parties. That is to say, 'The Moor has done his duty. The Moor can depart.'[1] Lukács was no longer needed.

Int: In retrospect, what were the ideological factors that made it necessary for the Moor to depart?

G.L.: Essentially the problem was to discover democratic solutions to these ideological questions. Ever since the Blum Theses I have followed a consistent line which I have never retracted. In the initial post-war period this was accepted by Rákosi and his followers. That is, they accepted it in the sense that they tolerated it. I do not wish to give the impression that my ideas ever became the official ideology. But equally, no one made any protest. Not even about the hare.[2] That was an idea that could be exploited by the Communist Party in its propaganda campaign among the social democrats. You should not forget that Rákosi and Gerö, too, were thoroughgoing pragmatists. And of course their opinions changed in tune with changes of opinion in Moscow. I do not believe that the change in attitude towards me necessarily came directly from Moscow. It was simply the case, as I have already explained, that the Moor had done his duty and could depart. I must add that my own assessment of the situation was incorrect too, since I had thought that in the wake of the Rajk affair (in 1949) my own life and freedom were at stake and that I should not take any great risk on purely literary issues. I should also mention, incidentally, that it was Révai who told me about the Rudas debate. He phoned me and asked whether I knew that Rudas had written a disgraceful article abusing me. Of course Révai then brought this debate into line with Rákosi's general policy. Where I went wrong—and I do not really reproach myself with it, since at the time of the Rajk trial it was not hard to go astray—was in not knowing that Gerö and Rákosi had received instructions from Moscow to the effect that only the Moscow emigration was trustworthy, whereas those who had remained in Hungary and the émigrés who had returned from the West were only to be relied on within certain definite limits. I did not know this and so made concessions which may have gone beyond what was strictly necessary. At all events, when talking about this period, I always feel self-critical and am convinced that on the Rudas issue I could have escaped with fewer concessions. In my own defence I can say that if Rajk could be executed, no one could have looked for a serious guarantee that he would not be executed too, if he offered real resistance.

Int: A key issue in the Rudas debate was the accusation that you had misinterpreted the class character of a people's democracy and disparaged the role of the proletariat in the people's democracy.

G.L.: In my own view, which goes back to the Blum Theses, a people's democracy is a form of socialism that grows out of democracy. In the opposing view, the people's democracy is a dictatorship from the outset, and it is moreover that version of Stalinism into which it developed after the Tito affair.

Int: I would like to put a question to you which may be completely undialectical and unhistorical. Looking at it from your present position, do you think it conceivable that the people's democracies might have developed naturally into socialism wholly by virtue of their own internal dynamics if the external political situation had not been so desperate?

G.L.: I think so, yes. But, of course, only if there had been no Stalinism in the Soviet Union. With Stalinist methods, any such development would have been unthinkable because even the slightest deviation from the official line would have been impossible. If we think of Rajk's case, we must not forget that Rajk was an orthodox supporter of Rákosi. It is untrue that he was in the opposition. I have recently had a rather unpleasant confrontation with Mrs Rajk who took great offence because in the essay I wrote for the volume on Rajk I said that he was an extremely likeable person, but there was no question of his having been in opposition. What they did to him was in reality a pre-emptive murder, and that remains true even if Mrs Rajk finds herself surrounded by a world, a view of the world, according to which Rajk was a member of the opposition. I have read the second volume of Marosán's book in manuscript. The whole episode is very fully described there. It is interesting that up to 1949 his sympathies lay mainly with Révai and Rajk. They were the people with whom he was in closest touch. He writes very frankly about Rajk and depicts him clearly as an orthodox follower of Rákosi. There are an incredible number of these legends and I simply do not know what evidence Mrs Rajk would produce to show that Rajk was in opposition. The fact is that they simply got rid of anyone who was suspected of not endorsing Stalin's line with sufficient enthusiasm. That was the crux of the whole Rudas debate. And Révai refers to the Blum Theses at the end of one of his articles as the fount of all my mistakes. The whole debate simply proves that the dictatorship which prevailed in the fifties was a dictatorship from the very start, and that it is a myth that it was preceded by a democratic phase. This was the connection between the Rudas debate and the Blum Theses. I also learned the lesson that if such absolutely orthodox people as Rajk could be executed, it was not possible to imagine any alternative. Such a fate seemed to lie in store for anyone whose opinions deviated from the orthodox line.

Int: Your self-criticism was also justified in one respect. For you had been mistaken in thinking that a people's democracy on the basis of the Blum Theses was a conceivable option.

G.L.: That is true although my self-criticism posed it as an option that *ought not to be*, whereas I actually saw it merely as something that *had not come to be*. This was the element of untruth in my self-criticism.

Int: What differences do you see between the Moscow trials and the Rajk trial?

G.L.: It was like this. It is often overlooked that in the thirties the trials took place in the shadow of the approaching war. This is not meant as an excuse for them, but it is an excuse, a justifiable excuse, for the reactions of decent people. There were people at that time who said that they would not support Hitler in any attack on Moscow, regardless of what might be happening in Moscow itself. None of this applies to the Rajk trial, because there was no comparable threat at the time. There was the Cold War, but that was not a sufficient justification.

Int: It was indeed to some extent a cause of the Cold War.

G.L.: No, I do not think so. Stalin helped the West greatly in bringing about the Cold War, but the underlying cause was Dulles's so-called rollback policy according to which the agreements of 1945 were to be gradually reversed by pressure and all sorts of other means. I would not deny that we played into their hands, but the fact that it may have encouraged our stupidity is beside the point. So here in Hungary—and not just in Hungary—the trials went on without any justification. I do not doubt that there were two genuine spies among the ten thousand that were arrested. But that was pure chance. Already in 1941, when I was being held in the Lyubianka, I had been accused of being the resident Moscow spy of the Hungarian police. When I was released I said in reply to Lifshitz's question, 'It was very funny.' Of course, that all happened in a much more favourable climate, for they were not guilty of any great atrocities towards me. Rajk and his people were ruthlessly tortured.

Int: Even though the charges against them were likewise 'very funny'...

G.L.: The accusations were indeed very funny and entirely fabricated. In my opinion an historical distinction must be drawn between two sets of purges. The trials of Radek, Bukharin and Zinoviev were later transformed into something quite different. Around 1937 or 1938 they turned into a completely unjustified wave of persecution and all the Hungarians who lost their lives—Sándor Bartha, Gyula Lengyel and so on—had for the most part done nothing at all to merit such a fate. On the other hand, there can be no doubt that Béla Kun really was Zinoviev's henchman. And Béla Kun was caught up in the wave that swept away Zinoviev and his followers. That is to say, Zinoviev had backing both in the Comintern and in Leningrad that had to be taken seriously. But this entire group had suffered a decisive ideological defeat and in my view Khrushchev was absolutely right to criticize the trials as superfluous, although of course that judgement does not undermine the distinction I am making and two years previously the people around Zinoviev were anything but unimportant. For if you read Deutscher's book, you can see that the Trotskyist organization was in being at this time and constituted a potential opposition. In contrast to that, I am quite unaware of any opposition under Rákosi, not even arising from the Tito affair.

Int: Let us go back to the period after your return home. What work did you do? Am I correctly informed in thinking that you were a member of the Central Committee?

G.L: No.

Int: Not even for a brief period?

G.L: Not even for a brief period. I had no official function of any sort. Of course the falsification of the record nowadays knows no bounds. For example, I have been told that in an unpublished discussion at the Sötér Institute, Szabolsci tried to associate me with the Rákosi system by claiming that I was a member of the Central Committee. But if you consult the records of the party congress, you can see quite clearly that I was never a Central Committee member during the Rákosi era.

Int: But even the members were unable to do anything to stop the Rajk trial...

G.L.: That is not the point. The point is whether I was a member or not. That is not a matter for discussion, it is a question of fact. I even know that at the time when I had the greatest influence on the intelligentsia, it was suggested to Gerö and Rákosi that I should be voted onto the Central Committee. Their reply was, and in particular Gerö made the point very strongly, that of the intellectuals belonging to the party apparatus I was the only one who could even be considered for such a post, but that even I could not be considered. There is no point in discussing the matter further since the whole thing is based on a lie.

Int: Did you already have a post at the university?

G.L.: Yes.

Int: And the editorship of *Forum*?

G.L.: I think I was made editor a year later. I cannot recall the exact date.

Int: Was it a nominal post or did it involve you in genuine editorial activity?

G.L.: It was genuine editorial activity, with a conscious effort to make my policy prevail. You must not forget that *Forum* was suspended in the wake of the Rudas debate.

Int: Who were the editors of *Forum*?

G.L.: Vértes and Darvas. *Forum* was based on the idea of a Popular Front, and so the main question was whether the Popular Front would lead to the dictatorship of the proletariat.

Int: Had you known the editors previously?

G.L.: I knew Vértes very superficially as a person of longstanding oppositional views. I thought he would be suited to promoting my literary objectives. Révai had reservations about Vértes to begin with. But when I insisted on having him, he withdrew his objections. And that gives you an idea of the climate in 1945 as contrasted, say, with 1948.

Int: Did you not have any prior contact with Darvas?

G.L.: My relationship with Darvas was primarily determined—and I was concerned to keep things as they were during the life of *Forum*—by my efforts to ensure that *Forum* would be an organ of the Popular Front and not of the Communist Party, one which would proclaim the truth of Communism, but within the framework of the Popular Front.

Int: You have not yet said anything about the third editor, Gyula Ortutay.

G.L.: Gyula Ortutay was, like Darvas, a representative of the left-wing bourgeois movements and I was able to work as well with him as with Darvas. Within *Forum* there was agreement in the sense that a close relationship existed between the Communist movement and the most radical part of the non-Communist movements. This came about partly through the radicalization of the non-Communists and partly through the democratization of the Communists. This agreement remained intact up to the Rudas debate.

Int: Which writers were you in touch with personally or politically after your return? Déry? Illyés?

G.L.: I became very friendly with Déry because I wholeheartedly approved of his socialist declarations, and also because I thought highly of his literary talent. Hence I became a personal supporter of Déry and was sorry when Révai's criticism rather pushed him into the background. With Illyés matters were more complicated because, unlike Déry, he was never really one of us. At that time Déry really considered himself a Communist writer, and *The Incomplete Sentence* and *The Answer* really are Communist works, typical of those days. Illyés, on the other hand, never budged from his old half-nationalist, half-socialist viewpoint. That is to say, personally I was always on good terms with Illyés, but I was never able to see eye to eye with him on politics.

Int: And Péter Veres...?

G.L.: With Péter Veres I always had a very polite relationship based on mutual respect. Of the Populists, Ferenc Erdei was the one I always regarded as being on our side.

Int: Did a personal friendship develop with him?

G.L.: Initially we got on very well, and even became friends. Later we drifted apart.

Int: Lajos Nagy?

G.L.: I always regarded Lajos Nagy as an important Communist novelist and my opinion of his works always remained very high.

Int: I believe you had known him from when you worked for *Nyugat*.

G.L.: I did not know him then. But I became very friendly with him early in the thirties, when he was staying with Illyés in Moscow, for the Writers' Congress. He thought I was insufficiently radical. We once had a conversation in which he asked how long I though Hitler's regime would last. I told him I thought it could be stabilized for another nine or ten years, and so forth. He became immensely indignant and asked me what things were coming to if even revolutionaries were so indifferent about when a revolution would break out.

Int: If I remember rightly, he said he was not such a good Communist that....

G.L.: ...he could be indifferent to when a revolution would break out.

Int: I believe that he was very disillusioned on his return from Moscow. Is that true?

G.L.: He was very disappointed with our regime.

Int: Did he express his opinions in private conversation while he was still in Moscow?

G.L.: Yes, he did.

Int: And Illyés?

G.L.: Illyés was an even greater opportunist than Lajos Nagy. Illyés was in fact fairly orthodox at that time.

Int: Do you recollect that Illyés, in his last response in *Népszabadság*,[3] claims that your assertion that he was never one of the writers to be persecuted was untrue because he had written the text of a protest together with Babits and

Schöpflin. Do you know anything about that?

G.L.: I do not have any reliable information about that, but there are two versions of the story. In one version he was the author of the protest, in the other he was just one of the signatories. The second version can of course easily be proved or disproved.

Int: I have a copy which makes it very clear that he was not a signatory. It is true that his claim is carefully formulated: 'After all, I was the author of the protest', which need not imply that he also signed it. The fact is that he was the author of a different protest, one which never reached the public. It is said that he did not sign the protest because it was due to appear in *Szép Szó* (The Beautiful Word) and he was unwilling to associate himself with it.[4]

G.L.: These are simply evasions. *Szép Szó* went in for exclusive things of that sort and I remember criticizing it years ago because the two trends were really incompatible. This also shows that Illyés's idea of unity was perhaps not as clear-cut as he pretends today.

Int: Illyés recently gave a talk in the Student Theatre in which he said that Hungarian literature is the literature of the Populists. What is extraordinary about that is that he bases his claim on the authority of Attila József. He asserts that Attila József formulated the programme of the Populists in *My Country*.

G.L.: If by the literature of the Populists we understand what Attila József meant by it, then we can certainly accept that as a point of view. In fact there aren't any important writers in Hungarian literature who do not have such a definition of the people. But that is not what Illyés meant. And I have never heard of Attila József ever having anything to do with the Populist movement in the narrower sense.

Int: Only to the extent that he quarrelled with them. Right up to the end of his life he refused to appear on a common platform with them.

G.L.: The position was that the rural Populists felt a profound mistrust of the workers following the collapse in 1919. This is an undeniable fact that should not have been swept under the carpet, for in the last analysis it was a consequence of the mistaken policy of the Soviet Republic towards the peasantry. If you research into the mistrust towards the Communists felt by representatives of the peasantry, it must not be forgotten that there were reasons for it. I do not wish to say that this fully justifies their mistrust. The point is that their lack of enthusiasm was not simply arbitrary or based on reactionary prejudices; it was based on their rejection of the rural policy of the Soviet Republic.

Int: Can we talk about some other writers? What was your relationship with Milán Füst?

G.L.: Well, that was a very simple matter. It was a party-political relationship. Milán Füst had been promised a doctorate by a university professor long before my time.[5] I was then a supporter of a popular front policy and thought that if a prominent member of the *Nyugat* generation had been promised a university lectureship, then that promise should be kept. There is even testimony, in a book about Milán Füst, that he was very pleased with the reference I had given about him to the faculty. The book goes on to assert that in my view it was completely unimportant to decide how good a lecturer he would be. That would not count politically. But it was absolutely vital to appoint him so as not to give the impression that we were unwilling to appoint an outstanding member of *Nyugat* to a university post.

Int: I once heard Milán Füst lecture. He was incomparably more capable and more amusing than Waldapfel and all the others put together.

G.L.: I can well imagine that. It is quite clear that Milán Füst was a genuine writer and poet and that on literary matters he was perfectly capable of saying very true things, alongside some false ones.

Int: In addition it was generally held that Milán Füst expressed his own personal opinion. At that time the only other person who said what he thought was yourself, Comrade Lukács.

G.L.: There can be no doubt that Milán Füst was an important writer of the *Nyugat* variety. I must only mention a curious thing in passing. There was a sense in which I was disappointed by him. I had always believed him to be an extremely arrogant man, full of his own importance as a writer. But before the award of the doctorate he would pay me regular visits, just like an ordinary student visiting the great professor. On each occasion he would bring Gertrud a bunch of flowers. In short I was greatly disappointed by him...

Int: Only today I heard from Miksa Fenyö that Füst was in the habit of kissing Osvát's hands.

G.L.: It is not impossible, but apart from that he was an extremely arrogant man within his own narrow circle. Still, I never doubted his achievements as a writer.

Int: Oszkár Gellért?

G.L.: Oszkár Gellért was a totally self-centred man and in dealing with him everything depended on the kind of relationship one had with Oszkár Gellért. To be quite honest, this never interested me greatly in the *Nyugat* days, and nor did it interest me later.

Int: What sort of personal and ideological relationships did you have with the other professors?

G.L.: I was pretty independent on the whole and did not concern myself much with the opinions of my colleagues.

Int: Before the Rudas debate the Philosophy Department had about eighty active students. The seminars on aesthetics were highly popular. After the debate only about five or six students were left.

G.L.: Naturally. To explain the situation I have to begin with a quotation from Béla Kun. When the Central Committee was set up in 1919, I was made a member and Rudas was left out. For the sake of peace I said to Kun, 'Look, what is the point of that? I shall carry out my duties whether I am a member of the Committee or not. But here is Rudas for whom membership is a desperately important matter.' Kun replied, and I remember exactly what he said to this day, 'What you say is ridiculous. I am your opponent. But there is no doubt that you have your convictions, and you proclaim these convictions within the communist movement, even when I disapprove of them. But you do have convictions and they are a force in the Party. But with Rudas it is different. You give him money and he writes.' That was Kun's opinion of Rudas in 1919.

Int: As early as 1919? That suggests that Béla Kun was a good judge of people.

G.L.: He was a cynical judge. He had a keen eye for people's negative characteristics but he was unable to discover their positive qualities.

Int: Which of your works appeared after 1945?

G.L.: Chiefly the books I had written between 1919 and 1945. After that *The Theory of the Novel* and *History and Class Consciousness* appeared in German without my permission. I had ceased to include these among my works, and I even had a dispute with Somlyó about this. He claimed that I had no right to disown my own life's work. But my view was that I had absolutely nothing to do with my life's work. It is up to history to decide whether it makes sense to talk of a life's work. Anyone who sets out to create a life's work is embarking on a lie from the outset.

Int: Nevertheless, there have been great artists who have made a conscious effort to produce a life's work, striving to achieve a certain unity in their works. In Thomas Mann you constantly have the feeling with every book that he knows the part it will play in his Collected Works.

G.L.: That is true, but for all that he repudiated the position he had taken in the First World War. And he would never have written *Dr Faustus* if he had remained convinced of the views put forward in his book on the war.[6] That is the whole point of 'And until you possess this maxim: Die and become!'[7] This is what Goethe perceived so clearly. Without that there is no human development. I do not say that you must change your mind every five minutes. But if you are confronted by weighty arguments, you must accept the need to change your mind. If you are not prepared to do that, then you lack intellectual integrity—one of the most prevalent failings nowadays.

Int: Tell me how your relations with Révai developed after 1945.

G.L.: After the Blum Theses Révai and I broke off relations completely. During the preparations for the Seventh Congress he told me privately that the Blum Theses would have to be treated as the precursor of the Seventh Congress. But of course he never said as much in public, and after that congress he never so much as alluded to the Blum Theses again. On the contrary, it was his contacts with populist movements that moved into the foreground. The situation was that there were disagreements on this point within the party. Andor Gábor, for example, sympathized with *Szép Szó*, whereas I, as you know, felt equally hostile to *Szép Szó* and to *Válasz* (The Answer),[8] and in that respect found myself on the same side as Révai.

Int: Did this harmony of interests persist beyond 1945? Up to the Rudas debate?

G.L.: Very much so. He warned me beforehand as a good friend, and then went and joined the other side. This stemmed from an aspect of Révai which made it impossible for him to imagine the Hungarian Party without himself in a leading position. In consequence he left nothing undone that might help to consolidate that position. His compromises should be ascribed not to any base motives, but to his desire to remain in the leadership. To this end he was willing to make the greatest concessions, including on the issue of the democratic currents within the people's democracy.

Int: Comrade Lukács, do you mean to say that his craving to remain in the leadership was motivated by factors other than ambition?

G.L.: I believe that personal factors were not decisive here. Révai has to be regarded as a tragic phenomenon, as a man who had great insight into many important and pressing problems, and yet made the wrong decisions because he thought that to decide otherwise might endanger his place in the leadership. And what would be left of the Hungarian Party without Révai to lead it?

Int: Your satirical and ironic remarks might lead one to conclude that Révai hoped to exert influence over Rákosi and Gerö.

G.L.: Révai believed that the party was always right. Hence he did not follow the party line for opportunistic or careerist reasons, but because the party was in the right and everyone simply had to support its point of view.

Int: How far was your friendship with him affected by such attitudes after 1949?

G.L.: After 1949 relations between us cooled considerably. Later, Révai was removed from the party leadership and relations between us improved once again.

Int: How do you explain Révai's great enthusiasm for the Populists? Was it purely tactical? Or did it involve a 'reconciliation with Hungarian realities'?

G.L.: That is very likely. Of all the leaders, Révai had the deepest knowledge of Hungary and stood closest to the dominant Hungarian ideologies. It is a near certainty that he maintained some relationship with the Populists.

Int: Did you ever meet László Németh?

G.L.: I met him only once, at Révai's where there was a Council of Four—myself, László Németh and Gyula Illyés. On that occasion there was an acrimonious dispute between László Németh and myself, because I accused him of having adopted an impossible position on Franco-German relations during the Second World War when he maintained that a rapprochement with Germany had demolished the France of the lawyers. Németh denied that he had ever written anything of the sort. The following day I sent him a postcard with exact references to what he had said and that was the end of our relationship.

Int: What is your opinion of the NEKOSZ movement?[9]

G.L.: I was wholeheartedly in favour of it as a people's movement, but I was critical of it because the wish to rise in the ranks of the leadership was very powerful among its members. I was chiefly involved with NEKOSZ students at university and it was clear to me that many of them did not primarily want to study; what they wanted was to prepare themselves for the leadership. They imagined that they would soon be the ones to assume the intellectual, political and ideological leadership in the United Party. I was never willing to accept that any section of the population had an a priori right to the leadership, and so I was unwilling to accept it in the case of NEKOSZ.

Int: What were your relations with the Social Democrats at that time?

G.L.: I never had any relations with them. I was a radical Hungarian Communist of a particular kind, in the sense that what I advocated was democracy within communism. But I never accepted the weakening of the idea of dictatorship which the Social Democrats desired. I stood between the two camps. I did not sympathize with the Social Democrats, and nor did I sympathize with those who wished to introduce communism by dictatorial methods. After 1945 a new situation had arisen. An opposition had formed within the Social Democratic Party that had to be taken seriously. This included Zoltán Horváth, Marosán and others I need not name. I had a direct alliance with them. What was characteristic of the period was that Rákosi accepted my attitude and raised no objection to the lectures I gave. He had in fact realized that it was easier to win over the intellectuals by my methods than by his. This then led to the union of the two parties, although my contribution to this was minute. But once the unification had been completed, Rákosi, Gerö and the rest thought that they would decide what was to be done, and not someone like myself who was completely superfluous and even detrimental. That is the background to the Rudas debate. It did not just coincide in time with the union of the parties; there was also a close internal connection between the two events.

Int: Subsequently the question of your relations with the Social Democrats ceased to be relevant, because they no longer existed.

G.L.: I am still on friendly terms with Marosán. I also had a good relationship with Zoltán Horváth. In fact I never had difficulties with the Social Democrats who were united with us, except that I thought them too liberal. When the parties merged, Marosán was asked by Rákosi whom he would like to instruct him in the foundations of communism. Marosán's choice fell on me.

Int: Comrade Lukács, who were the people who stuck by you in those difficult years?

G.L.: That is very hard to say. I must say that Vértes stuck by me. And of the writers, Ferenc Erdei was one who showed genuine interest in what I was trying to achieve.

Int: Was Déry influenced by the Rudas debate?

G.L.: No, but he was influenced by Rákosi's belief that his own importance in Hungary was not adequately recognized in Déry's novel *The Answer*. Hence Révai launched vehement attacks on *The Answer*.

Int: What was the reaction of the educated public during the Rudas debate?

G.L.: I think that people felt more sympathy for me than for Révai, because the aesthetic qualities of *The Answer* worked to his disadvantage. *The Answer* is, after, all, the best socialist novel yet written in Hungary. It was accepted among young people even though Déry had announced as soon as it began to be attacked that he would neither modify the novel nor continue it. At the same time, a very interesting and essential feature of the novel was that its hero did not become a Communist until after 1945. According to Déry's idea, a man of that type would only become a Communist after the establishment of the dictatorship. But the Rákosi-Révai camp was, of course, unwilling to concede the validity of this.

Int: Nevertheless, it is a very positive sign that the top leadership of a country should be willing to engage in such intensive discussion about the continuation of a novel.

G.L.: Behind that a very important question lay concealed. Rákosi and his followers were rewriting the past and trying to persuade people that the dictatorship had been an integral part of the liberation from the outset and that it had not been preceded by a democratic phase.

Int: There were very strange contradictions in Rákosi's and his supporters' views. On the one hand, they wanted people to believe that freedom had been achieved through the struggles of the Communist Party and the Communist Party had a great mass base. On the other hand, they justified their methods of government by claiming that the whole population was fascist. What they wanted to see in the novel was a synthesis of these two elements. But the novel that could harmonize two conflicting lies has yet to be written.

G.L.: Déry could not be fitted into such a framework, and unfortunately the result of the whole affair was that he left the ranks of socialist writers.

Int: Does that mean that you would hold these criticisms responsible for his highly sceptical and non-socialist development?

G.L.: Yes, I would. Of course, there were other reasons rooted in his personality. But if you read his autobiography, you can see the way he always makes his own personality into the focal point of the world. There was a period when his personality and the world converged, and it was out of this convergence that *The Unfinished Sentence* and *The Answer* arose. The criticism of *The Answer* put an end to it, and after that he wrote the later novels in which socialism is presented as a highly questionable, feeble and inauthentic phenomenon. It is terrible to see how many writers' careers have been destroyed by events since 1945.

Int: The career that suffered the most tragic disruption in my opinion was that of Juhász.

G.L.: There was also something tragic about Déry. But in the interim he wrote books such as *Two Women* which, when taken on their own, are enough to ensure that his reputation will survive. Or to take another example, think of the poem he published in a volume together with Illyés. I think that this is a marvellous work which places him in the front rank of lyric poets.

Int: That is true. I think of Juhász as a tragic figure because he was so immensely talented.

G.L.: Juhász was a product of the whole Hungarian crisis. He was a highly talented poet, one of the greatest talents of all. But Tolstoy, as an old man, was very wise when he took exception to the fetishization of talent. His point was that talent was an indispensable component in an artist's make-up, but it was just one among others, not the whole. It is possible that there are no greater talents in Hungary than Juhász. And the other extreme is no less interesting. In the case of Benjamin, for example, we find great poems, even though his talent did not seem to place him in the front rank of Hungary's lyric poets. His *Arany Ode* is one of the finest Hungarian poems. So I think that Tolstoy was right to object to the fetishization of talent.

Int: I have not yet asked about your relations with other writers who returned to Hungary after exile in Moscow. Could you say something about your relations with Béla Balázs, Andor Gábor, Béla Illés and Sándor Gergely after 1945?

G.L.: There were many points of disagreement with Béla Balázs and Andor Gábor. Yet I thought highly of them as writers. As for the others, the disagreements were present without the high opinion.

Int: Did you remain on friendly terms with Andor Gábor and Béla Balázs?

G.L.: With Andor Gábor, yes, but not with Béla Balázs, because relatively to his importance as a writer Béla Balázs had made greater and more far-reaching compromises than Andor Gábor. Hence in later years I was unable to retain the high opinion I had previously had of Balázs as a writer.

Int: I believe that after 1945 you took part in a number of international congresses?

G.L.: They were not really international congresses in the true sense of the word. They were peace congresses. I only took part in peace congresses.

Int: But were there not also philosophy conferences? In Geneva, for example?

G.L.: I only took part in the Geneva Conference as a result of a personal invitation. It had no significance for the party. The conference was very illuminating for me because I was able to see how widespread the American way of life still was in the West at that time. Although I was known personally and also as a writer to a number of people, my reception was a little like that which Montesquieu reports in the *Persian Letters*—'Monsieur est Persan? Comment peut-on être persan?' In other words, how could anyone who could speak a number of languages, and who was educated and cultured, possibly be a Marxist? I had a minor confrontation with Jaspers. The main issue was whether Marxism could be defended and propagated as an intellectually viable philosophy.

Int: Did you encounter Bloch after the war?

G.L.: I met him and it was partly due to me that he was appointed to a chair at Leipzig University. We remained friends even after he had left East Germany, although we did not meet again and had no further correspondence.

Int: Do you view leaving East Germany in a different light from leaving Hungary?

G.L.: Of course. I regard Bloch as a wholly admirable man of great integrity.

Int: Can we turn to the period starting in 1953?

G.L.: It started with my giving up all my literary duties following the Rudas debate. I even obtained a dispensation from the Central Committee, freeing me from all official obligations. This eliminated what might be called the negative consequences of the debate, since I took no part in the subsequent skirmishes. You remember that when the writers' attack on Rákosi started in the fifties, I took no part in that either, not from any very exalted motive, but simply for tactical reasons. I knew the party better than most, and I knew that if the writers all began to move in a particular direction, it would be regarded as an attempt to form a caucus. And if one of its members were threatened with expulsion for forming a caucus, then all of them would retreat. And this is what actually happened. Since I had no wish to retreat, I refused to involve myself from the outset. So my involvement in the literary revolts that preceded the events of 1956 was nil.

Int: Had you started work on *The Specificity of the Aesthetic* before 1956?

G.L.: Yes.

Int: Is it possible that one factor in your unwillingness to become involved was the fear that your work might suffer?

G.L.: I have never yet complained that political activity disrupted my work. On the contrary, political activity only ever stimulates my work, because it focuses the issues more sharply, makes it possible to see more clearly what people's real aims are, and so on.

Int: How did you see the future after the Twentieth Party Congress?

G.L: I can only repeat what I said at the time, when the issue came to the surface. It is not true that the whole matter can be reduced to the question of the personality cult. The problems go well beyond that issue. Reforms are essential. It is true, and I would not deny that I believed during the early phase that Imre Nagy would introduce those reforms. I found later on that I had to abandon such illusions.

Int: When did you first meet Imre Nagy?

G.L.: Very early on. It should not be forgotten that Imre Nagy was a prisoner-of-war in Russia. He went back to Hungary in the twenties and worked in the provinces. When I was in Budapest in 1929, we worked together on a number of occasions and our collaboration was fairly successful. Subsequently I refused to recognize his leading role, and so one day I was visited by some students. (You may have been one of them, I can no longer remember precisely.) They told me that it was wrong for us not to be on speaking terms. I replied that the way from Imre Nagy's door to mine was not a step further than from mine to his. It was up to him to take the initiative! It was not just a matter of personal pride. Had I been the one to pay him a visit, I would have been sucked into that Uncle Imre current that was so powerful in Hungary in those days. But if Imre Nagy had come to see me, I could have told him in confidence that it was not possible to make a revolution without any programme at all.

Int: Let us turn back for a moment to the period before 1953. At the time of the Rudas debate Imre Nagy was expelled from the Central Committee because of his agrarian programme. Did he and you not meet before 1953?

G.L.: Since both he and I belonged to the so-called second rung of the leadership, we used to meet in such places as Mátraháza which were reserved for people like us. We had a good conversational relationship, but it never went any further.

Int: Did you consider that Imre Nagy had no programme of any kind, or simply that he lacked an overall programme?

G.L.: Obviously he had a programme for reform in very general terms. But he had absolutely no idea how to implement it in particular spheres of government, what it involved in concrete terms, or what the specific rights and duties of individual Communists should be.

Int: Did he not have a specific agricultural programme?

G.L.: That was the sort of programme which did not entail any particular action. You must not forget that under Imre Nagy hardly any agricultural reforms were carried out.

Int: It is true that in the Imre Nagy Government, he was in a minority in the party, apart from a single week.

G.L.: That is so. But if I were to find myself in a minority in the party, either I would accept no responsibility or else I would lay down certain conditions for taking on the leadership. Imre Nagy failed to do this, and instead he remained the Grand Old Man of the state. Moreover, he formed a group which contained some of the worst of the reformers. On the other hand, there was no precise programme or a declared intention to carry out specific measures and abstain from others, and so forth. Hence we did not meet in the year when he was Prime Minister. I thought highly of his personal integrity and intelligence, and also of his expertise in the agrarian question. But I did not regard him as a real politician.

Int: Is it true that there were no real Marxists in the group he had formed?

G.L.: I cannot confirm that even today.

Int: Ferenc Donáth?

G.L: Ferenc Donáth was on friendly terms with Imre Nagy and was present at the meetings of the group. Szilárd Ujhelhi and others were also present. But I do not know what Donáth's attitude to the situation was at the time, because I only became friendly with him later, when he appeared to be very critical of Nagy.

Int: The fact is that you were not involved in this movement, but it is also true that when the discussions in the Petőfi Circle began, you were almost the first person who came to mind and people had great expectations of you. Can you say why you were prepared to play a political role?

G.L.: The fact is that I think of 1956 as a great movement. It was a spontaneous movement which stood in need of a certain ideology. I declared my willingness to contribute towards formulating this in a series of lectures. For example, I attempted to clarify whether our relationships with other countries had changed; whether, and on what conditions, collaboration and coexistence were now an actual possibility. So I had ideological intentions of that sort, but no other intentions at all.

Int: Did you make your contribution to the spontaneous movement in the Petőfi Circle before the events in 1956?

G.L.: No, not just in the Petőfi Circle. I also gave a lecture in the Party College which went roughly in the same direction.

Int: How was the lecture received?

G.L.: Politely.

Int: And after that, the party leadership...

G.L.: After that, whatever I did was wrong. They let the whole gang off the leash, all the disciples of Rudas, and they could write whatever they wanted about me.

Int: I was not thinking of the period after 4 November 1956. I also remember the polite hearing given to your lecture, for I was present myself. I am thinking of the period before October, some two or three weeks after the lecture. What action did the party leadership under Rákosi take?

G.L.: Nothing happened at all. They were in such a panic that they did not dare do anything.

Int: How were you affected personally by the events of October 1956?

G.L.: The first consequence was that I was voted onto the Central Committee. Secondly, within the Central Committee I found myself to a certain extent in opposition to Imre Nagy. Just to mention the most important issue: when Imre Nagy withdrew from the Warsaw Pact, Zoltán Szántó and I voted against doing so. We demanded that in future, matters of such crucial importance should not be made public before they had been fully aired within the party.

Int: Was the decision to leave the Warsaw Pact endorsed by the other members of the Committee?

G.L.: Yes.

Int: Were there other disagreements among the leaders?

G.L.: That was the decisive one, determining all other conflicts. But the question had to be faced at every point whether to make a decisive break with the old system or simply to reform it. I can say quite frankly that I was on the side of reform.

Int: So was Imre Nagy for a long time.

G.L.: Yes, but his point of view never emerged clearly.

Int: I believe that he too was in favour of reform. The problem was that he came under direct pressure from the various civil and military groups within the uprising. In my opinion he was simply dragged along by it.

G.L.: That is very possible. I do not want at all to suggest that Imre Nagy was a counter-revolutionary or a supporter of capitalism. I would not claim anything of the kind. I only say that he had no programme. He would say one thing one day, and the next day another.

Int: Comrade Lukács, were you opposed to withdrawing from the Warsaw Pact on principle, or were you influenced by tactical considerations, such as fear of Soviet intervention?

G.L.: Initially, of course, I was opposed in principle. I was quite simply in favour of Hungary's membership of the Warsaw Pact. But I also took the view that we ought not to give the Russians an excuse to intervene in Hungarian affairs. This consideration could not be ignored.

Int: Comrade Lukács, we know that in October 1956 you became one of the six members of the Party Central Committee. But we have not yet said anything about your official duties.

G.L.: I was given a ministerial post because Ferenc Erdei had been made something important and he had put my name forward for the Ministry of Education and the Arts.

Int: Did you have any specific ideas, any programme?

G.L.: No, no, nothing at all. I did not once set foot in the Ministry.

Int: As I remember it, you made a statement, possibly in *Szabadság* (Freedom), in which your programme seemed to consist in dissolving the Ministry.

G.L.: That is most unlikely.

Int: Not the section for schools, but the adult education department. I think you said something to the effect that the Ministry had a whole host of functions that made no sense at all. For instance, it was responsible for literature and film.

G.L.: That is quite possible. I may well have made a statement with that in mind.

Int: Were you subsequently criticized for having accepted a ministerial post?

G.L.: Of course.

Int: Were there specific criticisms, or just the stereotyped accusations?

G.L.: I can no longer remember. So many hostile things have been written about me in the course of my life, that I can no longer recall individual attacks.

Int: Were you surprised by the events of 4 November, or did you believe in the possibility of an agreement between the Soviet and Hungarian governments?

G.L.: That is a very difficult question to answer, because something happened to me that I have rarely experienced. I made a mistake for purely physical reasons. On 3 November I returned home late from a session of Parliament, and I had barely fallen asleep when the Szántós's rang up and said that Gertrud and I should go to their house. Once we were there, they said that we had to go to the Yugoslav embassy because the Russians were on their way. I confess that in my exhausted condition I acquiesced in their reasoning, even though—and I say this in defence of my actions—as soon as I had had a couple of hours' sleep in the embassy, I began to regret my decision. But by then it was too late and it was not possible to leave.

Int: Were there already at that stage disagreements among those who had sought refuge in the Yugoslav embassy? Or did they not emerge until you were all in Romania?

G.L.: Of course disagreements became quite clear in the embassy. You must not forget that people had gone there for a variety of reasons. Zoltán Vas, for instance, had fled to the Yugoslav embassy because he thought that his wife would arrive with the approaching Russian troops and haul him over the coals because he was already living with the woman who was to become his present wife. I only mention this to make the point that people's motives really differed quite widely. Our attitude right from the start was that we wanted to return home. A number of others wanted the same and, interestingly enough, this was accepted, in my own case as well as theirs. However, when we attempted to carry out our intention, we were put under arrest and interned in a Russian camp, or whatever.

Int: Who else was allowed to leave?

G.L.: Lots of people. I can remember Szilárd Ujhelyi, Zoltán Szántó and Zoltán Vas, for example. Apart from the group around Imre Nagy, there were a fairly large number of people who wanted to leave.

Int: What happened when you left the embassy?

G.L.: When we got into the car, we were joined by a police car and told to follow it. We turned into a side street and then had to get into other cars which took us to the Russian camp.

Int: How were you treated?

G.L.: Very well and very politely, right from the start.

Int: There was a rumour going the rounds in Budapest according to which you were all asked to surrender your weapons and you were said to have responded by handing over your fountain-pen.

G.L.: That is a legend. No one asked us to give up any weapons. Zoltán Szánto, Zoltán Vas and myself were the first to arrive in the Russian camp. I do not know whether there were any others in the group. Three or four days later everyone else arrived. After that we were all taken to Romania.

Int: Were you able to work there?

G.L.: In actual fact it was possible. We had access to the library and could read what we wanted. In that respect no obstacles were placed in our way. We were left very much to our own devices.

Int: And did you in fact do any work?

G.L.: I was able to catch up on some reading that had been made impossible before by my commitments to party work. Of course it is hard to describe such activities as work. But I cannot say that I remained unoccupied.

Int: I heard another anecdote according to which a Romanian prison warder was assigned to convert you ideologically.

G.L.: That is possible. I did in fact know a guard like that, but it was a completely harmless business.

Int: The story went that after a few weeks' discussion he had to undergo treatment in a psychiatric clinic.

G.L.: I can no longer recall anything about that. When I left Romania, he had not yet gone into a psychiatric clinic.

Int: Was he an intelligent man?

G.L.: At party level such people are thought to be intelligent. That is all, but it isn't very much.

Int: Did you make any efforts to bring about your return to Hungary?

G.L.: Yes, and this gave rise to a problem. My interrogators said to me that they knew I was no follower of Imre Nagy and so there was no reason why I should not testify against him. I told them that as soon as the two of us, Imre Nagy and myself, were free to walk around Budapest, I would be happy to make public my opinion of all of Nagy's activities. But I was not free to express an opinion about my fellow-prisoners.

Int: Did all the internees maintain this position?

G.L.: I believe so.

Int: There were rumours circulating in Budapest that Zoltán Szántó's behaviour was not beyond reproach.

G.L.: I do not know about that. I have no concrete evidence one way or the other, since everyone was interrogated separately and afterwards was able to describe his behaviour as he saw fit. I think it likely, however, that Zoltán Szántó made a statement unfavourable to Imre Nagy. There had been a meeting at which the entire emigration—that is, all the internees—had taken part. Zoltán Szántó had spoken and been highly critical of Imre Nagy, who was also present.

Int: Did these meetings take place under observation?

G.L.: Of course. These twenty or thirty people were... And then the Russians or Romanians were present too.

Int: The reason why I am asking about Zoltán Szántó is that I remember that your earlier friendship with him seemed to have been badly affected around this period.

G.L.: I did not agree with his conduct at this time and so it was natural for our relationship to cool to a certain degree.

Int: When we talked about Zoltán Szántó in 1956, you described him as the most talented Communist leader of the day.

G.L.: He was an excellent party worker, and early in the fifties[10] he played a very active part in the reorganization of the Hungarian Party. He was then pushed into the background by Rákosi and his people, and this resulted in a peculiar situation in which Szántó thought that his position was more important than it really was.

Int: Did he have any particular ideological importance?

G.L.: Ideologically, his position was always very correct.

Int: Can you tell me about the circumstances in which you were invited to return to Hungary in May 1957?

G.L.: I returned to Hungary at the end of March or early in April.

Int: Were any conditions imposed on you?

G.L.: No.

Int: What was your relationship with the party?

G.L.: When the party was reorganized and given its present name, I wrote a letter insisting on the continuation of my membership. I sent this to the Central Committee, mentioning how long I had been a member and how my entire party history was on record from the time I had joined. I said that there could be no reason to turn down my application for membership. Despite this my application was rejected, or rather I received no answer to my letter. The question of what to answer did not arise for another ten years.

Int: In the *Encyclopedia* that came out in 1962 József Szigeti claimed that you had been expelled from the party.

G.L.: That is untrue. But someone may very easily have written such things, because I was under a cloud until well into the sixties. It was all too easy to spread such rumours about me. But the fact is that I was not expelled from the party. All that happened was that there was no reply to the letter in which I applied for party membership.

Int: It is obvious that no reply was forthcoming because no one dared to say either yes or no.

G.L.: I am sure that there must have been some such reason. At all events, the problem emerged once more when I gave an interview to *L'Unità* in connection with the introduction of the new economic policy, in which I made a statement to the effect that I was in favour of this policy because it necessarily implied democratization of the party and a renewal of Marxism.

Int: Was this interview for *L'Unità* the start of your return to the public stage?

G.L.: Yes, up to a point. But you have to take things as they are. Right up to the time when the economic reforms were introduced I had continued to play a passive role in public. I was a kind of monument of revisionism, and during that entire period that role was not without a certain explosive potential.

Int: Were you still at work on the *Aesthetics* at this period?

G.L.: In the first period I finished the *Aesthetics*. Of course there was no prospect of having it published abroad, let alone in Hungary. So I wrote to Kádár, criticizing the government's publishing policy. In my opinion, every publishing house has the right to publish what it wants. And conversely, no publisher has the right to prevent other publishers from publishing books. So in my letter I protested to Kádár about the government's procedures. The result was that I received a summons. What was the name of the man in the Politburo? Szirmai. I was summoned by Szirmai and told that they would gladly give me an exit visa if I wanted it. I said to him, 'Look all the power is in your hands. You can do to me whatever you want. If a policeman puts his hand on my shoulder when I leave this room, I shall be a prisoner unable to do anything. But you do not have the power to compliment me out of Hungary just when it suits you.' After that, they just forgot the whole idea for a good year and a half.

Int: When did the plan for a German edition of your complete works come into being?

G.L.: A long time ago. Before 1956.

Int: Was it true that the reason for the dispute was ultimately that you wished to send the *Aesthetics* to Benseler?[11]

G.L.: That is so.

Int: Was it possible to publish other manuscripts abroad at this time?

G.L.: Everything that I managed to smuggle abroad was published.

Int: Were you never challenged about this?

G.L.: No one ever questioned it. After peace was re-established. I discussed the matter with Aczél. What I said to him was, 'Listen, as long as you forbid me to publish abroad, I shall continue to smuggle my works out without a qualm. I do not acknowledge your right to prevent the publication of my books in German. If you give me a guarantee that my writings can be published abroad, I shall relinquish my right to smuggle with the greatest pleasure.' This is what happened as matters started to simmer down.

Int: After your return to Hungary I believe that for a time you gave assistance to people who had got into difficulties.

G.L.: Yes, that goes without saying. I can no longer say whom we helped or what form our assistance took. I always tried to resist the force emanating from the government, and no one can maintain that I approved of the execution of Imre Nagy, and so forth. But it was also necessary to make distinctions of a largely tactical nature: it was essential to realize that there was no prospect of helping some people, whereas in other cases help was possible.

Int: What were you working on in this period apart from the *Aesthetics*?

G.L.: I was engaged in the preparatory work on my *Ontology*. The *Aesthetics* were actually intended as a preliminary stage of the *Ontology*, since in that work the aesthetic is treated as a moment of Being, of social Being.

Int: I believe that you had intended to follow up the *Aesthetics* with an *Ethics*.

G.L.: I had actually conceived the *Ontology* as a philosophical foundation of the *Ethics*. But in the upshot the *Ethics* was supplanted by the *Ontology*, which is concerned with the structure of reality and not merely of a separate form.

Int: You were also engaged on a number of political articles at this time: in fact you even wrote a political study about the relations between bourgeois democracy and socialist democracy. This work has not yet appeared in any language. It was written in connection with the events in Czechoslovakia.

G.L.: The events in Czechoslovakia only took place very recently. I took up an explicitly pro-Czech position. Making use of my prerogative as a party member, I wrote to Kádár saying that I could give my approval neither to his particular stance, nor to that of the party. That is what I wrote to him.

Admittedly, I also turned down an invitation to a philosophy conference in Vienna—and I still believe that I was right to do so—because it was obvious that, had I been present, every second word would have been interpreted in the light of the events in Czechoslovakia and I did not want that to happen.

Int: Did the Czech events change your attitude at all towards the Hungarian events of 1956? What I mean is that the intervention took place in Prague even though the Czechs clearly had no desire to withdraw from the Warsaw Pact. Can it be argued that Imre Nagy's withdrawal from the Warsaw Pact was simply the pretext for intervention in 1956?

G.L.: At that time it was not possible to answer such a question. As far as I was concerned, I felt sympathy for the Czechs, even though I wanted to write an article for a Romanian paper pointing out some of the internal contradictions in the Czech conception of democracy. (As it happened, I did not have the time to write the article.) In short, I was critical of the Czechs, but it was the criticism of a sympathizer.

Int: If I remember correctly, this article would have been connected with the Masaryk question.

G.L.: Under the dictatorship (in 1919) Czech troops under Masaryk had invaded Hungary. What I wanted to say was that I did not have a very high opinion of a democracy that intended to use democratic weapons against the dictatorship of the proletariat of another country.

Int: Were there any special debates at this time?

G.L.: What I always say in confidence to Comrade Aczél is that he is a very well-meaning and decent person, whom I greatly like and respect, but who wants to solve things so that everyone can be happy. Things simply do not work out like that. It is just not possible to stamp out smuggling and at the same time to keep the smugglers happy. When Aczél wrote a polemic in *Népszabadság*, attacking what I have referred to as the Révai tragedy, I told Aczél—and this did not appear in *Népszabadság*—that hundreds and thousands of people from the Rákosi era were still around. At one extreme there was Mihály Farkas, an unmitigated scoundrel, and at the other was András Hegedüs, who had been prime minister under Rákosi and who today is one of the most important reformist leaders. If we were to proceed from the assumption that everyone has had difficulties of one sort of another—there is no point in going into details—this would ultimately mean placing Mihály Farkas and András Hegedüs on a par with each other. That would be unjust. One of the prime tasks of the present is to reject people like Mihály Farkas with hatred, and to encourage people like András Hegedüs. Obviously I am speaking here of types and not individuals. Between these extremes there is a vast range of variations and it must be the task of art to depict them as they are in reality. In order to do that, we have to be shown the whole spectrum. If we neglect to do so, we arrive at a position that there has been great unpleasantness in the past, but that we should now draw a veil over it and simply forget what has happened. The fact is, however, that we should not forget the past. The whole problem has been treated in our literature in exemplary fashion, especially in Makarenko's great pedagogic novel. In that book the socialist method of education is shown to consist in the idea that forgetting should follow the experience of shame and catharsis. That is to say, catharsis has to precede any forgetting of an offence. If we really wish to bring about a socialist society, we cannot dispense with such educational processes. In the absence of education of this type we shall only produce a pseudo-socialism.

Or let us consider the problem of revolutionary terror. If by that we have Mihály Farkas in mind, we arrive at a completely untenable position. Whereas if by revolutionary terror we mean Ottó Korvin... Let me tell you a story to illustrate my point! When elections were held during the dictatorship, my wife—this was before our marriage—came to see me with a girl-friend and said that something terrible had happened. The girl-friend's brother, a teacher, had made a great electoral speech denouncing the elections as a piece of trickery, a great swindle, whereupon he had been arrested. 'What would become of him now?' she asked. 'Surely he would be hanged.' I promised to telephone Ottó Korvin the following morning. I did in fact phone him from the People's Commissariat, and all Korvin said was, 'Oh that lunatic; he has already been released.' In a different case, however, the Stenczel-Nikolényi conspiracy, both Korvin and I argued passionately in the Council of the People's Commissariat against the social-democrat view that the two men should be pardoned. We urged that they should both be executed because high-ranking police officers had been creating whole arsenals for the counter-revolution in their homes. Now, I maintain that these apparently incompatible positions are not contradictory in reality. Were I to obliterate the distinction between Korvin and Mihály Farkas and endorse the modern belief in universal forgiveness, I would have to sacrifice the authentic revolutionary hero, for that is what Korvin was. Nowadays Ottó Korvin has no reputation or prestige of any kind in Hungary, and this can largely be explained by the disappearance of the positive image of the revolutionary, thanks to the levelling down that results from this universal amnesty. Ottó Korvin is represented as a sort of watered-down Mihály Farkas, a moderate version of Farkas, but a Farkas all the same. I would be very pleased if people realized that my critical attitude here is essentially socialist. I do not judge these matters from the point of view of a so-called bourgeois humanism. I can imagine how one might decide for tactical reasons to let bygones be bygones. Remember that this was the attitude in 1867.[12] And when I was a child, the memory of the Thirteen of Arad was still very much alive.[13] The stark fact is that letting bygones be bygones is nothing more than a bureaucratic device. So I would be absolutely opposed to adopting such an attitude towards the Farkas era. For such an attitude has very real consequences, even if they are less dire than in former times. But if Zoltán Horváth had to endure house-arrest for over a year merely because he had spoken contemptuously of Kállai in a private conversation, that really points to the fact that the Farkas era is with us again.

Int: I believe that Aczél's criticism of you arises from his constant demand for a balanced view, so that whenever you start to say anything negative, he expects you to follow it up with a positive qualification—which is of course nonsense.

G.L.: It is certainly quite superfluous, for I would be perfectly willing to concede that Mihály Farkas was a good father to his children—I do not know whether that was the case, but it is not impossible. But I do not think it my task as a historian to take such compensating virtues into account. The situation is quite different if a person exhibits a dialectic of good and evil characteristics, as was undoubtedly true of Trotsky, for example. In that event it is necessary to lay bare the dialectic—not, of course, in order to balance out its positive and negative sides, but because without understanding it you cannot grasp the person's motivation. I remember how delighted we were in my youth that Endre Ady should have described István Tisza as a masculine variant of Elisabeth Báthory.[14] He did not mention a single positive characteristic of Tisza in extenuation, even though István Tisza was an intelligent, honest and sincere man. And in his description of Tisza as a masculine variant of Elizabeth Báthory, Ady was absolutely right.

Int: In Ady's case such passionately stated beliefs could be tolerated. We would never be allowed to get away with such assertions.

G.L.: But without such passion we shall never make progress. You can see something similar in Jancsó's film about Count Ráday, who doubtless also had his positive qualities. I would in fact deny that he had, but that is irrelevant here.

Int: Or in Jancsó's latest film, *Csend és Kiáltás* (Silence and Cry)...

G.L.: I liked that film very much. It is valuable for a variety of reasons and I cannot help thinking that we can expect great things from both Jancsó and Kovács in this realm. But for that to happen, it is essential that they be supported by friends of the film, so that the revelation of the negative sides of the past and the present can become a positive matter, of benefit to socialism.

Int: It is no accident that the Hungarian cinema should become successful at the moment it subscribes to a policy of honesty.

G.L.: It is a grotesque fact that Stalin should have written that the task of literature is 'to tell the truth'. Unfortunately he did not allow the truth to be told. I would be inclined to accept his formula and say: 'Tell the truth!'

Int: Now some personal questions. When you came back from Romania, was Révai still alive? Did you meet him?

G.L.: We did meet again, since this was at a time when Révai had been expelled from the Central Committee and found himself in a rather unhappy position. After a thirty-year friendship I could not have found it in myself to leave him in the lurch. Our contact was not excessively friendly or close, but we met once every four weeks.

Int: Had Révai not revised his views on anything?

G.L.: Révai had revised nothing at all—on the contrary, he was mainly concerned to assert the validity of his old views on every issue and to represent them as the only possible ones.

Int: When Déry came out of prison...

G.L.: Déry had not abandoned in prison his belief that it was possible to write a socialist novel in Hungary, but he did lose his faith during the debate triggered off by Révai. From that point on, all his writings up to and including his autobiography had very little or nothing to do with socialism, although they are of course all highly gifted works.

Int: Do you still maintain personal contact with him?

G.L.: I feel a liking for him personally and also for his wife. Hence we remained in touch, for the fact is that we have never done anything to each other's detriment. So why should we not see each other? However, I would not still defend the opinions I expressed about Déry's writings in the early thirties.

Int: Which writers have you been friendly with in recent years?

G.L.: I have continued to be on friendly terms with Déry and Illyés. Or, more precisely, I have had a good conversational relationship with them. Illyés was really a plebeian democrat, not a socialist. My impression is that he ceased to believe in anything and hence, despite their high quality, his latest writings are not remotely comparable to the great works of his youth. Of the other writers, mention should perhaps be made of László Benjamin, whom I met a number of times in the period after 1957. But with whom should I maintain a relationship? There are no writers whose work I would give much for. Apart from the three I have mentioned—and what I have said of Benjamin only applies to some of his poems—there is no such writer. Whose acquaintance ought I to cultivate?

Int: A few words now about your pupils. Which of them have you known the longest and of whom do you think most highly?

G.L.: First and foremost, Ágnes Heller, Ferenc Fehér and a few others.

Int: Márkus?

G.L.: Márkus is no pupil of mine. Márkus came back from Moscow with seventy-five per cent of his ideas fully formed. I do not say that I had no influence upon him, but I cannot call him my pupil.

Int: Vajda?

G.L.: Yes. Vajda was really Ágnes Heller's pupil, when she was still teaching at the university, and I took him over from her... He cannot really be called my pupil, because he was more or less mature when he came to me. Only Ágnes Heller and Ferenc Fehér were really my pupils from the very beginning.

Int: And among the musicologists?

G.L.: I also have pupils among the musicologists. Dénes Zoltay, for example. You will always find people around Bence Szabolcsi and around me whom I have influenced to a certain extent.

Int: Since we are talking about music, can I ask about the distinction you often draw between Kodály and Bartók.

G.L.: I consider Kodály to have made an outstanding contribution to the revival of old Hungarian music. The relevant works naturally represent the old idyllic Hungary. The *Cantata Profana*, on the other hand, is not the old, idyllic Hungary, but the rebellious Hungary. Apart from Kodály's early works, which I would not venture to judge, since I am no musician, I see no common ground between Kodály and Bartók.

Int: Bence Szabolcsi disputes this, I believe.

G.L.: That is so. But I do not regard him as a competent authority on this question, which is directly concerned not with music but with, for example, Kodály's belief that the revival of old Hungarian music is necessary. For Bartók Hungarian music is not superior to, or more rustic than, Egyptian music. For Bartók, if I may put it in this way, the revival of the world of the peasantry is important in the sense in which Lenin said of Tolstoy that, before the arrival of this count, there had never been a real peasant in Russian literature. Similarly, it could be said that no peasant had ever made his appearance in music, and that is what is so important about Bartók. Not that it was a Hungarian peasant or a Romanian peasant, or whatever, but that is was simply a peasant. He is the stag who does not wish to return to the world of men.[15] In my opinion this opens up a huge gulf between Kodály and Bartók, and I am not prepared to reduce them to a common denominator. It is true that a myth has formed around Kodály, and not unjustifiably so, because his works express the relationship of the old, pre-cultural Hungary to the peasantry. I do not want at all to put that in question. What I doubt is the presence of the international and revolutionary implications of that relationship. His peasants are not the peasants of the *Cantata Profana*; they are not the stags who refuse to return home. They are the peasants who perform country dances and represent an age-old musical tradition wihtout having a word to say in criticism of ancient Hungary. The position is similar in literature, where there is a comparable failure to distinguish between the tradition of Csokonai-Petöfi-Ady-Attila József and other traditions. So too in music, these distinctions are never made. People talk about Kodály *and* Bartók. It would be as if I were to say 'Ady *and* Babits'. I do not doubt that Babits was a true poet, but when he says at the end of the First World War, 'Let us not ask who was to blame, let us plant flowers!' and so forth, he is clearly prepared for reconciliation even with István Tisza. Endre Ady, on the other hand, would never become reconciled with Tisza. The gulf between Bartók and Kodály is just as fundamental as the distinction between Ady and Babits.

Int: In conclusion, would you like to say a few words about your last work, the *Ontology*?

G.L.: Following Marx I conceive of ontology as philosophy proper, but as philosophy based on history. Historically there can be no doubt that inorganic life came first and that organic life, in its plant and animal forms, evolved in ways we do not understand, although we know roughly when it happened. From this biological state, after innumerable transitions, there emerged what we know as human society whose essence is the teleological action of man: that is to say, work. This is the new master concept, because it includes everything within itself. It must not be forgotten that as soon as we speak of human life, we are bound to make use of all sorts of value concepts. What was the first value? The first product? Either a stone hammer is suited to its purpose or it is not suited to it. In the former case it will be valuable, in the latter case, worthless. Value and non-value are not found at the biological level of existence, for death is just as valid a process as life. There is no distinction of value between the two. The second fundamental distinction is the concept of 'Ought', which in Hungarian we call '*Legyen*'. 'That is to say, things do not change of their own accord, by virtue of spontaneous processes, but as a consequence of conscious choices. Conscious choice means that the end precedes the result. This is the foundation of human society in its entirety. The antithesis between value and non-value, between what has evolved and what has been made, makes up the whole of human existence.

Int: To what extent did Marx elaborate this theory himself?

G.L.: Marx established that historicity is the fundamental concept of social being, and as such of all beings. This I hold to be the most important part of Marxian theory. In the Paris Manuscripts Marx says that there is only one science, the science of history, and he even adds, 'a non-objective being is a non-being'. That is to say, an object without categorial attributes cannot exist. Existence means, therefore, that a thing exists in an objectively determinate form: the objectivity of the determinate form makes up the category to which the object in question belongs. It is this that distinguishes my ontology clearly from earlier philosophies. Traditional philosophy conceived of a system of categories which included the categories of history along with others. In the Marxist system of categories every object is furnished from the outset with attributes, with thinghood and with a categorial existence. A non-objective being is a non-being. And within the object history is the history of the changes which take place in the categories. The categories, therefore, are components of objective reality. Nothing can exist which is not in some sense a category. In this respect there is an extraordinarily sharp difference between Marxism and earlier world-views. In Marxism the categorial being of a thing constitutes its being, whereas in the old philosophies categorial being was the fundamental category within which the categories of reality were constituted. It is not the case that history unfolds within the system of categories, but rather that history is the system of categories in the process of change. The categories, therefore, are forms of beings. To the extent that they become ideas, they become forms of reflexion without losing their primacy or forms of being. In this way completely different groups of categories with their various contents come into being. We can illustrate this with reference to the celebrated incident in which Leibnitz explained to the princess that no two leaves are exactly alike. He might equally have said that no two pebbles are exactly alike. The uniqueness of objects is inseparable from their being and cannot be reduced to anything more fundamental. This means that the system of categories itself develops in such a way that the category of uniqueness evolves in an extraordinarily lengthy process from the uniqueness of a pebble to the point where the uniqueness of man is reached.

Gelebtes Denken
Notes Towards an Autobiography

Every autobiography: subjective; not a general human development out of a social context—but one within a given context showing how a man becomes himself or fails to do so.

Objectivity: the correct historicity. Memory: tendency to relocate in time. Check against the facts. Youth: Benedek; 1914 Simmel's letter to Marianne Weber. But the facts useful only as a check. Eliminate (a) bourgeois [?] interpretation. E.g. Zitta, p. 101.[1] (b) Party history. Trotsky (in my case too). But also possibility of ignorance bona fide: Victor Serge, p. 213; memory (written later). Contradiction with practice (time, also later). V.S. (a) date (p. 213) not right (wasn't in Russia in 28/29). But also as regards Vienna: (b) big un-published books (p. 212). Includes 'author of *History and Class Consciousness*': only book of this period, published 1923 (p. 211), (c) Landler, pp. 213–4; Kremlin. V.S.'s general tendency: later events earlier—such information to be checked wherever possible.[2]

Within this framework, inner development and development as expressed in practice, just as it subjectively was. Intention: to portray *my* development directly. The objective aspect: to show *how* reacted and *to what*. Aim: become what you are—to depict this accurately. In characterizing myself from this angle, my hope: to depict objective reality *at the same time*—without pretending to a comprehensive historical account. It will come right, if certain *essential* features are captured.

Not my life in any *immediate* sense. Only want to show how (in human terms) this particular intellectual tendency, this mode of thought (this behaviour pattern) emerged into life from life. Today, with hindsight: individuality neither the starting-point nor end-product. But: *how* personal characteristics, inclinations, tendencies, given the maximum opportunity to develop—according to circumstances—have become socially typical, or, to my present [way of thinking], have developed in accordance with the species or have striven to achieve species being.

No poet. Only a philosopher. Abstractions. Memory, too, organized to that end. Danger: premature generalization of spontaneous experience. But poets: able to recall concrete feelings, and above all the context in which they arose. That already means: at the right place at the right time. Especially: childhood. But there was there an important and enduring tendency—to put up with things.

Autobiography: concrete intention here: the correction of particular attitudes towards social life. Contemporary relevance, manipulation: the individual as the central issue. The apparatus constructs this individual (Gauloise cigarettes—to the point of artificially arousing feelings[3]). Fight against this: up to now in the form of objectivations: both aesthetic and generally philosophical.

Live here: over 80—subjective interest in reality maintained—at a time when the contact with early youth often lost. Long and even now, an undeniably industrious life—my right to attempt to justify this posture. This connected with the struggle for Marxism. Individuality and the problem of species being. This the point of conflict between particularity and the extent to which species identity is realized in practice. (Therefore: this antithesis never elevated to the transcendental sphere [negative attitude to everything religious: pure earthliness in overcoming particularity].) Also in this context—in which a practical standpoint on the intellectual questions of the time is implict—supplementation of and commentary on my achievement as a writer hitherto.

Subjectivity of autobiography as supplementation of and commentary on my own activites as a writer. In this respect subjectivity cannot be overcome. (Admittedly only in writing. In the last analysis: history. Its judgement irrevocable, i.e. revoked only by the further course of history itself.) Even this mode of presentation submits—with conviction—to such judgements.

I
Childhood and School

Of pure Jewish family. For that very reason: the ideologies of Judaism had no influence whatever on my intellectual development. Father: consul in Budapest. In other respects: episodic influence on childhood of insistence on conventional behaviour: participation in weddings, funerals, etc., of acquaintances: presence at ceremonies. Since no importance was attached even to the learning of Hebrew, all this without any reality for the child, a pure formality (hat on in synagogue, forgot that spoken or sung texts could be capable of any meaning). Hence integration of religion in ordinary social life: whether an (unknown) guest should be respectfully greeted, whether his questions (mainly quite meaningless to a child) should elicit a polite (seemingly interested) and, above all, prompt response. Normal childhood existence hedged about with this system of senseless formal obligations: characteristic for the earliest years of childhood.

Spontaneous rebellions. No direct memory. Maternal quote (referring to me at age 5 or 6) about how 'naughty' used to be: 'I never say hello to strangers, I didn't invite them.' Resistance at first—then submission with the conviction: of no concern to me; if I want the grown-ups to leave me in peace: submission, with the feeling that the whole business is quite meaningless; whether I actually formulated this myself in these terms at the time: no idea. The only certitude: no wild and rebellious child, no spontaneous blind revolt against order or obedience as such. Story about Nanny: Remember it to this day, also the fact that I heeded her words: kept my toys in order, later on: books, papers. I saw the sense of it all; no rebellion. Even where something was senseless—no more revolt; only the clear awareness: I must submit, even though the matter had no sense (formal submission, though I have since forgotten how I formulated it then). Memory: Paris—visits to art galleries. I: demanded to be taken to the zoo. The Versailles battle picture. Hence clearcut opposition: what really interests and benefits me; and what is purely formal submission to the stupidities of the grown-ups. (Guerrilla warfare with my mother: episodes of being locked in the dark room, when I was around 8. Father: set free without apologizing/conventional rules versus conventional rules.)

All this: very poor relationship with my mother. Clever and—what used to be called cultured in our circle of acquaintances (later observation), without any interest in the way things are in reality, what needs are genuine. That is to say, entirely conventional, and since she was able to live according to the rules of polite behaviour very competently, even with flair, she was highly respected. My father too (as a self-made man) revered her greatly; I felt a measure of respect for him as a child (his work and his intelligence), but was indignant about his reverence for my mother, and sometimes despised him for it (his blindness). We only found ourselves on better terms when, perhaps under pressure from me on occasion, he began to view my mother more critically. (But this was not until much later.)

In childhood my mother dominated the house, both its atmosphere and ideology. One aspect of this—almost the central point—my brother was regarded as a highly promising child; compared to him I was completely insignificant. Here again, the *division* into reality and conventional behaviour important. I was never inwardly affected by this judgement: all the facts contradicted it: learning to read.

Learning to read: the expansion of reality beyond the confines of the nursery. But here, from the outset: criticism on the basis of an 'etiquette' view of things. Especially writings about childhood. Great scepticism about 'Cuore'.[4] Here I discovered a great deal of conventional behaviour (school!), but also in historical fiction (as in the heroes of the Turkish Wars, for instance); heroism as such seemed full of convention. The bravery of the heroes in the Turkish Wars put me in mind of the intellectual superiority of my 'uncles' and 'aunts' in real life. But also and especially: a broadening and deepening. At 9 years: prose works (Hector and Achilles, *The Last of the Mohicans*). Both hostile to values at home (including Father's): success, the only criterion of what was right. Cooper particularly noteworthy: the vanquished are in the right, are authentic, in contrast to the victors, the representatives of conventional behaviour. This intensified 1 or 1½ years later: Tom Sawyer and Huckleberry Finn. An important extension: the truly real—not an abstract scheme, but individual: individual paths to reality. Highest form: learnt English at this time—*Tales from Shakespeare*: the immeasurable wealth, far beyond my grasp, of reality and an understanding of it. Read Shakespeare much too young to achieve any proper appreciation; read him again subsequently—not a refutation of my earlier reading but it increased my understanding.

Naturally, all this rather up in the air (reality at home—and the Mohicans); movement towards a real critique of existing state of affairs, linked with a view of the only correct way for me to behave—all that later on. Read the classics, from time to time. Not without an impact (though: hostile to Schiller), but no real rapport. The nearest I came: a feeble story about Spinoza by Auerbach: its theme: flying in the face of convention to achieve an independent grasp of reality: against religion, intensification of this effect.

To anticipate: school—I was not quite nine. Relief: not at home the whole day; together with boys my own age; I thought them superior to my brother and the children in our social circle. Hopes of the poor—despite the scepticism induced by my reading. These justified. Although in school itself (disillusionment about the poor) scarcely anything more than a passing friendship. For they too were dominated by convention in many ways—partly expected, but—as I rightly suspected—more relaxed, with more scope than at home. What I expected, turned out to be the case. Without fear: I found learning easy; in all areas. Even where I was and still am quite without talent (as in mathematics), this persisted up to the end of Gymnasium. Was always a model pupil, quite without making any effort. School occupied the morning, but the preparation for the following day never required more than an hour in the afternoon. I could therefore spend the afternoons quietly reading, for myself, on excursions with my bicycle, skating, etc. After about an hour's study, I was free. Hence increase of freedom at home, particularly after the first good reports. Of course, the 'ideology' at home still unshakeable. My mother employed tutors for me, since in her opinion my brother required no assistance; when after a few weeks the position was reversed and my brother spent until evening swotting with the tutor, only narrowly being saved from having to repeat a class, there arose the legend of his indolence and my diligence. The facts were drastic enough to refute this legend time and again and to render it ineffectual.

But as far as I was concerned: school was always the rules. Spontaneously: was a so-called model pupil. Social problem: a swot—despised. Long-term solution: practical solidarity with the middling and weaker pupil. Gradual success of this strategy during my school years. By the end: in the eyes of the teachers, I had the advantages of the good pupils (a wrong answer was regarded as an accident, without being ostracized by the class as a swot). Small sacrifices called for: e.g. later this took the form of my helping others with their translations—which even benefited my own work.

All in all: my years at Gymnasium, between childhood and production-oriented youth, were really just filled up instead of making an essential and concrete contribution to my development. My path: from the childish rejection of very slowly, gradually, intermittently, barely conscious, to an increasingly concrete criticism of society. Turning point: not until I was about 15. Came across Nordau's *Decadence* in my father's library. This called for a turn of 'only' 180° in order to discover Baudelaire, Verlaine, Swinburne, Zola, Ibsen and Tolstoy as leaders and guides. Criticism: protocol = convention, this an essential insight into what elements of modern society had to be opposed. Thanks to such experiences, thanks to such an insight—however abstract to begin with—into the nature of social milieu, the defence of the harmonious world of childhood can become a connecting thread to social practice, a guide to man in his search for self-discovery.

This radical transformation brought about by my reading—even though very hesitantly at first and mixed up with abstract and mistaken ideas. Certainly no accident that around this time: the first friendships worthy of the name. The most important (Leo Popper)—more of that later, since it went much deeper than this initial transition to my first phase of creative activity. In this transitional phase a) a school friend, Marcell Hammerschlag, from a musical family, who was undergoing similar experiences. Discussions about the problematic nature of R. Wagner; b) generally more important and longer lasting: Marcell Benedek. His father: I did not think highly of him as a writer—but as a model of an indomitable moral code of decency. Thanks to this friendship: transition from 'conscious' opposition to productivity. Our alliance: that of young writers taking their first steps. (My admiration for his verse technique, but accompanied by the feeling that I was his superior in my understanding of conflict.) (This undertone largely irrelevant; no question of rivalry; limits: the task itself.) Double beginning: criticism—already published: not without success. Bródy. Failed to make use of it: dogmatism (Merezhkovsky). More importantly—after leaving school—the Thalia. First 'movement', first 'leader' (Pethes).

II
Literary Beginnings

The Thalia leads me beyond my half-childish efforts. This not our achievement: the real impetus provided by Hevesi, the producer, and the actors: the real effect lay in the clarification of theatrical problems, as the first step towards a never-to-be-achieved revolution. Only its contours emerged.

For my part—to repeat—my first involvement in a movement. But my reservations proved lasting. However great my development subsequently, no fulfilment ever again as long as the framework remains that of the bourgeoisie.

Two important concretizations of my entrance into the world of literature. a) with Benedek, even before the Thalia, Bánóczi (characterization; later development), in the background (L. Popper). Discovery that I had no authentic gift as a writer. Not long after leaving school—destroyed *all* my manuscripts. This led spontaneously to a criterion: where does real literature start? b) illusions about the theatre destroyed. My experience in the Thalia demonstrated: no talent as a producer. The particular form of the transposition here—criticism and theory. A similar clarification to a). With that the road clear to becoming a critic, theoretician, literary historian: the greater impulse. Increasing knowledge: Germany. (The Anglo-French positivism propagated by the radicals without lasting effect.) Germany: disappointment with literary history, already from my brief visits to Berlin University (from Erich Schmidt downwards: Lotte's eyes—the knowledge of what is not worth knowing). On the other hand: Dilthey, Simmel—individual writers producing criticism:

Paul Ernst. Simultaneously, Marx. Superficially confirmed by Simmel—in reality distorted. For all that: the theoretical analysis of literature never quite abandoned a social perspective. Social Democratic theory: negative—even including Mehring in great measure. Powerful influence: Lessing, the correspondence between Goethe and Schiller, the Romanticism of the *Athenäum*[5]. Read: Schopenhauer and Nietzsche. Pushed into the background via Kierkegaard (known through Kassner, who was himself influential in this direction). Thus: first attempt at the theory of literature on the basis of a theory which stressed the importance of society (the influence of Marx visible), but making use of categories derived mainly from conservative aesthetic theory and literary history.

For all that, this development is nevertheless the continuation of what went before. New intellectual approaches do not obliterate the very real continuity: hatred of the vestiges of Hungarian feudalism, and of every kind of capitalism that thrives on that feudal foundation. (1906 Ady's *New Poems*.) A great jolt for me: the principles of what can really be called 'new'. This leads to a revolution of form: means to express this. Far less clear in German literature. But a) I dimly perceive that the pinnacles of German Classicism are connected with the French Revolution and Napoleon, b) that the present is a condition composed of half-hearted compromises on all important human issues. Henceforth: admiration for the radicalism of Scandinavian and Russian literature (start of Tolstoy's impact). Inner loyalty to the ideal of humanity (Peer Gynt and Peder Mortensgaard[6]). Opposed to 'superficial' positivism, even if radical, and 'inward' revolution (even though its outer form was not revolutionary). These tendencies only at the start. Without involvement in the Hungarian literary movement, without any unconditional affirmation of Ady's revolution: without doubt a blind alley. This double aspect present in the Thalia, the friendship with Béla Balázs (from 1908). For a time perhaps contradictory and confused motifs, but all with a single inner tendency: the search for a new form of revolution (later on Tolstoy and Dostoevsky).

Few writings in the transitional period—so, in summary, the drama book, written 1906–7, completed in January 1907. Attempted summary: Marxist tendency very much in the foreground. Sociological theory: drama as the product of a declining class (the past—especially the Renaissance—much schematic abstraction; Greece—the polis, but without any specific research of any profundity). Bourgeoisie: synthesis of the problems inherited from childhood and youth: a meaningful life impossible under capitalism; striving for such a life: tragedy and tragi-comedy, the latter plays a major role in the analyses; leads to the conclusion that modern drama is not just the product of crisis, but crisis is expressed in all its elements; even its immediate artistic features: a growing problematic.

Entered a competition organized by the Kisfaludy Society. Awarded the prize in February 1908.

In view of my profound contempt for the men in charge of the competition—had not reckoned with my winning; wanted—*à la* Schopenhauer—to publish the book without acknowledging the prize. Victory in flattering circumstances: shortly afterwards a brief crisis of despair (saved by L. Popper). Reception of the book: lukewarm praise: (Feleky's review the only exception). Despite this general improvement in my literary reputation; above all at home: my father—brief sketch of his attitudes at the time—becomes my Maecenas. Clever and feels the need for culture (early career aspirations), but wholly untheoretical: wants me to become a member of parliament in Tisza's Party. Ridiculed the idea. Not insulted. Continues to act the Maecenas—of course, successes necessary—but the recognition of important people suffices (Max Weber, Thomas Mann). This even lasts beyond the dictatorship.

Apart from that, total alienation at home. Mother especially; almost no communication, none at all with my brother (death). Letter during final illness. Only my father and—peripherally—my sister.

More important: at the same time as the prize: period of essay writing begins. My need: to grasp the many-sidedness of the phenomena (which do not yield to abstract theories). A feeling for the simultaneity of the various aspects of individual phenomena and the wish to seek out non-mechanical ways of connecting them with broad general substances (totalities). To comprehend this: Romanticism, Kierkegaard, Meister Eckhart, oriental philosophy. For the most part selecting arbitrarily what suits the immediate need (Kierkegaard the exception here). For all that, the general line (up to Marx) not abandoned. The illusion that I would discover a novel synthesis (Kierkegaard again).

Thus *Soul and Form* written during this phase. The first essay (Novalis) almost simultaneously with the prize (book on the drama). My essayistic phase not a rapprochement with the dominant (in many ways, of course, positivist) impressionism, indeed rather a sharpening of the contrast, because in the final analysis I aimed at objectivity (a much more emphatic stress on laws). Importance of Cézanne, parallel with Italian primitives (Giotto). My speech at the first exhibition of a comparable Hungarian painter who had already modelled himself on Matisse: my argument went directly against impressionism (i.e. modern subjectivism). Hence tendency to absolutize great art (rejecting every 'historically' orientated conservatism).

Kierkegaard phase: not without Regine Olsen. Irma Seidler, to whose memory *Soul and Form* was dedicated. As with the Kierkegaard precedent—spontaneous, certainly no conscious intention: framework of strict bourgeois conventions (breach: outcast. Zalai episode. At best: young women divorced early are tolerated—if they have no child from the relationship). So in this instance marriage the only way to achieve a sexual-erotic solution. In my case, on the other hand, absolute independence in order to produce, and for that reason silent rejection. Hence a 'great love' acted out in narrowest framework of dominant social 'respectability'. My attitude towards life at the time: cultivation of an 'essayistic' style of life; for her, justifiable dissatisfaction with the incomplete nature of the solution. Hence (at the end of 1908), her marriage with a painter colleague—which ended badly. The break—an important motif in this essayistic phase—makes visible the unity between the attempt to dissolve every mechanical system into its individual components and the perspective of a new dogmatism. This only contained implicitly in the essays. After her suicide (1911) (unhappy marriage, failure of her efforts to construct a new love life—not with me), end of the essayistic phase (1911). The dialogue *On Poverty of Spirit*: attempt to come to terms morally with my responsibility for her suicide. Background: the possibilities of distinguishing between different types of ethical position as a spiritual revival of the caste-system. The cul-de-sac here plainly visible.

III
Philosophical Prospect

Hence not by chance, my essayistic phase comes to an end. Ernst Bloch's role in this crucial. Contradiction: decisive—but not possible to express influence in concrete terms. Encounter in Budapest. Corrected the misunderstandings of our first conversation. Good relationship. My experience: a philosophy in the classical style (and not in the epigonal manner of today's university philosophers) proved possible for me by Bloch's personality and thus available for me as a possible path in life. But at the same time, the ultimate content and structure without any power to influence me. This confirmed some years later by Bloch himself (*Spuren* [Traces], p. 246). Already here: rejection of any human-like consummation (or even of the problem) in the humanized reality of nature. Here already the programme of *History and Class Consciousness*. Of course, it is still a long way from genuine Marx's historicism ('Pushing back the limits of nature' as the principle of progress). In Bloch's work the philosophy of nature already at the centre.

A natural consequence of this: for all the great fascination, there were always definite limits, on both sides. And in different ways, it has remained so. But I doubt whether I would ever have found my way to philosophy without Bloch's influence. (But essentially), even though my philosophy came into being thanks to his stimulation, no direct or concrete influence of any sort. Respect—but at a distance, particularly on philosophical issues. My respect for his personality, character—without limits (Bloch in the Stalin era, today). Whereas with Adorno: philosophy of compromises—with Bloch, the old classical type. First impression: correct. Outwardly: shift from the essay to aesthetics. (First draft in Florence in the winter of 1911–12.) Remarkable that without my being aware of it, my development with all its contradictions and setbacks moves right from the start towards ontology, bypassing logical and epistemological questions. Variation on Kant: 'There are works of art—how are they possible?' Instead of the form of judgement I see it as a move in the direction of ontology. (Of course it seems to me that the same tendency, in a primitive and distorted form, can also be seen as the foundation of the essayistic phase.)

With such plans I went to Heidelberg together with Bloch. Characteristic of this transitional phase is that under his influence the ontological foundation of aesthetics turned into its metaphysical critique (importance of the Lucifer principle): only with the return to Marx, with the construction of a historical world-view in his sense, was it possible to preserve the correct tendencies concealed in this fantastic and false line of thought and to isolate the core of truth in it (namely, the concrete specificity of the aesthetics in social being). Only after *History and Class Consciousness* had been overcome did the transformation of my views take concrete form: the genuine aesthetics of Marxism (in opposition to Plekhanov and Mehring). Therefore: it became possible to correct the prevailing view of the historic role of Marxism. (Later stage of my own Marxist development.)

But very far from that at the time. My understanding then was purely ideological. Even though, in consequence of the domestic situation in Hungary, the starting-point was provided by the need to oppose the vestiges of feudal ideology (Lenin: the Prussian road), and even though Russian literature (above all, Tolstoy and Dostoevsky) was always there to point the way. But such foundations did not suffice to establish a unified philosophical position. On the one hand, (works of art exist)—immanence, the immanent nature of art, works of art should not be judged by the light of alien criteria; sharply opposed to a) mere existence, mere subjective 'experience'—critical rejection of modern subjectivism and naturalism, naturalism not a preliminary, a preparatory stage of artistic realism—but *the* antithesis; b) rejection of every 'metaphysics' of art—such as that of Schopenhauer. Kierkegaard: rejection of art as life-principle in the name of an as yet highly contradictory and only gradually emerging ethic. Hostility towards 'the art of living' (already in the essays). Now, the 'Luciferian' nature of such a philosophical conception in the name of an ethical revolution which should lead to a genuine 'redemption' (the first, metaphyscial formulation of the humanization of man).

All this together with a number of partly correct insights (the homogeneous medium of artistic quality—L. Popper's ideas extended here), absolute immanence, the internal completeness of every work of art. The integration of each work into larger contexts (genre theory) is methodologically distinct from the abstract concepts or genera in the sciences. Whereas the genus is epistemologically stable and the individual fits into it, in the case of the arts (epic or dramatic, etc.) the universal is modified by each particular instance of it—without necessarily losing its universal validity (Shakespeare and the Greeks and up to Lessing).

These ideas were certainly fruitful in so far as they involved a search for new generalizing forms, but they did not advance radically beyond the world of the essays. Instead they were generalized and hardened out into completely false principles (such as the Lucifer principle). Although some ideas could be reconciled with the facts, they could not be fully developed within such a system (the sterility of aesthetics as a life-principle). Accordingly I had manoeuvred myself into a theoretical cul-de-sac. There was no direct way out. Thus, even at best I would have become no better than an interesting and eccentric non-staff lecturer in Heidelberg.

IV
Towards the Fateful Turning-Point

But this insight not taken any further: with the outbreak of war, society posed radically new problems. As shall be seen at once, these did nothing to point a way out of the intractable problems I already faced. But since they posed quite different problems for actual practical life, the war at least destroyed the ordinary texture of life and hence—even though I failed to grasp the significance of this change at the time—diverted the entire flow of modern inquiry into other channels. These proved in themselves to be no more free of theoretical contradictions than the old blind alleys. But they at least had the virtue that the new and increasingly critical social situation was able to force me to take a fresh look at the problems. (Relationship to Hungarian ideology before the war.) That was the effect of the war. It laid bare the falseness, the inhumanity in those static views which were threatening to congeal into a system: for the anti-humanitarianism which forms the central motive force in our lives and which entered my first philosophical efforts unconsciously, was given such a dominant, all-pervasive position in them that an intellectual confrontation could not be evaded. All the social forces that I had hated since early youth and tried to overcome intellectually, united to produce the first universal war, a war devoid of, and hostile to, ideas. Moreover, the war was not simply one determining factor of life, but universally determined it in its extensive and intensive totality. It was not possible to survive *alongside* this new reality, as was the case with earlier wars. It was universal: it absorbed the whole of life, whether you liked it or not.

From the outset I was on the side of those who opposed the war: a life simply abounding in inhumanity was to be imposed on all of us in order to preserve those forces which even before had seemed despicable in their universally accepted inhumanity. Even in its 'normal' state my homeland, the Hapsburg monarchy, appeared to me as a humanly meaningless apparatus destined for destruction. Now everyone was supposed to risk their neck and participate in universal murder in order to ensure that this obstacle to any true humanity would be further sustained by the strict, mindlessly regimented system of the German Empire. Each individual would have to become a murderer, a criminal or a victim simply to preserve this system in existence.

My emphatic repudiation of all this had nothing to do with pacifism. I have never regarded force in the abstract as an inhuman evil *per se*. Without Marathon, the Migration of Nations, without 1789 and 1793, the best of humanity, the things that make people human today could never have become reality. What has to be eliminated is not force in general, but the force of reactionary authorities, the force used by Wilhelm ll and his like, the force that prevents the humanization of man. And such force should be eliminated by force, if necessary. Furthermore, it had to be acknowledged that the Western form of democracy could not become the required counterforce. Admittedly, Jaurès against Wilhelm ll—that sounds almost sensible—but what about Jaurès's assassins? The Dreyfus Affair, the way it was hushed up, all that was carried out by more modern methods than were ever available to the Hohenzollern or Hapsburg regime. But in themselves are they any less reprehensible and anti-human?

So my condemnation of the war was neither pacifist nor Western and democratic in its inspiration, but was motivated instead by Fichte's idea that this was 'the age of absolute sinfulness'. In this I remained truer to my previously held convictions than could be claimed for the many adherents of the antinomic philosophies of life and action of the time. War emerged as the central negative feature of the existing system. The content of my hatred: the continuation of my youthful attitude towards feudal Hungary (Ady's influence). My point of view different now only to the extent that the 'revolution' of Tolstoy and Dostoevsky opened up a utopian perspective and erected a moral standard. Hence, the recourse to Fichte not consistent. But no influence on that utopian perspective. The depiction of the phenomena: that of the *Geisteswissenschaften*. What it all comes to: left-wing ethics combined with right-wing epistemology. This characterizes the level of the Marxism I had reached at the time.

Theory of the Novel as the expression of this eclectic philosophy of history.

Life: remain outside it. Because anything more than the protest represented by *The Theory of the Novel* was impossible for me at the time. Sympathy for Liebknecht and Jaurès without the smallest opportunity to follow their example. Heidelberg: help from Jaspers (very much against his better judgement) not wholly successful [?]. Budapest, instead of the front; mail censor; after a year: released, returned to Heidelberg.

Private life—comparable confusion thanks to the war. J. Grabenko, summer 1913 (a friend of the Balázs's). Love + friendship. Both form the basis of a good—always terminable—relationship.

Independent literary life: on appropriate basis. Heidelberg situation: marriage necessary. War. J. Grabenko: Russian, her only protection: Hungarian citizenship. Material basis: one year. Predictable (J. thought it an actual possibility even in this form): her love affair with a musician. Living together as a threesome: tested the loyalty of the relationship. Marriage though with inner separation. The correct solution: amicable divorce, not until after the war.[7]

Despite all the friendly forms of coexistence during War, concurrent dissolution of that modernist theory with whose help we had striven to shape our lives in a way that was humanly authentic and 'modern' at the same time. When Lena visited me during the dictatorship after her separation from her musician, we were still capable of an understanding and friendly relationship, but neither of us felt our central human interest was involved. Respect and sympathy, without being-together in inner core of our lives. I always thought highly of her penetrating, clear-sighted intelligence, her ability to grasp the essence of a person with a single glance. (Béla Kun, Vautrin, etc.) But the centre of life lay elsewhere.

Opposition to the war: centre of my interest shifted from aesthetics to ethics (lectures in Budapest, spring 1917). Circle in Budapest (almost completely isolated in Heidelberg since Bloch. Even with Max Weber no real common ground on these issues). The Budapest circle was also very mixed ideologically. General foundation: the old opposition (Ady: attitude towards the war: our viewpoints converge). Predominance of morality: Béla Balázs and the war: from ethical motives (solidarity with the human victims)— wanted to be at the front himself. (In the background a conformism I rejected; reconciliation with the Hapsburg Monarchy.) But such differences of opinion no barrier. Private society. Later emerged as the Free School of the Humanities. (In agreement with *Huszadik Század*.) Its importance exaggerated—because of the role played, much later—by Mannheim and later, Hauser in exile.

At home, the decisive year 1917–18: reaction to the Russian Revolution. My own path: contradictory fascination, with lapses: 1918 Communist Party.

Life: lectures 1918 (ethics: Gertrud), our earlier acquaintance (Lena's account of our meeting). 1917–18: growth of a new attachment: unfathomable, but I had the feeling that for the first time in my life, I was in love: complementarity, solid basis for life (a touchstone for my ideas)—not opposition. Immediate topics of conversation were secondary. The true content was always: whether what I thought and felt was real, i.e. whether it expressed my true individuality (subjectively: genuine; objectively: in conformity with the species). Her activity as a touchstone, which at first took the form of spontaneous gestures, emphases, gradually became a new way of life: a permanent double check on authenticity.

I do not know whether the inner transformation of my thought (1917–19) would have been possible without this double check. Not just because—for the first time in my life—I had to make an ideological decision and change my entire life, but also because now ideological alternatives of quite a different nature. Above all, ethics (practical conduct) did not simply entail a prohibition on any action which my own system of values condemned as sinful, but implied now a dynamic balancing act in practice whereby something that might be sinful when taken on its own might yet form an inevitable part of right action, or, conversely, an ethical limitation (held to be universally valid) might sometimes become a barrier to right action. Not a simple opposition: universal ethical principles versus the practical exigencies of specific actions. This was no doubt the general background, but it never operated in a rigid manner. In the subsequent process of decay (to the point of bureaucratization) a frequent motif was: a mode of action which—exceptionally—was permitted, hardens out into a general guideline for action. (In the case of quite abject, mechanized

---

bureaucrats such sclerosis is a very common basis for a more widespread human degeneration. And, on the other hand, the unique nature of particular choice in times of crisis can become the basis for a cynical degeneration.)

Of course, in 1918–19 all of this only appeared on what seemed to be a distant horizon and was not concretely experienced as a dilemma by people in the process of transforming themselves. (Even though it did sometimes become visible on the horizon in the event of specific alternatives.) Hence, precisely because decisions immediately brought with them weighty social consequences, indivdual decisions and the resulting actions had to be thought through, more carefully differentiated and nuanced than in the case of decisions taken before this crisis. The determining social moments were of course clear and robust. But transposed in changing of individual life through such determination.

But even these social determinants: interacted directly with individuality. For my part: culture. Continuation of the Ady line (implications of the false solution to the agrarian problem—recognized subsequently, in Vienna. Crucial point here: no real knowledge of Lenin; whole problem of the emigration. Importance of my stay in Vienna. In contrast, culture: Lenin + action + the appropriate continuation of the Ady line; adequate.)

Gertrud's importance in this transition: for the first time in my life. Different from previous occasions (Irma, Lena): my policy always clear; relationship—even love—always within the given line of development. Now with every decision, Gertrud strongly involved: particularly in human, personal decisions. Her reaction often decisive. Not that I would not have turned to communism without her. That was something that was contained in my previous development, but nevertheless the complex questions surrounding the actual decision and the highly important personal implications of that choice would quite certainly have had a different outcome but for her. And with that much of what has been most essential to me in the whole course of my life.

And long before a spiritual bond had developed between us, this irresistible need for harmony, this need for her approval, had become a central issue in our relationship. Ever since I first met G. the need to be approved of by her has been the central question of my personal life. And since one of her characteristics was a kind of instinctive rigour in intellectual matters—to say nothing of ethical questions—that is sometimes found in Gottfried Keller's women characters, there were occasional periods of estrangement at this time. My relationship with her differed from earlier ones in that I found these periods unbearable. (Previously such differences of opinion, even on humanly important issues, belonged to the charm of the relationship: the fact was that we were different people and differences of opinion were simply part of the attraction.) With G., too, I did not really think in terms of a total identification. It did not exist and could not be achieved without a distortion of the facts of the relationship. Rather, what was at stake was my need to fuse my intellectual and practical aspirations with the contemporary world situation in such a way as to make my efforts bear fruit (not just objectively and practically right, but also favourable to my personal development). At this point the situation pointed to something qualitatively new: the choice between two world systems. No one—with the exception of Lenin (in quite a definite sense)—has understood that the two processes are ultimately identical: that is, the social development of the new man is in effect a synthesis of all the individual aspirations to come to terms with the novel reality in an honest revolutionary way. Although there were many participants in the Hungarian Revolution who had also been active—sometimes in relatively important positions (locally at least)—in the Russian Revolution, my efforts to obtain a clear picture of Lenin proved vain. Everyone revered the 'infallible' political leader, but even Béla Kun said to me in a private conversation that, despite everything, he thought that Bukharin was the true theoretician of the Revolution. Not until I went to Vienna did I have an opportunity to gain a real understanding of Lenin, and to find myself in a situation where I could begin to gauge the dimensions of his intellectual, practical and moral achievement.

In such circumstances, in Budapest, where fateful decisions had to be made (whether to join the Communists or remain in a 'left-socialist' position), G.'s reaction was decisive in the final analysis, even though she remained reluctant to speak her mind on the grounds that she had never considered these issues before. But whenever she reacted by refusing to involve herself, saying that she had scarcely thought about the matter, and when she remained modestly passive in the face of my changes of direction, she nevertheless managed to convey such clear disapproval that I found myself compelled again and again to examine the issues once more. On the other hand, whenever her tacit and reserved approval became apparent, I always felt I had received a great fillip and was encouraged to make further advances in the same direction. (That such support was more in evidence in the initial stages of my resolve to join the Communists was a function of the nature of the decisions that had to be made. Even though it was never stated in so many words, an important aspect of our growing compatibility sprang from the link to my old ideological hostility to the remnants of Hungarian feudalism and the fact that I increasingly found it possible to envisage close collaboration with democratic tendencies, without drawing any nearer to the liberalism which I hated and despised even then.)

My moving towards the Communists was the greatest turning-point in my life. Whereas hitherto at best a loose ideological collaboration had been possible—as in the fine arts—now an alliance was forged in which the practical preparations for the dictatorship of the proletariat, the implementation of the demands for democractic reforms, laid the basis for cultural achievement under the dictatorship of the proletariat. Field of activity enlarged: to include above all educational reform. All the remnants of feudalism to be swept away: the assumption that reforms would be carried out self-evident. This would not only involve the broad masses and determine specific modes of transition. It also guaranteed a) broad mass participation, b) taking the threads from the revolutionary past, from this the growth of socialism: hence socialism not alien, not an 'import', c) its historical character, d) anti-bureaucratic: there would be no 'official' art in the name of development (Kassák group).

This political line alien a) to the average Communist, b) to the Social Democrats. I was considered a radical Communist without having any of their dogmatism. For that reason no need to defend the cultural reforms; they were simply accepted unofficially. (The Social Democrat people's commissars were indifferent to such reforms.) For my part: the connections with old radical aspirations of the masses important precisely on such issues. Concentrated on culture. Did not admit mistakes. Agrarian question: even where I came into contact with it in the army (brief discussion of the army commissariat), I did not realize its central importance until I went to Vienna.

V
Apprenticeship in Life and Thought

After the fall of the Republic: Korvin and I (suspicions about Kun), illegality, escape to Vienna. Debates about Lenin's teachings. For me: this was when I really studied Marx properly. Philosophy of Marx: rejecting all forms of Revisionism (Kant, etc.): Hegel. General direction: unified philosophical foundations of Marxism (no 'completion' necessary). Revolution the essential element of Marxism. My interpretation at that time: ultra-left: radicalism, continuation of the November days. Inwardly failed to register that the revolutionary movement had faltered, hope sustained by means of organized 'actions'. At the same time, I was suspicious of the bureaucratic dogmatism of the Comintern (Zinoviev—Kun thought of as his supporter and disciple). Periodical: *Kommunismus* (acknowledged Lenin's criticism).

The Hungarian crisis. Relationship to Landler. The theoretical importance of 'minor' causes of the party split. My attention shifted from the 'great' questions (their existence perhaps only postulated) to the actual problems of the movement—here: the effect revolutionizes. Politics educates behaviour (importance of reality). Theoretical double life: example, the March Action (1921) versus Hungarian politics. Its growing importance. Hungarian Socialist Workers Party—republic—democratic dictatorship. (Both still intertwined in *History and Class Consciousness*.)

Spring 1920, Gertrud in Vienna. Lived with her sister with the children in Hütteldorf; I stayed in Vienna for the time being. Only together on our free days. In this way her form of life (family, three children) becomes the determining factor for me as well. My involvement in raising children (with her): daily need to get to grips with specific human problems. Had thought such a life impossible for me—now Gertrud. a) no disruption preventing me from concentrating on my work, no distraction by everyday events. Isolation. b) meals together as an occasion for conversation with the children. Recognition of their problems, attempts to resolve them (ethics, many issues seen in a new light). Gertrud—a synthesis of patience and impatience; great human tolerance combined with hatred of everything base. New attitude: hostile to ethics on Kantian lines; now, the alternatives no less rigorously formulated, but my inherent tendency to an abstractly motivated inhumanity overcome: hence a new and direct approach to childhood problems (completely open discussions).

All this but a minor part, a mere premise of my harmonious relationship with G. Her irrepressible development in Vienna, her rapprochement with comrades-in-arms (Gábor, Lengyel), her study of Marx, never a beginner, at the heart of economic problems from the outset. Amazingly quick: accumulation (Luxemburg—Bauer—Bukharin). Even at that stage: an intimate knowledge of the most important problems of theory. Although she retained her particular point of view through various metamorphoses—failed in the attempt to achieve a normal synthesis in economics, the quality of an individual 'adventure' survived; a) not the Varga Institute, to acquire the routine and then leave it behind, b) even when just taking notes, her individuality persists. Whereas I was often a bungling dilettante—she in fact achieved a grasp of the most crucial matters, the matters essential for living, without any need of any communicable, systematic theorization (her relationship with Ferkó. Painless renunciation of production for herself: fulfilment through her son.)

Thus economics became the vehicle for the extension of her judgement of the world to broader areas of society, without ever becoming subjectivized and also without diluting her individuality and generalizing from her particular judgements. The influence which she exerted by virtue of her way of living and thinking became ever more powerful. Although, thanks to her outstanding grasp of economic questions, she was in the right in our discussions of some important problems—this was not the essential point (after all that would have amounted to no more than a stimulating friendship). The reality was: the more the ontological element in my thought came to the fore, the more important it became to achieve a wholly authentic starting-point and attitude (mimesis never photographic): if a thing has true being, the authenticity of the subjective impulse must be present (Being is never reached through untruth). Hence emphasis: first appearance often in form barely expressible in language. Here: the weightiness of authenticity. But this also human and vital: rejection not necessarily a sign of absolute negativity, but often reflects the intrusion of false (inauthentic) nuances in the first intuition. Correction possible—once again with her help. In addition: the same interest in (the same critical attitude towards) totalizations (the latter emerged gradually, more complete and substantial in the *Aesthetics* than in *History and Class Consciousness*). Crucial for the whole enterprise: the method and contents of the Hungarian factional struggles. Landler: the other stroke of luck in this transition. His personality. Its political impact on me. Once again, the living interaction between the individual and the general. Reality as principle (from Landler, the slogan of the Republic). Both together: in philosophy—search for totality; a generality which includes elements of particularity—historically (hence: in reality).

This the point where theory, politics and history reveal themselves as different forms of manifestation of the same movement of being. Theory and history: general tendency, what the majority of human beings (or the most influential class) will do (direction of their activities). On such a foundation—politics: amounts to the question of how to influence the direction and intensity of such foreseeable activity, both qualitatively and quantitatively. In every case inferences about the future based on processes defined 'post festum'. This impossible in purely scientific terms; could only be done if it were possible to make predictions about the future based on extrapolations from a 'post festum' understanding of the dominant forces at work in the present. This is a hundred per cent impossible in principle: even if it is scarcely perceptible in concrete instances, historical change is always structural change (with human change as its foundation) and hence also substantive change. Such inferences from processes which have been analysed post festum (and whose true causality has therefore not necessarily been understood) always contain *in addition* changes in the content of those processes; individual deviations from the general tendency. Proportion is vital here.

Hence correctness in theory, history and politics arises from an individual standpoint—but goes beyond this in the direction of reality. (Inauthenticity to be rejected, but authenticity no guarantee of truth.) Hence a new attitude towards reality: epistemologically directed standpoints gradually overcome. This process of intellectual re-orientation: characteristic of the twenties. Crucial: my life with Gertrud. Testing ground: Hungarian politics. Above all in the struggle against general (abstract) sectarian tendencies: *History and Class Consciousness* still a mixture. But important: radicalism the (ultra-left) continuation of the Marxist line: problems created by contemporary society not soluble within it. Lenin: this became obvious in 1914. Diminution of acute revolutionary tension no proof that these foundations no longer valid. This the theoretical basis of opposition to Zinoviev's Comintern policy. (Back to a purely bourgeois policy, one that is revolutionary only in theory: this the basis of my opposition.)

VI
The First Breakthroughs

The practical point of departure: republic or Soviet republic in the Hungarian context. The former: genuine dilemma: necessity of coming out in opposition to the basic principles of the Horthy period, both in theory and practice. The latter may admittedly offer a general perspective, yet be devoid of any inherent obligation to act. Opposition to bureaucratization: such attitudes, which are compatible with innumerable courses of action, have lost their authenticity, both subjective and objective. This—negatively—true of *History and Class Consciousness*: the denial of any 'dialectic of nature' (simultaneously a model whereby the workings of economics can be understood): *History and Class Consciousness* the attempt to free the necessities of the world for authentic action. Even though the Blum Theses signal a radical change of direction in political terms, they nevertheless constitute the fulfilment of this development. Written for the Second Congress of HCP, their thrust is that in the light of the profound crisis afflicting the Horthy regime, the revolutionary perspectives opened up point not towards the dictatorship of the proletariat, but to what Lenin in 1905 called 'the democratic dictatorship of the workers and peasants'. (Caution: e.g. the Sixth Congress of the Comintern, and other analyses)—scandal. Period of the consequences (my political destruction; Manuilsky in Berlin. Break-up of the Landler faction. Révai on the Theses).

Double effect: politically, an annihilating defeat. Danger: expulsion from the Comintern. Korsch's fate. Impotence at a time when the fascist threat was at its greatest. On the other hand, it provided the stimulus for the further development of theory and the opportunity to make it more effective. This duality: give up political activity and concentrate on ideological impact. The reason for this reaction to the period of consequences, undoubtedly there: Kun's intention to destroy me and ability to do so (to silence me). Anything else just an avoidance, a localization of this, without any clarity: how much truth actually contained in these hopes (in this theoretical perspective).

Principle: the period of consequences can be biologically necessary (e.g. cancer today). Socially, a tendency with very high negative probability. The only question: are these probabilities not susceptible to external influence—within certain definite limits? (Lenin, Third Congress: there are no hopeless situations.) In this instance, there was an optimal objective: viz, that the issue should remain internal to the Hungarian Party. (Objectively: maximum impotence on this very point at the level of practical action.) So, if I wished to salvage my prospect of future activity—radically different activity, no longer political, but essentially ideological—the only way was to attempt to restrict the inevitable criticism to the Hungarian Party. The important thing was to deflect attention from the Theses as a document with claims to general theoretical validity which just happened to have originated in Hungary. Hence unconditional surrender on the Hungarian front (where anyway prospects of success were more or less nil), so that Kun would lose interest in the matter and have no wish to force the issue in the Comintern—all the more since new problems (problems of power) had arisen. For my part, I disappeared from the Hungarian movement. Once I was forgotten, a continuation or intensification of criticism became superfluous. Circumstances facilitated this. Hence the criticism of the Blum Theses gradually faded. When Kun's fall in 1935 (at the Seventh Congress) made collaboration with Hungarians possible once more, I had long since been forgotten.

The positive side: re-think *History and Class Consciousness*. The result: what was important about it, was not its hostility to materialism but its completion of historicism in Marxism, and with that, ultimately, the universality of Marxism as a philosophy: philosophical debate (against Deborin). Against the 'orthodoxy' of Plekhanov and Mehring: both 'revisionist' since they both tried to 'supplement' Marxism with elements of bourgeois philosophy, e.g. in aesthetics.

Here my alliance with Lifshitz. The Sickingen Debate (he worked on Marx's early thought): aesthetics an organic part of Marxist theory, arising solely from its own premisses. Hence, Marxism a universal theory (in the thirties, *Literaturnii Kritik* an important trend; anti-RAPP, anti-modernism, etc.). In my case, moreover, movement in the direction of a general ontology which would be unified in the final analysis, for all its internal diversity; ontology as the true philosophical foundation of Marxism.

Therefore it is the philosophical unity of Marxian theory that points the way to its universality. Hence an old branch of philosophy in a new context: revival of ontology. Old epistemological questions, 'x exists, ... how is it possible?' When taken to logical conclusion, becomes 'x exists, ... what historical necessities brought it into being?' What historical factors had and still have a real function in the development of social being?

Only from this point of view: the antithesis of epistemology and ontology—do you achieve the elimination of every idealist approach. If for Marx ideology is not false consciousness, but the attempt to answer all questions arising from economics for being as such—then everything can be regarded as a developmental form of being. This can only be carried through if (see *The German Ideology*) history is seen as the universal foundation. The so-called dialectics of nature are no longer to be regarded as running parallel to dialectics of society (a parallel rejected in *History and Class Consciousness*), but as their pre-history.

The programme at its origins not yet clearly thought out. Provisionally restricted to aesthetics and to an attempt to prove that the Marxian theory of social development is *at the same time* the theory of the origin, development and effect!?!, i.e. the essence of the aesthetic; it actually exists; it can (if understood) be developed, but never manipulated. Simultaneously against both 'modernism' and Stalinist manipulation.

VII
Extension of the Field of Conflict

Immediately: social genesis in the foreground as a way of explaining essence and value (importance of mimesis in this connection); teleological, positing as its precondition; the meaning of partisanship in mimesis (everyday life).

In the transition to other realms (starting with *The Young Hegel*), the question is still 'scientifically' limited: the task was to demonstrate that the most subtle intellectual reactions of philosophy to the world arise in the last analysis from the appropriate generalization of the primary life-reactions to the realm of economics. Hence as early as Hegel, the demand to place the concept of genesis in the forefront of the history of thought ('genesis' here more than 'origin', primary consciousness). *The Destruction of Reason* is the social history of a typical perversion of thought. From that point on: move towards the universality of history. Knowledge of essence and historical knowledge: profound convergence (species being historically). Art as species being (the permanent reproduction of tragedy in the history of the different ideologies): the self-awareness of universal historicity. Hence even at that stage: opposition to Stalinist ideology general, not just confined to aesthetics. (Of course, most of these writings could not then be published, including the book on Hegel.)

Remarkable: my isolation (*Literaturnii Kritik* ceases to appear; *International Literature* often very problematic) after the Seventh Congress of the Comintern: Hungarian possibilities: Popular Front tendencies even in Moscow literature—movement towards a correct assessment of the intellectual currents within the Horthy regime and the potential for ideological resistance to fascism. The possibility of renewing old democratic traditions (Ady) in a Marxist form. Critique of the quarrel between 'urbanist' (bourgeois-democratic) tendencies and 'populist' (peasant-democratic) ones; continuation of the opposition to the vestiges of feudalism calculated to view the non-identity of democracy and merely bourgeois democracy as real difference of strength between [the two tendencies]. Extension of the field of activity: the conflict extended almost imperceptibly, by no means yet a direct and conscious turn against the Stalinist system, although the narrow bureaucratic inflexibility of that system emerged more and more clearly (see 'Tribune or Bureaucrat')[8]. Initial impulse: Leninist differentiation as opposed to Stalin's mechanical uniformity. Similarly, increasingly pronounced emphasis on Engels's 'triumph of realism' as opposed to ideological regulation from 'above'. The fact is that in art, for art, there can be no such absolute directedness. What is decisive is not the writer's design or intention (which can be disciplined), but his shaping of his material, which remains subject to the laws governing the 'triumph of realism'. Therefore, ideology can influence attitudes—mainly indirectly.

This the reason why it is essential to probe the question of genesis, mimesis—in terms of : what? how? By providing an account of the genesis of mimesis, the 'triumph of realism' is freed of every trace of irrationalism: in it the truth of history breaks through. The question of genesis goes beyond literature: a general problem of ideology: Hegel and the French Revolution (more specifically: Hegel and the capitalist economy). Real theory of ideology: ideology (Marx's definition): the culmination of the contradictory impact of the economy on life, modes of action, human consciousness: the unified historical process: truth of action: inner synthesis of individual and historical development of man. The significance of the age of Goethe and Hegel. Balzac already: only prelude to Marx's philosophy. Later development up to *The Destruction of Reason*.

Conflicts sharper: philosophical works cease to appear. (Likewise literature. End of *Literaturnii Kritik*.)

Period of the great extermination of cadres. My position (parallel: Bloch). Good luck in the face of catastrophe (a) Bukharin-Radek 1930; (b) the Hungarian movement; (c) my apartment. Good luck nevertheless in situation of 1941.

Internal inconsistency of the period: the years of the great trials—at the same time the Seventh Congress of the Comintern: Popular Front. Great contrasts jostling each other (indeed intertwined with each other). Objectively, the beginning of the end of the time of crisis.

Possibilities. Hungarian analysis of the democratic movement (thanks to the Seventh Congress). (For People's democracy—critique of liberalism.) Criticism of the Blum Theses forgotten.

Personally, not without difficulties (two arrests). Despite this, my relationship with Gertrud at its most human and harmonious. No 'beautifying', no 'optimism'. But feeling that I was approaching not just what I imagined to be my right path—(Marxism as historical ontology—but also the ideological perspectives which would make it possible to make some of these tendencies a reality.

VIII
Attempts at Self-Realization In Hungary

Homecoming with high hopes. Their justification (very ephemeral): the tactics of Rákosi and Gerö. This made possible a principled and successful propaganda policy of democratic transition over a period of years. (Freedom for myself—because of their indifference to ideological matters.) Beneficial results for process of readaptation: homecoming in the true sense (although—for objective reasons—few old friends and comrades; Gertrud: yes; superficial collaboration in alliance with a few people).

Nevertheless a homecoming. Again: as Gertrud was with me. Very important: contacts and conversations. My first students. Discover myself through teaching (Gertrud's influence). Character: seminar-like: official opinions not decisive at that period. Hence gradually: a highly promising young generation. Standards higher all the time—their foundations: Gertrud, mode of teaching (seminar). Possibility of continuation of tendencies of youth—of course much modified yet rooted in fundamental principles. (Marxism: change in emphasis, but no actual break in development, as with many people). Many intellectuals accept *my* Marxism as (subjectively) authentic, not simply learnt up or assumed. Hence fruitful dialogue possible. On good terms with the most important people: Déry and Illyés.

Tolerated (silence): only political and social contacts of importance (hence gave my vote for the CP). Involvement on individual issues here: my position on literary questions tolerated. Even possible to conduct discussions—with suitable caution.

Although I could already detect anti-democratic trends in politics (e.g. the agrarian question, the distribution of land), I still had confidence in the value of the cultural politics I was permitted—for tactical reasons—to engage in. Even the real turning-point (the merging of the workers' parties) did not alert me to the threat (Révai's warning about Rudas's attack on me). Start of the Rajk affair: clear revival of the Stalin purges (why even worse this time?). Discussion of these circumstances determines: my aim—to draw in my horns without succumbing to the Rajk purges. (An error but comprehensible.) Retreat. I confine myself to becoming a mere ideologist—but henceforth only as an individual, no longer with an official post. No social function. Academy: collaboration with Forgarasi, who acted as mediator. Hence complete freedom for myself; even possible to repudiate official trends.

IX
'Merely an ideologist'

Dual development (unity: provided by Gertrud). a) An increasingly determined opposition to the Rákosi system and an increasingly clear insight into the situation, and identification with my earlier tendencies in favour of a democratic Hungary; b) hence opposed not only to Rákosi, but also to everyone who sought renewal through introduction of bourgeois democracy. Hence independent of (indeed isolated from) the opposition of the period. Expected little of Imre Nagy. During his first, brief period of leadership—[9] no contact with him (his lack of programme). This remained true even after the Twentieth Congress. His very first intervention: essential that there should be no 'cult of personality' (whose principles, as became evident later, endure in collectives with undiminished force). Crucial: the breach with a domestic and foreign policy conducted along autocratic and merely tactical lines. The principles of Marxism: the democratic reorganization of production (the internal connection between democratization and the quality of production). Capitalism effective in certain tendencies of the market where it is impossible to manipulate total production centrally. But it would be an illusion to believe that such elements of the market could lead socialist production along the right, democratic path.

So my position was clear: opposition to Rákosi, to any illusions of a particular, internal reform of his regime, and opposition also to bourgeois liberal reforms (which were widely advocated even in circles close to Imre Nagy). (Tendency in that direction also to be found among the orthodox followers of Rákosi.) Nagy: no programme. Hence my position was purely ideological. The demands of the Twentieth Congress put to public opinion so as to create a general mood that they could become a political reality.

My position remained constant throughout the entire Nagy period. No rapprochement except late in November: nevertheless, he had the power (or the popular support) to keep the spontaneous (and highly heterogeneous) movement running along socialist lines. Hence my membership, indeed my acceptance of a ministry, in order to help. Attempted reorganization of the party (Donáth-Szántó). Overwhelmed by events. The question of guilt (without a clear programme). Hence at the end a major concession: Warsaw Pact.

Yugoslav embassy: brutal error. The period of consequences. Retention of my point of view emerges as a way out. Return home (relationship to the party); easy meat for the sectarians. I stick to my guns. In publications abroad (not possible in Hungary) I continued my criticism of Stalin in increasingly concrete form. My first positive statement on economic reform: the situation has changed. ('Positive' = the possibility of democracy and a return to Marxism.) With that, despite my acceptance into the party (details), I have the possibility of maintaining my polemic against continuity in general support of tendencies (inconsistently carried out). Maintain my position, with varying emphasis. (Replacing the indicative with the optative.) The tendency towards democracy already making itself apparent, relatively speaking. I approve of this tendency (for all the obstacles and difficulties in its path), view it as a possible foundation; hence not opposition but reform. But reform has the task of providing a genuine solution to the basic problems of democracy. Keep coming back to this example: Lenin versus Trotsky on trade unions. (Indifference or wildcat strikes. Poland as symbolic of the threat to all the people's democracies.) Hence everywhere the same problem: how to effect the transition to genuine, socialist democracy (democracy of everyday *life*) or permanent crisis. Not yet resolved (the Soviet Union crucial here). This the future perspective for the whole world, precisely because there are incipient signs of crisis in capitalism. (The Stalinist preference for tactical rather than strategic methods: confuses real problems, remote from any solution: Arab World, Israel.)

Both great systems: in crisis. *Authentic* Marxism the only solution. Hence in the socialist states Marxist ideology must provide a critique of the existing state of affairs and help to promote reforms, which are becoming ever more urgent.

Subjectively—attempts to formulate the principles of Marxist ontology. For this purpose the *chief basis*: autobiography, subjective addenda, illustration, explanation, etc. Of course, there have to be individual human premises on which to base a theorization of ontological problems. Hence there must be a convergence: man's progress towards species being as a solution to the great problems of the age. (Individuality as the consequence of the increasingly pure social relationship of the individual to society. Pseudo-immanence; in reality: species being.) Autobiography documents the subjective tendencies (in course of development) as they progress towards the practical realization of one's own species being (= the *real* unfolding of individuality).

Here we have the deepest truth of Marxism: the humanization of man as the content of the process of history which realizes itself—in a myriad of varieties—in each individual human life. If follows that each individual—regardless of whether he is conscious of this or not—is an active factor in the overall process whose product he also is. Progress towards species being in individual life represents the true convergence of two real but inseparable paths of development. The direction and the result: the direction (the role of individual decision; historical + [indivisible] profoundly personal). Result. Talent: this too is not simply 'given'. Depends on direction—it is of crucial importance whether genuine talent is *able* to develop. Conduct of life as a struggle between (genuine!) curiosity and vanity—vanity as principal vice: it nails people firmly to their particularity. (Frustration as fixation at the level of particularity.)

[Sketch in Hungarian]

1. Psychology of my early years. Last years at school. (Nordau—essays) Kerr. *Magyar Szemle* (Hungarian Review). Background!?! plays.
2. Thalia. End of the drama. Study. German culture (Kant—literary history).
3. Book on drama. *Soul and Form*. Relationship with *Nyugat* and *Huszadik Század*. Ady. Béla Balázs.
4. From war to the revolution. Struggle between idealism and Marxism. The

dictatorship (chance elements): new relationship: Hungarian reality, Hungarian life.

5. Exile in Vienna. International sectarianism—reality in Hungary. Landler. Hungarian Socialist Workers Party. Blum Theses.

6. Moscow turning-point. Marx and literature. Berlin. Moscow (*Literaturnii Kritik*).

7. *Üj Hang* (The New Voice). Choice: Hungarian.

8. 1945–1949.

9. After the Rudas debate. New significance of internationalism.

Appendix
Interview with *New Left Review*

Recent events in Europe have posed once again the problem of the relation of socialism to democracy. What are the fundamental differences for you between bourgeois democracy and revolutionary, socialist democracy?

Bourgeois democracy dates from the French Constitution of 1793, which was its highest and most radical expression. Its defining principle is the division of man into the *citoyen* of public life and the *bourgeois* of private life—the one endowed with universal political rights, the other the expression of particular and unequal economic interests. This division is fundamental to bourgeois democracy as a historically determinate phenomenon. Its philosophical reflection is to be found in de Sade. It is interesting that writers like Adorno are so preoccupied with de Sade,[1] because he is the philosophical equivalent of the Constitution of 1793. The ruling idea of both was that man is an object for man—rational egoism is the essence of human society. Now it is obvious that any attempt to recreate this historically past form of democracy under socialism is a regression and an anachronism. But this does not mean that the aspirations towards socialist democracy should ever be dealt with by administrative methods. The problem of socialist democracy is a very real one, and it has not yet been solved. For it must be a materialist democracy, not an idealist one. Let me give an example of what I mean. A man like Guevara was a heroic representative of the Jacobin ideal—his ideas were transported into his life and completely shaped it. He was not the first in the revolutionary movement to do this. Leviné in Germany, or Ottó Korvin here in Hungary, was the same. One must have a deep human reverence for the nobility of this type. But their idealism is not that of the socialism of everyday life, which can only have a *material* basis, built on the construction of a new economy. But I must add immediately that economic development by itself never produces socialism. Khrushchev's doctrine that socialism would triumph on a world scale when the standard of living of the USSR overtook that of the USA was absolutely wrong. The problem must be posed in a quite different way: one can formulate it like this. Socialism is the first economic formation in history which does not spontaneously produce the 'economic man' to fit it. This is because it is a transitional formation, of course—an interlude in the passage from capitalism to communism. Now because the socialist economy does not spontaneously produce and reproduce the men appropriate for it, as classical capitalist society naturally generated its *homo economicus*, the divided *citoyen/bourgeois* of 1793 and de Sade, the function of socialist democracy is precisely the *education* of its members towards socialism. This function is quite unprecedented, and has no analogy with anything in bourgeois democracy. It is clear that what is needed today is a renaissance of soviets—the system of working-class democracy which arose every time there was a proletarian revolution, in the Paris Commune of 1871, the Russian Revolution of 1905 and the October Revolution itself. But this will not occur overnight. The problem is that the workers are indifferent here: they will not believe in anything initially.

One problem in this respect concerns the historical presentation of necessary changes. In recent philosophical debates here, there has been considerable argument over the question of continuity versus discontinuity in history. I have come down firmly for discontinuity. You will know the classical conservative theses of De Tocqueville and Taine that the French Revolution was not a fundamental change in French history at all, because it merely continued the centralizing tradition of the French State, which was very strong under the *ancien régime* with Louis XIV, and was taken even further by Napoleon and then the Second Empire. This outlook was decisively rejected by Lenin, within the revolutionary movement. He never presented basic changes and new departures as merely continuations and improvements of previous trends. For example, when he announced the New Economic Policy, he never for one moment said that this was a 'development' or 'completion' of War Communism. He stated quite frankly that War Communism had been a mistake, understandable in the circumstances, and the NEP was a correction of that mistake and total change of course. This Leninist method was abandoned by Stalinism, which always tried to present policy changes—even enormous ones—as logical consequences and improvements of the previous line. Stalinism presents all socialist history as a continuous and correct development; it would never admit discontinuity. Now today, this question is more vital than ever, precisely in the problem of dealing with the *survival* of Stalinism. Should continuity with the past be emphasized within a perspective of improvements, or on the contrary should the way forward be a sharp rupture with Stalinism? I believe that a complete rupture is necessary. That is why the question of discontinuity in history has such importance for us.

Would you also apply this to your own philosophical development? How do you judge today your writings of the twenties? What is their relationship to your present work?

In the twenties, Korsch, Gramsci and I tried in our different ways to come to grips with the problem of social necessity and the mechanistic interpretation of it that was the heritage of the Second International. We inherited this problem, but none of us—not even Gramsci, who was perhaps the best of us—solved it. We all went wrong, and today it would be quite mistaken to try to revive the works of those times as if they were valid now. In the West, there is a tendency to erect them into 'classics of heresy', but we have no need for that today. The twenties are a past epoch; it is the philosophical problems of the sixties that should concern us. I am now working on an ontology of social being which I hope will solve the problems that were posed quite falsely in my earlier work, particularly *History and Class Consciousness*. My new work centres on the question of the relationship between necessity and freedom, or as I express it, teleology and causality. Traditionally, philosophers have always built systems founded on one or the other of these two poles; they have either denied necessity or denied human freedom. My aim is to show the ontological inter-relation of the two, and to reject the 'either-or' standpoints with which philosophy has traditionally presented man. The concept of *labour* is the hinge of my analysis. For labour is not biologically determined. If a lion attacks an antelope, its behaviour is determined by biological need and by that alone. But if primitive man is confronted with a heap of stones, he must choose between them, by judging which will be most adaptable to use as a tool; he selects between *alternatives*. The notion of alternatives is basic to the meaning of human labour, which is thus always teleological—it sets an aim, which is the result of a choice. It thus expresses human freedom. But this freedom only exists by setting in motion objective physical forces, which obey the causal laws of the material universe. The teleology of labour is thus always co-ordinated with physical causality, and indeed the result of any other individual's labour is a moment of physical causality for the teleological orientation (*Setzung*) of any other individual. The belief in a teleology of nature was theology, and the belief in an immanent teleology of history was unfounded. But there is teleology in all human labour, inextricably inserted into the causality of the physical world. This position, which is the nucleus from which I am developing my present work, overcomes the classical antinomy of necessity and freedom. But I should emphasize that I am not trying to build an all-inclusive system. The title of my work—which is completed, although I am now revising the first chapters—is *Towards an Ontology of Social Being*, not *The Ontology of Social Being*. You will appreciate the difference. The task I am engaged on will need the collective work of many thinkers for its proper development. But I hope it will show the ontological bases for that socialism of everyday life of which I spoke.

England is the only major European country without a native Marxist philosophical tradition. You have written extensively on one moment of its cultural history—the work of Walter Scott; but how do you view the broader development of British political and intellectual history, and its relations to European culture since the Enlightenment?

British history has been the victim of what Marx called the law of uneven development. The very radicalism of Cromwell's Revolution and then the Revolution of 1688, and their success in assuring capitalist relations in town and countryside, became the cause of England's later backwardness. I think your review has been quite right to emphasize the historical importance of capitalist agriculture in England, and its paradoxical consequences for later English development. This can be seen very clearly in English cultural development. The dominance of empiricism as an ideology of the bourgeoisie dates only from after 1688, but it achieved tremendous power from then on, and completely distorted the whole previous history of English philosophy and art. Take Bacon, for example. He was a very great thinker, far greater than Locke, of whom the bourgeoisie later made so much. But his significance was entirely concealed by English empiricism, and today if you want to study what Bacon made of empiricism, you must first understand what empiricism made of Bacon—which is something quite different. Marx was a great admirer of Bacon, you know. The same happened to another major English thinker, Mandeville. He was a great successor of Hobbes, but the English bourgeoisie forgot him altogether. You will find Marx quoting him in *Theories of Surplus Value*, however. This radical English culture of the past was concealed and ignored. In its place, Eliot and others gave a quite exaggerated importance to the metaphysical poets—Donne and so on—who are much less significant in the whole developing history of human culture. Another revealing episode is the fate of Scott. I have written about Scott's importance in my book *The Historical Novel*—you see he was the first novelist who saw that men are changed by history. This was a tremendous discovery, and it was immediately perceived as such by great European writers like Pushkin in Russia, Manzoni in Italy and Balzac in France. They all saw the importance of Scott and learnt from him. The curious thing, however, is that in England itself Scott had no successors. He too was misunderstood and forgotten. There was thus a break in the whole development of English culture, which is very visible in later radical writers like Shaw. Shaw had no roots in the English cultural past, because nineteenth-century English culture was by then cut off from its radical pre-history. This is a deep weakness of Shaw, obviously.

Today, English intellectuals should not merely import Marxism from outside, they must reconstruct a new history of their own culture: this is an indispensable task for them, which only they can accomplish. I have written on Scott, and Agnes Heller on Shakespeare, but it is the English essentially who must rediscover England. We in Hungary had many mystifications about our 'national character', such as you have in England. A true history of your culture will destroy these mystifications. In that perhaps you are helped by the depth of the English economic and political crisis, that product of the law of uneven development of which I spoke. Wilson is doubtless one of the most astute and opportunist bourgeois politicians anywhere today—yet his government has been the most utter and disastrous fiasco. That too is a sign of the depth and intractability of the English crisis.

How do you view now your early literary-critical work, particularly The Theory of the Novel? *What was its historical meaning?*

The Theory of the Novel was an expression of my despair during the First World War. When the War started, I said Germany and Austro-Hungary will probably defeat Russia and destroy Czarism: that is good. France and England will probably defeat Germany and Austro-Hungary and destroy the Hohenzollerns and Hapsburgs: that is good. But who will then defend us from English and French culture? My despair at this question found no answer, and that is the background to *The Theory of the Novel*. Of course, October gave the answer. The Russian Revolution was the world-historical solution to my dilemma: it prevented the triumph of the English and French bourgeoisies which I had dreaded. But I should say that *The Theory of the Novel*, with all its mistakes, did call for the overthrow of the world that produced the culture it analysed. It understood the need for a revolutionary change.

At that time, you were a friend of Max Weber. How do you judge him now? His colleague Sombart eventually became a Nazi—do you think that Weber, had he lived, might have become reconciled to National-Socialism?

No, never. You must understand that Weber was an absolutely honest person. He had a great contempt for the Emperor, for example. He used to say to us in private that the great German misfortune was that, unlike the Stuarts or the Bourbons, no Hohenzollern had ever been decapitated. You can imagine that it was no ordinary German professor who could say such a thing in 1912. Weber was quite unlike Sombart—he never made any concessions to anti-semitism, for instance. Let me tell you a story that is characteristic of him. He was asked by a German university to send his recommendations for a chair at that university—they were going to make a new appointment. Weber wrote back to them, giving them three names, in order of merit. He then added: any three of these would be an absolutely suitable choice—they are all excellent; but you will not choose any one of them, because they are all Jews. So I am adding a list of three other names, not one of whom is as worthy as the three whom I have recommended, and you will undoubtedly accept one of them, because they are not Jews. Yet with all this, you must remember that Weber was a deeply convinced imperialist, whose liberalism was merely a matter of his belief that an efficient imperialism was necessary, and only liberalism could guarantee that efficiency. He was a sworn enemy of the October and November Revolutions. He was both an extraordinary scholar and deeply reationary. The irrationalism which began with the late Schelling and Schopenhauer finds one of its most important expressions in him.

How did he react to your conversion to the October Revolution?

He is reported to have said that with Lukács the change must have been a profound transformation of convictions and ideas, whereas with Toller it was merely a confusion of sentiments. But I had no relations with him from that time on.

After the war, you participated in the Hungarian Commune, as Commissar for Education. What assessment of the experience of the Commune is possible now, 50 years later?

The essential cause of the Commune was the Vyx Note and the policy of the Entente towards Hungary. In this respect, the Hungarian Commune is comparable to the Russian Revolution, where the question of ending the War played a fundamental part in bringing the October Revolution into existence. Once the Vyx Note was delivered, its consequence was the Commune. Social-democrats later attacked us for creating the Commune, but at that time after the war, there was no possibility of staying within the limits of the bourgeois political framework; it was necessary to explode it.

After the defeat of the Commune, you were a delegate at the Third Congress of the Comintern in Moscow. Did you encounter the Bolshevik leaders there? What were your impressions of them?

Look, you must remember that I was a small member of a small delegation—I was not an important figure in any way at the time, and so I naturally did not have long conversations with the leaders of the Russian Party. I was introduced to Lenin, however, by Lunacharsky. He charmed me completely. I was able to watch him at work in the commissions of the Congress as well, of course. The other Bolshevik leaders I must say I found antipathetic. Trotsky I disliked immediately: I thought him a poseur. There is a passage in Gorki's memories of Lenin, you know, where Lenin after the Revolution, while acknowledging Trotsky's organizational achievements during the Civil War, says that he had something of Lassalle about him. Zinoviev, whose role in the Comintern I later got to know well, was a mere political manipulator. My assessment of Bukharin is to be found in my article on him in 1925, criticizing his Marxism—that was at a time when he was the Russian authority on theoretical questions, after Stalin. Stalin himself I cannot remember at the Congress at all—like so many other foreign communists, I had no awareness whatever of his importance in the Russian Party. I did speak to Radek at some length. He told me that he thought my articles on the March action in Germany were the best things that had been written on it, and that he approved of them completely. Later, of course, he changed his opinion when the party condemned the March affair, and he then publicly attacked it. By contrast with all these, Lenin made an enormous impression on me.

What was your reaction when Lenin attacked your article on the question of parliamentarism?

My article was completely misguided, and I abandoned its theses without hesitation. But I should add that I had read Lenin's *'Left-Wing' Communism: An Infantile Disorder* before his critique of my own article, and I had already been wholly convinced by his arguments on the question of parliamentary participation there: so his criticism of my article did not change anything very much for me. I already knew it was wrong. You remember what Lenin said in *'Left-Wing' Communism*—that bourgeois parliaments were completely superseded in a world-historical sense, with the birth of the revolutionary organs of proletarian power, the soviets, but that this absolutely did not mean that they were superseded in an immediate political sense—in particular that the masses in the West did not believe in them. Therefore Communists had to work in them, as well as outside them.

In 1928-29 you advanced the concept of the democratic dictatorship of the workers and peasants as the strategic goal for the Hungarian Communist Party at that date, in the famous Blum Theses for the Third Congress of the HCP. The Theses were rejected as opportunist and you were expelled from the Central Committee for them. How do you judge them today?

The Blum Theses were my rearguard action against the sectarianism of the Third Period, which insisted that social democracy and fascism were twins. This disastrous line was accompanied, as you know, by the slogan of class against class and the call for the immediate establishment of the dictatorship of the proletariat. By reviving and adapting Lenin's slogan of 1905—democratic dictatorship of the workers and peasants—I tried to find a loophole in the line of the Sixth Comintern Congress, through which I could win the Hungarian Party to a more realistic policy. I had no success. The Blum Theses were condemned by the party, and Béla Kun and his faction expelled me from the Central Committee. I was completely alone inside the party at that date; you must understand that I did not succeed in convincing even those who had shared my views in the struggle against Kun's sectarianism inside the party. So I made a self-criticism of the theses. This was absolutely cynical: it was imposed on me by the circumstances of the time. I did not in fact change my opinions, and the truth is that I am convinced that I was absolutely right then. In fact, the course of later history vindicated the Blum Theses completely. For the period of 1945–48 in Hungary was the concrete realization of the democratic dictatorship of the workers and peasants for which I argued in 1929. After 1948, of course, Stalinism created something quite different—but that is another story.

What were your relations with Brecht in the thirties, and then after the War? How do you assess his stature?

Brecht was a very great poet, and his later plays—*Mother Courage, The Good Woman of Szechuan* and others—are excellent. Of course, his dramatic and aesthetic theories were quite confused and wrong. I have explained this in *The Meaning of Contemporary Realism*. But they do not change the quality of his later work. In 1931–33 I was in Berlin working with the Writers' Union. About that time—in mid-1930, to be precise—Brecht wrote an article against me, defending expressionism. But later, when I was in Moscow, Brecht came to see me on his journey from Scandinavia to the USA—he went through the Soviet Union on that trip—and he said to me: There are some people who are trying to influence me against you, and there are some trying to influence you against me. Let us make an agreement not to be provoked by either into quarrelling. Thus we always had good relations, and after the war whenever I went to Berlin—which was very often—I always used to go and see Brecht, and we had long discussions together. Our positions were very close at the end. You know, I was invited by his wife to be one of those to speak at his funeral. One thing I do regret is that I never wrote an essay on Brecht in the forties: this was an error, caused by my preoccupation with other work at the time. I had great respect for Brecht, always. He was very clever and had a great sense of reality. In this he was quite unlike Korsch, whom he knew well, of course. When Korsch left the German Party, he cut himself off from socialism. I know this, because it was impossible for him to collaborate in the work of the Writers' Union in the anti-fascist struggle in Berlin at the time—the party would not permit it. Brecht was quite different. He knew that nothing could be done against the USSR, to which he remained loyal all his life.

Did you know Walter Benjamin? Do you think he would have evolved towards a firm revolutionary commitment to Marxism, had he lived?

No, for some reason I never met Benjamin, although I saw Adorno in Frankfurt in 1930 when I passed through before going to the Soviet Union. Benjamin was extraordinarily gifted, and saw deeply into many quite new problems. He explored these in different ways, but he never found a way out of them. I think that his development, had he lived, would have been quite uncertain, despite his friendship with Brecht. You must remember how difficult the times were—the purges in the thirties, then the Cold War. Adorno became the exponent of a kind of 'non-conformist conformity' in this climate.

After the victory of fascism in Germany, you worked in the Marx-Lenin Institute in Russia with Ryazanov. What did you do there?

When I was in Moscow in 1930, Ryazanov showed me the manuscripts which Marx had written in Paris in 1844. You can imagine my excitement: reading these manuscripts changed my whole relation to Marxism and transformed my philosophical outlook. A German scholar from the Soviet Union was working on the manuscripts, preparing them for publication. The mice had got at them, and there were many places where letters or even words were missing. Because of my philosophical knowledge, I worked with him, determining what the letters or the words that had disappeared were: one often had words beginning with, say, 'g' and ending with, say, 's' and one had to guess what came between. I think that the edition that eventually came out was a very good one—I know because of collaborating in the editing of it. Ryazanov was responsible for this work, and he was a very great philologist: not a theorist, but a great philologist. After his removal, the work at the Institute declined completely. I remember he told me there were ten volumes of Marx's manuscripts for *Capital* which had never been published—Engels of course, in his introduction to Volumes Two and Three says they are only a selection from the manuscripts Marx was working on for *Capital*. Ryazanov planned to publish all this material. But to this day it has never appeared.

In the early thirties, there were of course philosophical debates in the USSR, but I did not participate in them. There was then a debate in which Deborin's work was criticized. Personally, I thought much of the criticism justified, but its aim was only to establish Stalin's pre-eminence as a philosopher.

But you did participate in the literary debates in the Soviet Union in the thirties.

I collaborated with the journal *Literaturnii Kritik* for six or seven years, and we conducted a very consistent policy against the dogmatism of those years. Fadeyev and others had fought RAPP and defeated it in Russia, but only because Averbakh and others in RAPP were Trotskyist. After their victory, they proceeded to develop their own form of RAPPism. *Literaturnii Kritik* always resisted these tendencies. I wrote many articles in it, all of which had some three quotations from Stalin—that was an insurmountable necessity in Russia at the time—and all of which were directed against Stalinist conceptions of literature. Their content was always aimed against Stalin's dogmatism.

You were politically active for ten years of your life, from 1919 to 1929, then you had to abandon directly political activity altogether. This was a very big change for any convinced Marxist. Did you feel limited (or perhaps on the contrary liberated?) by the abrupt change in your career in 1930? How did this phase of your life relate to your boyhood and youth? What were your influences then?

I had no regrets whatever about the ending of my political career. You see, I was convinced I was utterly right in the inner-party disputes in 1928-29—nothing ever led me to change my mind on this; yet I completely failed to convince the party of my views. So I thought: if I was so right, and yet so wholly defeated, this could only mean that I had no political abilities as such. So I gave up practical political work without any diffculty—I decided I had no gift for it. My expulsion from the Central Committee of the Hungarian Party in no way altered my belief that even with the disastrously sectarian policies of the Third Period, one could only fight effectively against fascism within the ranks of the Communist movement. I have not changed in this. I have always thought that the worst form of socialism was better to live in than the best form of capitalism.

Later, my participation in the Nagy Government in 1956 was not a contradiction of my renunciation of political activity. I did not share the general political approach of Nagy, and when young people tried to bring the two of us together in the days before October, I always replied: 'The step from myself to Imre Nagy is no greater to take than the step from Imre Nagy to myself.' When I was asked to be minister of culture in October 1956, this was a moral question for me, not a political one, and I could not refuse. When we were arrested and interned in Romania, Romanian and Hungarian party comrades came and asked me for my views on Nagy's policies, knowing my disagreements with them. I told them: 'When I am a free man in the streets of Budapest and he is a free man, I will be happy to state my judgement of him openly and at length. But as long as he is imprisoned my only relationship to him is one of solidarity.'

You ask me what my personal feelings were when I gave up my political career. I must say that I am perhaps not a very contemporary man. I can say that I have never felt frustration or any kind of complex in my life. I know what these mean, of course, from the literature of the twentieth century, and from having read Freud. But I have not experienced them myself. When I have seen mistakes or false directions in my life, I have always been willing to admit them—it has cost me nothing to do so—and then turn to something else. When I was 15 or 16, I wrote modern plays, in the manner of Ibsen and Hauptmann. When I was 18, I reread them, and found them irretrievably bad. I decided there and then that I would never become a writer, and I burnt these plays. I had no regrets. That very early experience was useful to me later, because as a critic, whenever I could say of a text that I would have written it myself, I always knew this was infallible evidence that it was bad: it was a very reliable criterion. This was my first literary experience. My earliest political influences were reading Marx as a schoolboy, and then—most important of all—reading the great Hungarian poet Ady. I was very isolated as a boy, among my contemporaries, and Ady made a great impact on me. He was a revolutionary who had a great enthusiasm for Hegel, although he never accepted that aspect of Hegel which I always, from the start, myself rejected: his *Versöhnung mit der Wirklichkeit*—reconciliation with established reality. It is a great weakness of English culture that there is no acquaintance with Hegel in it. To this day, I have not lost my admiration for him, and I think that the work Marx began—the materialization of Hegel's philosophy—must be pursued even beyond Marx. I have tried to do this in some passages of my forth-coming Ontology. When all is said and done, there are only three truly great thinkers in the West, incomparable with all others: Aristotle, Hegel and Marx.

Biographical Notes

ACZÉL, György (b. 1918), a key figure in Hungarian cultural politics since the Revolution of 1956. At present Deputy Prime Minister.

ADY, Endre (1877–1919), the greatest Hungarian lyric poet of his time.

ALEXANDER, Bernát (1850–1927), Hungarian philosopher and aesthetician.

ALAPARI, Gyula (1882–1944), Hungarian Communist journalist and politician. Killed in Sachsenhausen.

AMBRUS, Zoltán (1861–1932), writer, theatre critic and Director of the Hungarian National Theatre.

ANDRÁSSY, Count Gyula (1860–1929), conservative Hungarian politician.

ANTAL, Frederik (1887–1954), art historian of Hungarian origin. Gained his doctorate in Vienna where he studied with Dvořak. After the collapse of the Hungarian Soviet Republic, during which he worked in the Museum of Fine Arts, he emigrated to Berlin and, in 1933, to England where he lectured at London University.

AVERBAKH, Leopold (1903–1937), Soviet critic, head of the Russian Association of Proletarian Writers.

BABITS, Mihály (1883–1941), lyric poet, a leading figure on *Nyugat*, the journal founded in 1908, and later its editor-in-chief. Although he was regarded as the principal exponent of *l'art pour l'art*, he became a resolute opponent of political indifferentism in literature at the end of the thirties.

BALÁZS, Béla (pseudonym of Herbert Bauer) (1884–1949), Hungarian writer, film theoretician and scriptwriter. A supporter of the Hungarian Soviet Republic, he was forced to emigrate in 1919. Lived in Vienna, Berlin and the Soviet Union, returning to Hungary in 1945. Wrote libretti for Bartók.

BÁNÓCZI, László (1880–1926), President of the Thalia Society, the revolutionary Hungarian theatre of the turn of the century.

BARTHA, Sándor (1898–1939), Hungarian writer belonging to the avant-garde group around Kassák. Emigrated in 1919. Victim of Stalin's purges.

BARTÓK, Béla (1881–1945), Hungarian composer and pianist. Emigrated to the USA in 1940.

BAUER, Ervin (brother of Béla Balázs) (1890–1942), Hungarian doctor and biologist, married to the writer Margit Kaffka. Emigrated in 1919. Victim of Stalin's purges.

BECHER, Johannes R. (1891–1958), German poet and writer. Began as an expressionist; joined the German Communist Party; co-founder and head of the German League of Proletarian Revolutionary Writers from 1928 to 1932. Left for exile in the Soviet Union. Minister of Culture in the GDR from 1954.

BENEDEK, Elek (1859–1929), Hungarian writer and dramatist known for his collection of folk-tales.

BENEDEK, Marcell (son of Elek Benedek) (1885–1970), Hungarian writer, literary historian, critic, and translator.

BENJÁMIN, László (b. 1915), one of the most important poets of the school of Socialist Realism and one of the so-called 'workers' poets'. His poetry had always been noted for its social concerns and after the revolution he wrote propaganda for the Communist Party. He gave his unstinting approval not only to its ideology and its major objectives, but also to all of its individual tactical manoeuvres.

BEÖTHY, Zsolt (1848–1922), an important Hungarian literary historian of the positivist school of literary history and criticism. Started as a novelist and critic and subsequently became Professor of Aesthetics at Budapest University. Made use of Spencer's evolutionary theory and Taine's concept of race in an attempt to conserve a populist trend in style. Literature was always national, he maintained, and could only be authentic if it expressed national character, the 'soul of the nation'. He found the Hungarian national character embodied most perfectly in the gentry. From the 1890s Beöthy became the implacable opponent of all progressive aspirations.

BERCSÉNYI, Miklós Count (1665–1725), Hungarian magnate and Field Marshal. With Rákóczi led the peasants' revolt against the Hapsburgs.

BLUM, Lukács's undercover name in the illegal Communist Party.

BÖHM, Vilmos (1880–1949), with Weltner a member of the right wing of the Hungarian Social Democratic Party at the turn of the century. Minister of War in Károlyi's coalition government. During the Hungarian Soviet Republic was People's Commissar for the Army and Commander-in-Chief of the Hungarian Red Army.

BOLGÁR, Elek (1883–1955), Hungarian Communist lawyer, economist and historian.

BREDEL, Willi (1901–1964), German Communist writer, in exile in the Soviet Union from 1934; political commissar during the Spanish Civil War; President of the Academy of Arts in East Germany from 1962.

BRÓDY, Sándor (1863–1924), the most important Hungarian novelist of the early part of the century. Extremely influential, he took a lively interest in all the modern movements. He was most closely associated with Naturalism and Art Nouveau. Originating in the small-town Jewish bourgeoisie, he became known for a number of novellas by the title of *Nyomor* (Destitution) which aimed to exemplify the programme of Naturalism. They aroused great enthusiasm and also violent criticism.

CSOKONAI, Vitéz Mihály (1773–1805), the most important Hungarian poet of the Enlightenment, also a dramatist and philosopher.

CZIGÁNY, Dezsö (1883–1937), a member of the progressive group of painters 'The Eight' around 1919.

DARÁNYI, Ignác (1848–1927), conservative Hungarian politician.

DARVAS, József (1913–1973), one of the outstanding representatives of the Populists. Came from a poor peasant family in the lowlands. *The Chronicle of a Peasant Family* (1939) is one of the most successful literary works dealing with village life. Became a Communist functionary after 1944.

DEÁK, Ferenc (1803–1876), major Hungarian politician responsible for the compromise with Austria in 1867 that resulted in the Dual Monarchy of Austria and Hungary.

DEBORIN (pseudonym of Joffe Abram Moiseevich, 1881–1962), Soviet philosopher and editor-in-chief of the journal *Under the Banner of Marxism*, 1926–1930.

DÉRY, Tibor (1894–1979), one of the most important of recent Hungarian prose writers. Took part in the preparations for the 1956 uprising, received a lengthy prison sentence in 1957 and was pardoned in 1960.

DIENES, Valéria (1879–1978), Hungarian mathematician and philosopher, disciple of Bergson.

DOBI, Ferenc (Dobacsek) (1880–1916), actor, member of Hungarian Theatre and the Thalia Society.

DOHNÁNYI, Ernst (1877–1960), Hungarian composer and pianist. Studied in Budapest with Thoman and Koessler and later with E. d'Albert. In 1919–20 was Director of the Budapest Conservatoire, and after that conductor of the Philharmonic Society until 1944. From 1948 lived in Argentina and from 1949 at Florida State University. As a pianist Dohnányi specialized in modern music, in particular Bartók's works for the piano, while as a composer he remained in the late Romantic tradition.

DOKTOR, János (b. 1881), one of the founder-members of the Thalia Society, known mainly for his roles in Ibsen's plays.

DONÁTH, Ferenc (b. 1913), Communist politician and an expert on agriculture. In 1945 became Secretary of State in the Ministry for Agriculture. Arrested and imprisoned in 1951; rehabilitated in 1955. A supporter of Imre Nagy, he was arrested again and sentenced in 1957: amnestied again in 1960.

DUCZYNSKA, Ilona (1896–1980), Hungarian journalist and translator; founder-member of the Galileo Circle. Took part in the Zimmerwald Conference. Later in the war she was imprisoned in Hungary for making anti-war propaganda. After the Revolution of 1918–19 she went into exile where she married the economic historian, Karl Polányi, and lived in Toronto.

DVOŘAK, Max (1874–1921), Czech art historian. Studied history with Goll in Prague and then transferred to art history in Vienna where he succeeded Alois Riegl in the Chair and became one of the chief representatives of the Vienna School until his death.

ERDEI, Ferenc (1910–1971), belonged to the left wing of the Populists, maintaining links with the workers' movement. In the thirties the Populists developed an extensive sociological literature known as village research which laid emphasis on a strictly objective representation of reality. He did not himself produce any imaginative literature. Became Minister of the Interior, 1945; Minister of State, 1948; Minister for Agriculture, 1949–53; Minister of Justice, 1953-54; Deputy Prime Minister, 1955–56; General Secretary of the National Popular Front, 1964-69; and General Secretary of the Hungarian Academy of Sciences, 1970–71.

ERNST, Paul (1866–1933), German writer, dramatist and essayist.

FADEYEV, Alexander A. (1901–1956), novelist. One of the main exponents of Soviet cultural orthodoxy from the thirties. In 1947 he was appointed General Secretary of the Soviet Writers Union.

FEHÉR, Ferenc (b. 1933), a pupil of Lukács, research-fellow at the Hungarian Academy of Sciences, 1970–73. In 1973 he resigned from his post as an expression of solidarity with colleagues who had been dismissed. Since 1977 he has lived mainly in the West.

FELEKY, Geza (1890–1956), Hungarian journalist and aesthetician.

FÉNYES, Adolf (1867–1945), Hungarian painter who studied in Budapest,

Weimar and Paris became one of the leading personalities in the Szolnok artists' colony.

FERENCZY, Béni (1890–1967), sculptor. After a brief period in the Nagybánya artists' colony he studied in Florence, Munich and Paris with Bourdelles and Archipenko. After the fall of the Soviet Republic he settled in Vienna from where he returned to his native land in 1938. Sculptured in bronze from 1930. Professor at the Budapest University for the Plastic Arts, 1946–1950.

FERENCZY, Károly (1862–1917), Hungarian painter. Studied in Rome, Munich, Naples and Paris. In 1902 helped to found the Nagybánya Art School. Created a new style which he described as 'colouristic Naturalism on a synthetic foundation'. Father of Béni and Noemi Ferenczy.

FERENCZY, Noemi (1890–1957), Hungarian painter and tapestry maker, awarded the Grand Prix at the World Exhibition in Paris in 1937. Twin sister of Béni Ferenczy.

FENYÖ, Miksa (1877–1972), liberal patron and literary critic. One of the founders of *Nyugat*. Emigrated in 1948 and died in Vienna.

FISCHER, Ernst (1899–1972), Austrian Marxist literary critic. From 1934 to 1945 in exile in the Soviet Union. Expelled from the Austrian Communist Party in 1969 because of his critical stance. See his *Necessity of Art*, Harmondsworth 1963.

FISCHER, Ruth (real name, Elfriede Gohlke, 1895–1962), former leading official in the German Communist Party. Member of the Central Committee of the KPD, 1923–26. Spokeswoman for the ultra-left. Expelled in 1926. After 1933 she lived in Paris and from 1941 in the USA. Wrote a number of anti-communist books.

FOGARASI, Béla (1891–1959), Hungarian Marxist philosopher. A leading cultural official in the Hungarian Soviet Republic. Professor in the Soviet Union, 1930–1945. From 1945 Professor of Philosophy at Budapest University. In 1953 appointed Principal of the Economics Institute in Budapest.

FORGÁCS, Rózsi (1866–1944)? a leading actress in the Thalia Society. Hebbel's Maria Magdalena was one of her leading roles. She also gave outstanding performances of Ibsen, Strindberg, Gorki and Wedekind.

FRISS, István (1903–1978), Hungarian Communist economist.

FÜLEP, Lajos (1885–1970), Hungarian art historian, highly influential in the emergence of the Hungarian school of art history at the turn of the century. During the Hungarian Soviet Republic be became a professor at Budapest University.

FÜST, Milan (1888–1967), poet and writer, collaborator on *Nyugat*. In 1947 he became Professor of Aesthetics in Budapest.

GAÁL, Gábor (1891–1954), member of the Hungarian Communist Party, commissar of the Red Army. After the collapse of the Hungarian Soviet Republic he fled to Vienna and then to Berlin. In 1926 he returned to Cluj (Romania) where he edited the Hungarian-language journals *Korünk* (Our Age) from 1928, and *Utünk* (Our Way) from 1946.

GÁBOR, Andor (1884–1953), Hungarian satirist and journalist. After 1919 he emigrated to Vienna and then to Berlin. Co-editor of *Linkskurve*. From 1933 he lived in Moscow. He later became the chief editor of the satirical journal *Ludas Matyi* in Budapest.

GELLÉRT, Oszkár (1882–1967), poet who contributed to *Nyugat*.

GERGELY, Sándor (1896–1966), Communist writer who emigrated to Moscow.

GERGELY, Tibor (1900–1978), Hungarian painter and graphic artist. Emigrated in 1919; died in the USA.

GERÖ, Ernö (1898–1980), First Secretary of the Communist Party from July to October 1956 after Rákosi had been dismissed and had left for the Soviet Union.

HAMBURGER, Jenö (1883–1936), Hungarian Communist, political commissar in the Hungarian Red Army in 1919. Lived in the Soviet Union from 1922.

HARKÁNYI, Ede (1879–1909), Hungarian writer.

HATVANY, Lajos Baron (1880–1960), writer, critic and patron of the arts, son of a big industrialist. The fortnightly journal *Nyugat* was finally established on a secure financial basis as a result of his support. His book, *The Knowledge of What is Not Worth Knowing*, appeared in Budapest in 1908 and Berlin in 1912.

HAUSER, Arnold (1892–1978), art historian of Hungarian origin. Worked for the education ministry during the Hungarian Soviet Republic. Emigrated to Berlin and moved to London in 1939. From 1951 he taught art history at Leeds University. His major work, *The Social History of Art*, appeared in London in 1951. Returned to Budapest in 1977.

HAY, Gyula (1895–1944), Hungarian Communist journalist. Executed by members of the Hungarian fascist Arrow Cross movement. Brother of Julius Hay.

HAY, Julius (1900–1975), dramatist who emigrated to Berlin in 1919 and later to Moscow (1933). In 1945 he returned to Hungary where he received a long prison sentence for his activities in the 1956 uprising. Amnestied three years later, he died in Switzerland.

HEGEDÜS, András (b. 1922), one of the leaders of the NEKOSZ movement. He adapted to the Stalinist line and made a career in the party. After the first fall of Imre Nagy in 1955 Hegedüs was made Prime Minister by Rákosi. Today he is one of the most prominent dissidents in Hungary and one of the best-known East European sociologists. See his *Socialism and Bureaucracy*, London 1976.

HELLER, Agnes (b. 1929), Lukács's pupil and assistant. Numerous publications. In 1973 she was dismissed from her post at the Academy of Sciences, since when she has lived mainly in the West. See her *The Theory of Need in Marx*, London 1976.

HERCZEG, Ferenc (1863–1964), a writer known for his historical novels and plays written in the tradition of the great Hungarian Romantics.

HIROSIK, János, Hungarian Communist, in charge of nationalities policy during the Hungarian Soviet Republic. Left the party in 1933.

HORTHY, Miklós (1868–1957), Rear-Admiral and Hungarian politician. In 1919, with the support of the Entente, he launched counter-revolutionary troops against the Soviet Republic which he put down with much bloodshed. Imperial Administrator from 1920. His rule came to an end in 1944 after the Arrow Cross coup d'état. The Western Allies arrested him in Bavaria as a war criminal, but did not hand him over to the Hungarian Government.

HORVÁTH, János (1878–1961), literary historian and professor at Budapest University. His stimulating personality enabled him to exercise a powerful influence on the younger generation of scholars and teachers.

HORVÁTH, Zoltán (1900–1968), left-wing Social-Democrat politician and historian. Imprisoned from 1949 to 1956.

IGNOTUS, (Hugo Veigelsberg) (1869–1949), Hungarian critic, co-founder and chief editor of *Nyugat*. His views reflected the liberalism of the well-to-do middle class.

ILLÉS, Béla (1895–1974), the most important Hungarian prose-writer among the Communist émigrés. Returned to Hungary in 1945.

ILLYÉS, Gyula (1902–1982), Hungarian poet, dramatist and novelist. After the fall of the Hungarian Soviet Republic he went to Paris, studied at the Sorbonne and then returned to Hungary in 1926. He belonged to the *Nyugat* circle and in the mid-thirties associated himself with the Populists. Especially known for his book *People of the Puszta* (1936).

JANCSÓ, Miklós (b. 1921), Hungarian film director. He studied law, ethnography and art history before enrolling at the Academy for Film from which he graduated.

JÁNOSSY, Ferenc (b. 1914) son of Lukács's second wife, Gertrud Bortstieber. Lived with Lukács in the Soviet Union, where he was arrested in 1942 and spent three years in a Siberian camp. By profession an economist. Returned to Budapest after 1945.

JÁSZI, Oszkár (1875–1957), theoretician of Hungarian bourgeois radicalism. Leading journalist of the radicals around 1912, together with Ady. Publisher of *Huszadik Század*, which was banned after the fall of the bourgeois-democratic regime in 1919. In exile he lived first in Vienna and later in the USA.

JOFFE, Adolf A. (1883–1927), Russian revolutionary. A friend of Trotsky, he joined the Bolshevik Party with him in 1917. He became a member of the Central Committee and served as ambassador in Berlin, Vienna and Tokyo. Committed suicide in protest at Trotsky's expulsion from the party. His funeral was the last great public demonstration of the Left Opposition.

JÓZSEF, Attila (1905–1937), with Ady the greatest Hungarian poet of the twentieth century. Member of the illegal Communist Party. In his theoretical writings he attempted to harmonize Marxism with psychoanalysis, which led to his expulsion from the party. Committed suicide.

JÓZSEF, Jolán, (1899–1950) sister of Attila József about whose life she has written an unreliable biography.

JUHÁSZ, Gyula (1883–1937), Hungarian poet who wrote deeply moving poems about love and nature. He was an impressionist associated with *Nyugat*. Committed suicide.

KÁDÁR, János (b. 1912), one of the leaders of the Hungarian Communist Party after 1945. Interior Minister in 1949. Arrested in 1951, rehabilitated 1954. Became head of government after the crushing of the uprising in 1956. At present First Secretary of the Hungarian Socialist Workers Party.

KAFFKA, Margit (1880–1918), Hungarian writer who belonged to the *Nyugat* circle.

KÁLLAI, Gyula (b. 1910), Hungarian politician and journalist, member of the Central Committee of the Hungarian Socialist Workers Party.

KARINTHY, Frigyes (1887–1938), the most celebrated of Hungary's humorous writers, whose works have earned him an immense popularity. Both a satirist and a moralist, his best-known work is *That's How You Write* (1912), a collection of parodies of his fellow writers. Belonged to the *Nyugat* circle.

KÁROLYI, Mihály Count (1875–1955), a liberal and later socialist politician. Before 1919 one of the largest landowners in Hungary. During the First World War leader of the Independent Party. He was opposed to the war and in favour of a pro-Anglo-French policy. After the outbreak of the bourgeois revolution, he became Prime Minister in October 1918 and President in November. He spent the years from 1919 to 1946 in exile in Paris and London. During 1947–49 he was Hungarian ambassador in Paris. Resigned during the Rajk trial and went into exile a second time. His remaining years were spent in the south of France.

KASSÁK, Lajos (1887–1967), Hungarian poet, painter, and writer of fiction. A leading proponent of avant-garde tendencies in Hungarian literature. During the First World War he edited the Activist and Futurist journals *Tett* (Deed) and *Ma* (Today). During the revolution of 1919 Kassák was involved in the conduct of artistic affairs, but he came into conflict with Béla Kun on the issue of party influence in literary matters. He was arrested in the counter-revolution but was soon freed and fled to Vienna where he played a major role in the activities of the émigrés. In the twenties Kassák turned to graphic art, producing non-figurative constructivist 'picture architecture' and collages.

KASSNER, Rudolph (1873–1959), Austrian essayist and cultural philosopher.

KERNSTOK, Károly (1873–1940), Hungarian painter, and prominent member of the Hungarian avant garde. One of the founders of the group of 'The Eight', whose outlook was progressive both artistically and socially. He was active in the Hungarian Soviet Republic, after which he remained in Germany until 1925 and came under the influence of the German Expressionists.

KODÁLY, Zoltán (1882–1967), with Bartók the most important representative of modern music in Hungary. A student of folk music, he collected old Hungarian folksongs which were later published in a number of volumes by the Hungarian Academy of Sciences. Kodály was also an important educationalist and it is thanks to him that the study of music has become such an important feature of the Hungarian school system. From 1907 until his retirement he was professor at the Academy of Music in Budapest.

KORÁNYI, Sándor Baron (1866–1944), Professor of Medicine in Budapest. Author of books on neurological diseases in children.

KORVIN, Ottó (1894–1919), in 1918 leader of the Revolutionary Socialists, one of the founders of the Communist Party of Hungary and member of the Central Committee. In the Hungarian Soviet Republic he was in charge of the political section of the People's Commissariat for Internal Affairs. After the fall of the Soviet Republic he remained in Budapest to reorganize the illegal Communist Party, in the course of which he was arrested and executed.

KOSZTOLÁNYI, Dezső (1885–1936), Hungarian poet, fiction-writer and journalist. His writings are noted for their mastery of style. His volumes of poems and stories started to appear in 1907. Member of the *Nyugat* circle.

KOVÁCS, András (b. 1926), head of the filmscript department of the *Hunnia* Studio (1951–1958). Played a leading role in the reorganization of the Hungarian film industry in the fifties.

KRISTOFFY, József (1857–1928), Hungarian ambassador in Moscow in 1941. The Soviet Government made use of him to inform the Hungarians that they wished to make no demands on Hungary and had no aggressive intentions. Molotov informed Kristoffy, but the latter's telegram arrived late in Budapest and the Government did not present it either to Parliament or to the Imperial Administrator.

KRÚDY, Gyula (1878–1933), one of the most important Hungarian writers of his day. Started as a provincial journalist, but moved to Budapest in 1911 where his story cycle *Sinbad* and his novel *The Red Coach* were published. Of independent character, he is not associated with any literary grouping.

KUN, Béla (1886–1939), Communist politician and leader of the 1919 Hungarian Soviet Republic. After its fall he lived in exile, first in Vienna and later in the Soviet Union where he was one of the leading figures in the Comintern under Zinoviev. Executed under Stalin in one of the great purges.

KUNFI, Zsigmond (1879–1929), leading Social-Democrat politician. People's Commissar for Culture in the Hungarian Soviet Republic. Emigrated to Vienna. Committed suicide.

LANDLER, Jenő (1875–1928), Hungarian revolutionary. At first a left-wing Social Democrat and leader of the railwaymen's union, he became a member of the National Council in November 1918. Under the Hungarian Soviet Republic he served as People's Commissar for Internal Affairs and Commander-in-Chief of the Red Army. After the fall of the Republic he emigrated, joined the Communist Party of Hungary. A member of the Central Committee from 1919, he was leader of the illegal Communist Party of Hungary in emigration in Vienna.

LASK, Emil (1875–1915), German neo-Kantian philosopher. Appointed Professor of Philosophy in Heidelberg in 1910. Killed at the front.

LENGYEL, Gyula (1888–1941), People's Commissar for Foreign Trade in the Hungarian Soviet Republic. Victim of Stalin's purges.

LESZNAI, Anna (1885–1968), nicknamed Máli, poet, writer and craftswoman. In her early poems she was one of the first to speak with the voice of a liberated woman. The influences of Art Nouveau and Symbolism were balanced to a certain extent by a tendency towards neo-classicism. Emigrated in 1919. Died in the USA.

LEVINÉ, Eugen (1883–1919), Russian Social Revolutionary, later German

Communist. Imprisoned after the 1905 Revolution. Executed after the defeat of the Bavarian Soviet Republic, in which he had played a prominent role.

LIEBERMANN, Max (1847–1935), German painter.

LIFSHITZ, Mikhail (b. 1905), Soviet aesthetician and philosopher. Author of *The Philosophy of Art of Karl Marx* (1933).

MAKARENKO, Anton Semyonovich (1888–1939), Soviet educationist and writer. He had great success with the education in work-colonies of young people whose lives had been disrupted by war and civil war. His most famous book was *The Road to Life: A Pedagogical Poem* (1933–35).

MANNHEIM, Karl (1893–1947), sociologist of Hungarian origin, studied in Budapest, Freiburg, Berlin, Paris and Heidelberg. A pupil of Max Weber. In 1926 he became a *Privatdozent* in Heidelberg, in 1930 a Professor in Frankfurt, in 1933 he emigrated to England where he continued to teach. In 1942 he was made Professor at the Institute of Education in London.

MANUILSKY, Dimitri Z. (1883–1950), Russian revolutionary, arrested and exiled in 1905 for agitation at the University in St Petersburg. He fled to Paris where he joined the Mensheviks. In 1917 he became associated with the group around Trotsky and with them he joined the Bolsheviks. He was a member of the Secretariat of the Comintern under Stalin; subsequently he was Dimitrov's deputy in the Committee. As Zhdanov's confidant he had great power. In and after the Second World War he was Foreign Minister of the Ukraine and a UN delegate.

MÁRFFY, Ödön (1878–1959), Hungarian painter who had studied in Paris (1902–1904). He was strongly influenced by Cézanne and the Fauves. In 1908 he helped to found the artists' groups *Mienk* (Ours) and 'The Eight'.

MÁRKUS, György (b. 1934), Hungarian philosopher. Studied in Moscow until 1957. From 1959 he worked in the Institute of Philosophy at the Hungarian Academy of Sciences. In 1968 he was expelled from the party, and in 1973 he lost his job at the Academy. Since 1977 has been living mainly in the West.

MAROSÁN, György (b. 1908), left-wing Social Democrat until 1948. Imprisoned in 1950. Rehabilitated in 1956.

MASARYK, Jan (1886–1948), Czech statesman. Foreign Minister under Beneš in the Czech Government-in-Exile in London. Later served as Foreign Minister in Czechoslovakia (1945–48). Son of Tomas Masaryk.

MASARYK, Tomas Garrigue (1850–1937), Czech statesman who, together with Beneš, was influential in the establishment of an independent Czechoslovak state. President of Czechoslovakia, 1918–1935.

MEREZHKOVSKY, Dimitri Sergeyevich (1865–1914), Russian writer, the representative of a neo-Christian symbolism. After the Revolution he emigrated to Paris. One of the founders of Russian Symbolism.

MOLNÁR, Ferenc (1878–1952), Hungarian writer of social comedies. He emigrated to the USA in 1940. Noted for his extraordinary mastery of dramatic technique, theatrical effects and witty dialogue.

MÓRICZ, Szigmond (1879–1942), author of novels, stories and plays. With Babits edited *Nyugat* (1933–38). In 1938 founded a new journal, *Kelet Népe* (Nation of the East). Highly popular as a playwright in the inter-war period.

NAGY, Imre (1896–1958), agricultural expert and politician who joined the Communist Party as a prisoner of war in Russia in the First World War. He worked in the illegal Communist Party (1921–28) and lived in exile in the Soviet Union (1929–44). Between 1944 and 1953 he obtained ministerial posts in various governments; for a brief period he was President of the National Assembly and a university professor. In 1955 he was sharply criticized for right-wing deviations and expelled from the party, only to be rehabilitated a year later. In October 1956, in the middle of the popular uprising, he was appointed Prime Minister and led the revolution. Exiled to Romania and executed in June 1958.

NAGY, Lajos (1883–1954), writer of realist fiction. His works are noted for their social criticism.

NÉMETH, Laśzló (1901–1975), writer of fiction, essays and plays. Also a critic and translator. In 1925 a story of his was awarded a prize by *Nyugat*. Editor of *Tanu* (The Witness), 1932–35. In 1934 he founded a journal with the title *Válasz* (Answer). After 1945 he was given a provincial grammar school with which to experiment. Translations from Russian, 1948–1956. He was the author of 20 plays, several volumes of critical essays, and autobiographical works.

NEMES-LAMPÉRTH, József (1891–1924), Hungarian painter, member of the artists' colony in Nagybánya which devoted itself to *plein-air* painting. Modern Hungarian painting is largely the product of this colony. Other painters were drawn to Paris, chief among them was Rippl-Rónai. Nemes modelled himself on the German Expressionists.

NORDAU, Max (pseudonym of Simon Südfeld) (1849–1923), doctor, writer and politician. His father was Rabbi Gabriel ben Asser Südfeld of Budapest. His international reputation was established in 1883 with his book *Conventional Lies of our Civilization*. He became a committed Zionist.

OCSKAI, László (ca. 1680–1710), a highly placed officer who committed treason in the Hungarian Wars of Liberation against the Hapsburgs. In 1710 he was taken prisoner and executed.

ÓDRY, Arpád (1876–1937), Hungarian actor. Lifelong member of the National Theatre, general manager of the Studio Theatre and principal of the Actors Academy of Budapest.

ORTUTAY, Gyula (1910–1978), ethnographer, politician, and member of the left wing of the Agrarian Party. He was director of Budapest Radio 1945–47; Minister for Religion and Education 1947–50; director of the Hungarian Museums and Monuments 1950–53; Rector of Budapest University 1957–63; General Secretary of the National Front, 1957–64. Until his death he remained director of the Ethnographic Research Unit of the Hungarian Academy of Sciences.

OSVÁT, Ernö (1877-1929), literary critic and editor of *Nyugat*.

PÉTERFY, Jenö (1815–1899), one of the most influential Hungarian literary critics during the 1880s. Extraordinarily cultured and knowledgeable about philosophy, music and art, he taught at various middle schools. Committed suicide.

PETHES, Imre (1864–1924), Hungarian actor.

PETÖFI, Sándor (1823–1849), Hungarian poet and leading figure of the 1848 Revolution. He became an editor in 1844 and lived as a freelance writer from 1845 on. He fell in action in Transylvania as a major in the Hungarian Revolutionary army.

PIKLER, Gyula (1864–1937), Hungarian jurist, sociologist and psychologist. Professor of Literature at Budapest University 1903–19. Founder and president (1905–19) of the Society for the Social Sciences.

POGÁNY, József (1886–1938), Hungarian Marxist journalist and literary critic, worked on the Social-Democratic daily, *Népszava* (The People's Voice). He became a Communist in 1919, and during the Hungarian Soviet Republic was People's Commissar for Defence and Education. After the collapse of the dictatorship he went to the Soviet Union and was active in the Comintern. Victim of Stalin's purges.

POGÁNY, Kálmán (1882–1951), Hungarian art historian.

POLÁNYI, Karl (1886–1964), social philosopher and economic historian. Chairman of the Galileo Circle, 1908. After the bourgeois revolution of 1918 he went into exile and settled in England; after the Second World War he went to Canada and later taught for many years at Columbia University in

New York. Married to Ilona Duczynska.

POPPER, Dávid (1846–1913), cellist, studied at the Prague Academy of Music; solo cellist at the Court Opera in Vienna. From 1880 he was Professor for the cello at the Academy of Music in Budapest.

POPPER, Leo (1886–1911), Hungarian art critic and aesthetician who wrote in German. Dávid Popper's son.

PROHASZKA, Ottokár (1858–1927), Catholic bishop of Székesfehérvár. Writer. University professor from 1904. One of the leaders of the Christian-Socialist movement. Involved in the foundation of the Catholic People's Party. After the First World War, he was a member of parliament and chairman of the Christian 'Unity Party'. His Complete Works appeared in 1929 in 15 volumes. Because of his modern ideas three of his books were put on the Index by the Holy See.

RAJK, László (1909–1949), joined the Hungarian Communist Party in 1930. During the Spanish Civil War he was political commissar in the Hungarian Battalion of the International Brigades. After escaping from a French internment camp in 1941 he become leader of the illegal Communist Party in Hungary. In 1945 he became a member of the Central Committee and the Politburo. From 1946 to 1949 he was Minister of the Interior and then Foreign Minister (1948–49). Condemned to death for 'Titoism' in a show trial and executed. Rehabilitated in 1956.

RÁKOCZI, Ferenc II (1675–1735), Prince of Transylvania, leader of the War of Liberation against the Hapsburg dynasty (1703–11). A general and a writer he died in Turkish emigration.

RÁKOS, Ferenc (1893–1963), lawyer, writer and literary translator. In 1910 he joined the Social Democratic Party of Hungary. Became a member of the illegal Communist Party in 1918, and was president of the Revolutionary Court in 1919. After the fall of the Soviet Republic, he emigrated to Vienna and in 1925 went to the USSR. From 1938 to 1946, he was in labour camps and internal exile. Rehabilitated in 1956. Director of the New Hungarian Publishing House, 1951–56. Director of the Political Section of the Public Prosecutor's Office 1956–60.

RÁKOSI, Mátyás (1892–1971), Communist politician. Deputy Commissar in the Soviet Republic in 1919. Arrested and imprisoned for illegal activities, 1925. Released from prison in 1940, he went to the USSR. Returned to Hungary in 1945 as leader of the Communists. General Secretary of the Communist Party of Hungary and Prime Minister (1945–56). Overthrown in 1956. Lived in retirement in the Soviet Union until his death.

RÉVAI, József (1898–1959), politician, literary critic and Communist ideologist. Worked as a journalist during Hungarian Soviet Republic. In exile in Vienna; returned to Hungary but was arrested. Subsequently in Moscow. In 1945 he returned to Hungary where he was part of the inner circle of the Communist Party leadership. Editor-in-chief of the Party organ, *Szabad Nép*; Minister of Culture from 1949 to 1953.

RIPPL-RÓNAI, József (1861–1927), Hungarian painter, graphic artist and craftsman. A pupil of M. Munkácsy. Thanks to his great range and his close links with French painting, Rippl-Rónai was able to make a vital contribution to the introduction of modern painting in Hungary.

RITOÓK, Emma (1868–1945), writer, philosopher, translator.

ROLAND-HOLST, Henriette (1869–1952), Dutch Communist.

RUDAS, László (1885–1950), Hungarian politician and journalist. Founding member of the Hungarian Communist Party and editor of its principal organ, *Red News*, during the 1919 Soviet Republic. In exile in the Soviet Union, he taught at the Comintern party college and, during the Second World War, at the international anti-fascist school. Returned to Hungary in 1944 and became director of the Central Committee college, and later also of the College for Economic Sciences.

SALLAI, Imre (1897–1932), journalist, member of the Galileo Circle. Arrested in 1918. Founder-member of the HCP. People's Commissar for Internal Affairs in the 1919 Soviet Republic. Emigrated to Vienna and, in 1924, to Moscow. In charge of the secretariat of the illegal Hungarian Communist Party. Arrested and executed in 1932.

SCHÖPFLIN, Aladar (1872–1950), literary historian, critic, novelist and playwright. One of the most important members of *Nyugat*; editor-in-chief of the Franklin Society, the foremost literary publishing house in Hungary before the Second World War.

SEGHERS, Anna (1900–1983), realist writer. Joined the German Communist Party in 1928. Married a Hungarian, László Radvany. After 1933 her books were banned and she emigrated to France until 1940. Active on the Republican side in the Spanish Civil War. Spent the war years in Mexico. Moved to East Germany in 1948, where she held a number of leading positions, including the presidency of the Writers Union.

SEIDLER, Ernö (1886–1940), Hungarian Communist politician. Emigrated in 1919. Founder-member of the Galileo Circle and of the HCP. Victim of Stalin's purges. Brother of Irma Seidler.

SEIDLER, Irma (1883–1911), Hungarian painter. An early love of Lukács.

Committed suicide. Sister of Ernö Seidler.

SINKÓ, Ervin (1898–1967), Hungarian writer. In emigration in Vienna, Yugoslavia, France and the USSR. Held a chair in Hungarian Literature at Novi Sad University, Yugoslavia, after the war. He developed a powerful intellectual and moralizing prose style. In *The Optimists* he depicted the period of the Hungarian Soviet Republic, and in *Novel of a Novel* he described the literary policies of Moscow and the Comintern in the mid-thirties.

SOMLÓ, Bodog (1873–1920), lawyer and sociologist. Studied in Cluj, Leipzig and Heidelberg. Professor at Cluj (1898–1918) and Budapest (1918–19). Editor of *Huszadik Század*, a journal devoted to the social sciences. In 1901 he founded the Society for Social Sciences.

SOMLYÓ, György (b. 1920), Hungarian poet and essayist.

STROMFELD, Aurel (1878–1927), erstwhile colonel in the Hungarian General Staff. In the First World War Chief of the General Staff. Under the Soviet Republic he remained in the background, but when the Red Army got into difficulties in April 1919, he took over the supreme command and for this he was sentenced to three years imprisonment after the fall of the Republic.

SZABÓ, Ervin (1877–1918), Hungarian politician and scholar. From 1911 he was Director of the Metropolitan Library; a left-wing Social Democrat. Translated and published the works of Marx and Engels in Hungary. In the First World War he was intellectual leader of the anti-militarist movement.

SZABOLSCI, Bence (1899–1973), Hungarian musicologist, and pupil of Kodály. Since 1947 Professor at the Budapest Academy of Music. Fundamental studies on the subject of musical ethnology. Edited the writings of Béla Bartók.

SZABOLSCI, Miklós (b. 1921), literary historian, editor, university professor in Budapest, member of the Hungarian Academy of Sciences.

SZAMUELY, Tibor (1890–1919), Hungarian journalist and revolutionary. In 1915 he became a Russian prisoner-of-war and helped to organize the international POW movement. He returned to Hungary in 1919 and became a member of the Central Committee of the Communist Party of Hungary. Editor of *Red News*. During the Hungarian Soviet Republic he was a deputy People's Commissar for War. Was captured on 2 August 1919, while attempting to cross the Austrian border; committed suicide.

SZÁNTÓ, Zoltán (1893–1977), writer and politician. War service until 1918. Took part in the bourgeois revolution of 1918 and became a founding member of the Communist Party. Lived in exile in Vienna (1920–26). After that he was active in the underground Communist movement in Hungary. He spent the years 1927–35 in prison. After his release he lived in Czechoslovakia and the Soviet Union. He returned to Hungary in 1945 where he filled various party and state offices.

SZERÉNYI, Sándor (code name Sas) (b. 1905), Hungarian Communist. First Secretary of the party from 1929 to 1931.

SZIGETI, József (b. 1921), Hungarian philosopher. Former pupil of Lukács.

SZIRMAI, István (1906–1969), Hungarian Communist journalist, in the party leadership from 1957.

SZOMAHÁZY, István (1864–1927), author of numerous popular plays and operettas.

TISZA, István Count (1864–1918), Hungarian bourgeois politician. Prime Minister, 1903–5 and 1913–17. Murdered in 1918.

TIHANYI, Lajos (1885–1938), a painter and a founding member of the group 'The Eight' in 1909. He was associated with the avant-garde circle around the journal *Ma* (Today). After the fall of the Hungarian Soviet Republic he emigrated to Vienna, Berlin and from 1923 he lived in Paris. In 1933 he joined the group, 'Abstraction-Création'.

TOLNAY, Charles de (1899–1981), Hungarian art historian. He taught at the Sorbonne, 1933–39. In 1939 he went to the United States where he held posts at Princeton and Columbia. From 1965 he was Director of the Casa Buonarotti in Florence.

TÓTH, Árpád (1886–1928), Hungarian poet, member of the *Nguyat* circle. Noted for his highly elegiac tone, his melodious use of language and formal perfection. One of the most important Hungarian translators (Milton, Wilde, Baudelaire, Maupassant, Flaubert and Chekhov).

UJEHLYI, Szilárd (b. 1915), Communist politician, Secretary of State (1947–48). Arrested and imprisoned after the Rajk trial, he was subsequently rehabilitated. In 1967–68 he was in charge of the State Publishing House and in 1968 he was director of the film department in the Ministry of Education.

USEVICH, Elena Feliksovna (1893–1968), Russian literary critic. Party member since 1915. Took part in the October Revolution and the civil war. Graduated from the Institute of Red Professors in 1932. Her book publications began in 1932. She also wrote many articles on problems of Soviet literature.

VÁGÓ, Béla (1881–1939), Hungarian Social Democrat, later Communist politician. Took part in the Hungarian Soviet Republic. Victim of Stalin's purges.

VAJDA, Mihály (b. 1935), a pupil of Agnes Heller. Worked in the Philosophical Institute of the Hungarian Academy of Sciences, 1961–73. In 1973 he was dismissed and expelled from the party, since when he has lived mainly in the West.

VARGA, Jenö (1879–1964), Hungarian economist. Member of the Academy of Sciences of the USSR, where he lived after the collapse of the Hungarian Soviet Republic. A member of the CPSU from 1920. Active involvement in the Comintern. Director of the Institute for World Economics and World Politics, 1927–42. Shortly before his death he moved away from Stalinism and wrote a critique of the Soviet economy, which was only published abroad after his death.

VAS, Zoltán (b. 1905), Hungarian Communist. From 1924 to 1940 in prison in Hungary. In the Soviet Union till returning to Hungary in 1945 where he was active as a party functionary and in the government. In 1956 he worked with the Imre Nagy group. After 1956 mainly active as a writer. His memoirs, published in Hungary in 1981, caused a sensation.

VEDRES, Márk (1870–1961), Hungarian sculptor, trained in Munich and Paris. His early works reveal the influence of Rodin. During the Hungarian Soviet Republic he lectured at the College of Art. After the fall of the Republic he lived in Florence.

VERES, Péter (1897–1970), novelist, story-writer, journalist and politician; Peasant Party ideologist. Came from a poor peasant family, educated himself and lived from his work as an agricultural labourer until 1945. While still a young man, he joined the agrarian socialist movement and wrote for populist and socialist journals and newspapers. He established his reputation as a writer with his autobiographical novel *Settling Accounts*. He was chairman of the National Peasant Party (1945–49), Minister of Reconstruction (1947), Minister of Defence (1947–48), and President of the Hungarian Writers' Union (1954–56). After 1950 Veres devoted himself exclusively to writing.

WALDAPFEL, József (1904–1968), Hungarian literary historian.

WELTNER, Jakab (1873–1936), Hungarian Social Democrat politician.

WILDE, Janos (1891–1971), Hungarian art historian. Lived in emigration after 1919, mostly in England.

WITTFOGEL, Karl August (b. 1896), German Expressionist playwright and Communist literary critic in Weimar Germany. Emigrated to the USA; author of *Oriental Despotism* (1939).

WOLFNER (FARKAS), Pál (1878–1921), Hungarian writer, sociologist and conservative politician.

YUDIN, Pavel Fyodorovich (1889–1968), Soviet philosopher and loyal supporter of Stalin. Director of the Philosophical Institute of the Soviet Academy of Sciences, 1938–44; editor-in-chief of the journal of the Cominform, 1946–53; ambassador to China, 1953–59; member of the Central Committee of the CPSU, 1952–61.

ZALAI, Béla (1882–1915), Hungarian philosopher. Killed in the First World War.

ZHDANOV, Andrei Alexandrovich (1896–1948), Soviet politician, the son of a school inspector. In 1912 he joined the revolutionary movement and, in 1916, the Bolsheviks. He took part in the October Revolution. He was secretary of the Leningrad Party (1934–44). As a member of the supreme War Council on the Leningrad front in the Second World War, he played an important role in the defence of the city. He had been a member of the Central Committee since 1930, and of the Politburo from 1939. His name is associated with a number of theoretical works which formulated the cultural policies of 'socialist realism'.

ZOLTAI, Dénes (b. 1928), pupil of Lukács specializing in the aesthetics of music.

Notes

Notes to Eörsi: The Right to the Last Word

[1] See biographical notes, pp. 183ff

[2] *New Left Review*, No. 68, July-August 1971. See appendix to this volume.

[3] Two Hungarian philosophers, György Bence and Janos Kis, are the first to my knowledge to have written about the religious elements of Lukács's thought. They did so in an as yet unpublished study, written immediately after Lukács's death, in which they attempted to clarify their attitude towards him.

Notes to Chapter One: Childhood and Early Career

[1] Berthold Auerbach (1812–82) was a German Jewish writer whose *Spinoza* appeared in 1837. He is now known mainly for his later stories of village life (*Trans.*).

[2] Edmondo de Amicis (1846–1907) was an Italian writer known principally for his collection of short stories *Cuore* (Heart), 1886, which is still widely read by children in Eastern Europe (*Trans.*).

[3] Passages marked with an asterisk are literal extracts from an interview given by Georg Lukács to István Eörsi and Erzsébet Vezér on 26 November 1966. This interview was published in Emlékezések I (Recollections I) of the Petőfi Literary Museum. Lukács read and approved the text. Since the present selection is arranged chronologically, it was not possible to publish the interview as a continuous text.

[4] Bang (1857–1912) was the outstanding representative of Danish Impressionism (*Trans.*).

[5] English translation in *The Hungarian Avant-Garde*, Arts Council of Great Britain catalogue, 1980 (*Trans.*).

[6] English translation in *The Philosophical Forum*, Vol, 3, nos. 3–4, Spring-Summer 1972 (*Trans.*).

[7] Lukács is mistaken here. Bloch was in Heidelberg from 1910 to 1914.

[8] Ugosca, the smallest territory in the Hapsburg Empire, also had the right to object to the coronation of the emperor.

[9] The Novalis article was included in *Soul and Form* (Trans.).

[10] In *Wilhelm Meister's Apprenticeship* (*Trans.*).

Notes to Chapter Two: War and Revolution

[1] See the 1962 preface to *The Theory of the Novel*, London 1971 (*Trans.*).

[2] In his memoir of the Rajk affair Tibor Déry forgot that in 1949 he himself had written an article against László Rajk, a minister in the post-war Hungarian government who was executed in 1949 after a show trial.

[3]Vautrin is the master-criminal who appears in many novels by Balzac (*Père Goriot*; *Illusions Perdues*). He ends as a minister responsible for police and public health and is assassinated by a forger (*Trans.*).

[4]It is symptomatic of Lukács's attitude to his early works that he has shown so little interest in the fate of the manuscript. It has in fact survived complete and was published after his death as the *Heidelberger Philosophie der Kunst*, Neuwied 1974.

[5]That is, the Hungarian Soviet Republic of March-August 1919. Lukács refers to this throughout as the (proletarian) 'dictatorship' (*Trans.*).

[6]Georg Lukács, *Political Writings, 1919-1929*, London 1972 (*Trans.*).

[7]The reference is to Friedrich Hebbel's play *Judith* and relates to the morality of her murder of Holofernes (*Trans.*).

[8]Little chrysanthemums or 'autumn roses', of which there were great supplies in town for the coming All Saints' Day, were worn in the lapels of demonstrators and soldiers during the revolution of October 1918. The epithet also pointed to the bloodless nature of the revolution (*Trans.*).

[9]Headquarters of the Hungarian Communist Party.

[10]Leading representatives of the Social Democrat right wing.

[11]See *Political Writings: 1919-1929* (*Trans.*)

Notes to Chapter Three: In Exile

[1]Ignaz Seipel was the conservative Chancellor of Austria from 1926 to 1929 (*Trans.*)

[2]Lukács refers to pressure from the German Social Democratic Party leadership, which was against joint SPD-KPD resistance to the forcible break-up of the coalition by the central government (*Trans.*).

[3]See *Political Writings: 1919-1929*.

[4]The Hungarian Socialist Workers Party (MSZMP) was founded on 14 April 1925, following a decision of the Hungarian Communist Party in Vienna the previous November. It formed the legal counterpart in Hungary of the illegal Hungarian Communist Party operating from Vienna (*Trans.*).

[5]The idea and the phrase come from Lenin, *The Proletarian Revolution and the Renegade Kautsky* (1918), *Collected Works*, Vol. 28.

[6]Schweinitzer was deputy head of the Budapest police and chief of the political section.

[7]Abridged English translation, *Born 1900*, London 1974 (*Trans.*).

[8]*The Philosophy of Art of Karl Marx*, London 1973 (*Trans.*).

[9]For an English translation see *Essays on Realism*, London 1973 (*Trans.*).

[10]Brecht's later plays, starting with *The Life of Galileo* and including *Mother Courage* and *The Good Woman of Szechuan*, were begun in the 1938-39 period. Although Lukács could not have known these during the thirties, he did know *Fear and Misery in the Third Reich*, which was published in 1938 and on which he commented during the Expressionism debate (*Trans.*).

[11]The Russian Association of Proletarian Writers.

Notes to Chapter Four: Back In Hungary

[1]A quotation from Schiller's *Fiesco* (*Trans.*).

[2]Lukács is here referring to his well-known metaphor according to which Marxism is the Himalayas of the world's ideologies, but a hare roaming the Himalayas should not be so foolish as to imagine that he is taller than an elephant in the valley.

[3]'The People's Freedom': the official Hungarian Party daily (*Trans.*).

[4]*Szép Szó* was a left-oriented bourgeois periodical (*Trans.*).

[5]This was the second doctorate, which normally carried with it the offer of a university post.

[6]Lukács is referring to Thomas Mann's *Reflections of a Non-Political Man* (*Trans.*).

[7]From Goethe's 'Selige Sehnsucht'. The poem continues: 'You will be but a dismal guest on the

gloomy earth!' (*Trans.*)

[8]*Válasz* was the journal of the Populists (*Trans.*).

[9]NEKOSZ: The Faculty of Workers and Peasants.

[10]Lukács is mistaken here. He presumably means 'early in the twenties'.

[11]Frank Benseler was the editor at Luchterhand responsible for Lukács's *Collected Works*.

[12]The revolution of 1848–49 in Hungary was put down with particular brutality, but the restored Austrian monarchy nevertheless found itself unable to contain its own internal tensions. These were exacerbated by the defeat at the hands of Prussia in 1866, when the Austrians were forced to accept a compromise with Hungary. This resulted in the establishment of the Dual Monarchy in 1867 on the basis of a plan formulated by Ferenc Deák.

[13]On 6 October 1849 thirteen Hungarian generals were executed on the orders of Heynau, the counter-revolutionary Austrian commander.

[14]According to legend Elisabeth Báthory (who died in 1614) used to bathe in the blood of murdered girls in order to beautify her skin.

[15]Bartók's *Cantata Profana* tells the story of a father who taught his nine sons to perform no useful work but only to hunt. One day, while out hunting the magic stags, they are turned into stags themselves. Their father begs them to return home, but they refuse, saying that their antlers will not allow them to pass through the doorway and henceforth only the forest will be large enough to contain them (*Trans.*).

Notes to *Gelebtes Denken*

[1]Victor Zitta, *Georg Lukács's Marxism*, The Hague 1864, p. 101 gives a satirical account of Lukács's activities as Commissar for Culture under the chapter-heading 'Terror-stricken Yogi as Commissar' (*Trans.*).

[2]Victor Serge, *Memoirs of a Revolutionary*, Oxford 1963. Serge obviously admired Lukács greatly: 'In him I saw a first-class brain which could have endowed Communism with a true intellectual greatness if it had developed as a social movement instead of degenerating into a movement in solidarity with an authoritarian power' (p. 187). However, his brief references include a number of factual errors. He reports a chance meeting in Moscow, allegedly in 1928–29, when he claims that Lukács 'did not care to shake my hand in a public place, since I was expelled and a known Oppositionist'. He also mentions Lukács as the author of 'a number of outstanding books which were never to see the light of day' (*Trans.*).

[3]The reference is to advertisements which link smoking Gauloises to masculine sex-appeal.

[4]That is, *Heart*, the novel by Edmondo de Amicis.

[5]*Athenäum* (1798–1800), edited by August Wilhelm Schlegel, was the principal journal of the German Romantic movement (*Trans.*).

[6]A character in Ibsen's *Rosmersholm* (Trans.).

[7]This paragraph was written in Hungarian and appears in that form in the German edition (*Trans.*).

[8]In *Essays on Realism*, London 1980.

[9]From July 1953 to 1954 (*Trans.*).

Notes to Appendix: Interview with *New Left Review*

Note to Appendix: Interview with *New Left Review* Morality', in Adorno and Horkheimer, *Dialectic of Enlightenment*, London 1979 (*Trans.*).